TOXIC SHOCK

Toxic Shock

A Social History

Sharra L. Vostral

NEW YORK UNIVERSITY PRESS
New York

NEW YORK UNIVERSITY PRESS
New York
www.nyupress.org

References to Internet websites (URLs) were accurate at the time of writing. Neither the author nor New York University Press is responsible for URLs that may have expired or changed since the manuscript was prepared.

Library of Congress Cataloging-in-Publication Data
Names: Vostral, Sharra Louise, 1968– author.
Title: Toxic shock : a social history / Sharra L. Vostral.
Description: New York : New York University, 2018. |
Includes bibliographical references and index.
Identifiers: LCCN 2018012210| ISBN 9781479877843 (cl : alk. paper) |
ISBN 9781479815494 (pb : alk. paper)
Subjects: LCSH: Toxic shock syndrome. | Toxic shock syndrome—Social aspects. |
Tampons—Complications.
Classification: LCC RG220 .V67 2018 | DDC 614.5/797—dc23
LC record available at https://lccn.loc.gov/2018012210

New York University Press books are printed on acid-free paper, and their binding materials are chosen for strength and durability. We strive to use environmentally responsible suppliers and materials to the greatest extent possible in publishing our books.

Manufactured in the United States of America

10 9 8 7 6 5 4 3 2 1

Also available as an ebook

To everyone who has ever used a tampon

CONTENTS

ABBREVIATIONS

ASTM   American Society for Testing and Materials
BWHBC   Boston Women's Health Book Collective
CDC   Centers for Disease Control
CMC   carboxymethylcellulose
CMDA   Center for Medical Device Analysis
EIS   Epidemic Intelligence Service
FCC   Federal Communication Commission
FDA   Food and Drug Administration
FFDCA   Federal Food, Drug and Cosmetic Act
HHS   Health and Human Services
ICD   implantable cardioverter defibrillator
IUD   intrauterine device
JAMA   *Journal of the American Medical Association*
MDA   Medical Device Amendments
MMWR   *Morbidity and Mortality Weekly Report*
MRSA   methicillin-resistant *Staphylococcus aureus*
NCL   National Consumers League
NEJM   *New England Journal of Medicine*
NIH   National Institutes of Health
OBOS   *Our Bodies, Ourselves*
OMB   Office of Management and Budget
P&G   Procter & Gamble
RBGH   recombinant bovine growth hormone
TSS   toxic shock syndrome
TSST-1   toxic shock syndrome toxin-1

Introduction

Toxic Shock Syndrome

I became aware of toxic shock syndrome (TSS) after my first period in 1982, while in eighth grade. During a subsequent menstrual cycle, I caught a cold and became increasingly worried that I had contracted TSS. This was not such an outlandish conclusion on my part. TSS was the third most reported-on news story in 1980, behind the Iranian hostage crisis and the presidential election. The *NBC Nightly News* was a dinnertime staple, I had a subscription to *Seventeen* magazine, and I flipped through my mother's *Good Housekeeping*, and all had reported on this new illness. I absorbed reports of current events, and news sources warned that a tampon plus a fever equated to a scary disease, possibly even to death. My mother, a nurse, quickly rebuffed my concerns. She was a longtime Tampax user who trusted the safety of the product. I suspect she interpreted my concerns as the manifestations of an overreactive teenager. Despite her assurances, the message I received was loud and clear: TSS was a possible side effect from wearing tampons, and I must be vigilant to monitor my body for any sign of potential disease when I used them.

As I grew older and continued to use tampons, I neither contracted TSS nor died from using a tampon. My experience with them was incongruous with the warning label on the box, and I always wondered about these heavy-handed labels. Was I being reckless by disregarding the warning? Or was TSS still lurking, and only I could save myself from corporate malfeasance? For how long could I use tampons and not fall ill, thus have my cake and eat it, too? As an adult who has spent many years contemplating TSS, I am more sympathetic to the conundrum. While it is true that a confluence of corporate interests, epidemiological studies, women's health activism, and women's desires to use tampons influenced the politics of tampon-related TSS, there is one important common denominator. All were influenced by the belief that tampons are inert. This faulty premise and the consequences of assuming that tampons are inert provided the backdrop for the new illness. The prevailing notion of the inert nature of tampon technology explains why the devastating outcome of women's deaths were so difficult to study and understand; this traditional way of thinking about disease, technology, and women's bodies was insufficient in encountering what came to be identified as tampon-related TSS. Though it is not recognized as such, tampon-related TSS was a paradigm shift in the way that illness manifests because the supposedly inert tampon interacted with a common bacterium to cause sickness in otherwise healthy women. No longer was an infection the origin of disease, or a faulty product the direct cause of injury. Together, a new pathway to an illness formed, in which a supposedly inert tampon became interactive, and a bacterium, once held in bodily equilibrium, grew dominant and produced toxins. *Toxic Shock: A Social History* makes a case for understanding tampon-related TSS as the result of biocatalytic activity between technology and bacterium. Moreover, though women were the primary consumers, the bacterium became the unintended user. This unusual disease process challenged standard approaches to public health and required women to evaluate technological risk. It likely portends increasing incidence of injury related to medical devices used and worn within the human body.

Tampon-related TSS is unique in that it is contingent on both bacterium and technology interacting with one another. TSS is unusual in that it is an illness that strikes otherwise healthy individuals and is predominantly associated with a human-made technology. Many people had a difficult time accepting this relationship, believing that tampons were inert. And those who recognized that something was afoot could not necessarily prove scientifically the mechanisms by which TSS manifested. Because hundreds of thousands of women who menstruated used tampons, and many carried the requisite bacterial strain of *Staphylococcus aureus*, scientific findings about TSS were urgent. Health practitioners, corporate scientists, federal policy makers, and feminist political advocates shaped and defined the terms of the emergent illness. They both articulated and challenged notions of risk, the results of which changed the conceptualization of tampons from benign to dangerous, affecting all tampon users. Moreover, this tampon technology shares a legacy of silence and coded language linked with menstruation, at best tolerated and at worst shamed. Thus, presumptions about menstruation came to bear on tampon technologies, the conditions of illness, and how women should be warned about potential risk.

This book is a multifaceted history of tampon-related TSS as understood through distinct lenses: (1) technology and bacterium; (2) medicine and epidemiology; (3) communication and journalism; (4) law and litigation; and (5) policy and politics. TSS remains at the center of each chapter, but the conceptualizations, approaches, methods, and assumptions that different professionals and organizations brought to bear on this emerging health crisis demonstrate reactions to the revelation that tampons were not inert and, moreover, had the potential to cause irrevocable damage. Epidemiologists, corporate scientists, lawyers, and women's health advocates each asserted different positions about how the emerging illness was related to supposedly inert tampons and how TSS affected menstruating women. The chapters are arranged thematically and overlap chronologically to address the ways that TSS was identified, crafted, constructed, and politically contained. My goal is not to complicate matters but to explain the history of a complicated illness by exploring it through different viewpoints, because a linear history restricts the narrative.

TSS was identified with the bacterium *Staphylococcus aureus* in 1978, and the illness was later linked with tampons in 1980. Toxic shock syndrome was an urgent epidemiological event because of the feared potential to harm hundreds of thousands of young women. Though the epidemic never emerged, it is better characterized as a health crisis that instilled fear due to unknown elements and the inability of health providers to offer immediate explanation, relief, and a cure. Medical science failed to produce a quick and accurate resolution to the illness, compounding fears because tampons were simultaneously ubiquitous and also indecorous. According to Arthur Reingold, an epidemiologist at the Centers for Disease Control (CDC), 70 percent of women used tampons in 1980, and a potential national recall of all tampon brands would have affected hundreds of thousands of women.[1] News reports and press releases in the media unveiled women's intimate bodily menstrual management practices, presumably inappropriate to air yet necessary to speak of when warning women about the dangers, including death, associated with tampons.

This is a story about technology and bacterium, and also about the interrelatedness of these two active components in precipitating illness. Indeed, TSS is frightening because the majority of menstruating women in the United States use tampons, and women cannot willfully control their periods or the makeup of their vaginal microflora. Though menstrual periods are one of the variables to the illness, eliminating them (though currently they can be pharmaceutically managed with synthetic hormones) is both impractical and not entirely desirable. When tampons are avoided, the options are to use sanitary pads, which is a nonstarter for many due to their discomfort. Menstrual cups are gaining in popularity, but they are an expensive up-front investment and do not work for all women. For many, tampons are nonnegotiable and the only method to manage periods well enough to hide them. This is important because there are no privileges to be gained for heavy periods or stains on clothing. As Gloria Steinem glibly points out in her 1978 essay "If Men Could Menstruate," they "would brag about how long and how much," with slang such as "He's a three-pad man!" to boast about bodily performance and rationalize power justifications.[2] With no such social benefits extended to women, tampons offer a pragmatic means to absorb menstrual fluid, keep bloodstains off of clothing (for the most part), and leave the body unencumbered, unlike sanitary pads. Thus, the fear of contracting TSS during a period due to tampon use is an entirely legitimate concern, despite the fact that it occurs in "1 to 17 per 100,000 menstruating women and girls per year" and can be treated with antibiotics if diagnosed early enough.[3] In light of these statistics, the hype and concern seem overblown, while in other ways the risk is poorly clarified and contributes to ongoing misunderstandings that plague the worried well.

In part, the Rely tampon, culpable for most of the TSS cases until 1980, is no longer produced and sold, eliminating that particular risk factor while lulling many into a false sense of security. Though other tampon brands triggered TSS and may have even contained similar material components, Rely tampons, which were developed and manufactured by Procter & Gamble (P&G), shouldered the brunt of the responsibility for the outbreak, with epidemiologic data strongly correlating TSS with them. As such, I have put the bacterium of *S. aureus* and the Rely tampon at the center of this book, and I trace technological innovations, epidemiology, product liability, and health policy through them both as the story's main protagonists. This history explains the intertwined techno-bacteriological illness of tampon-related TSS and traces the unfolding health crisis, the definition of the illness, the shaping of knowledge distribution, and the gendering of health policy.

More broadly, this book raises questions about the way certain bodies are subjected to risk while others are not, and about why we are willing to tolerate harm for some people. We operate under a collective illusion and even desire that technologies related to bodies are safe. When something goes wrong, it is preferable to blame user error, presuming things have been vetted technically, scientifically, and medically, because then the problem can be rationalized as an aberration rather than systemic. This, unfortunately, is not the case. Corporations have a large financial stake in making sure the status quo of products is maintained, and women, too, have been compliant by ignoring known risks in favor of technoscientific menstrual management. So deeply ingrained is this narrative of technological progress that journalists often ask me to predict the next menstrual management technology on the horizon. I tell them that what we need is not another technological fix, but a more compassionate attitude toward menstruation. My response is unsatisfactory to them because it challenges the uplift narrative and the hopes of a capitalistic solution for socially conscientious menstrual management. It is also unsatisfactory because it asks women to be better consumers, resist the mantra that "new is better," and reject further synthetic and nonnatural fibers to be worn within the body. A deep understanding of tampons and their relationship to women's bodies is vitally important: it can have life-or-death consequences. A reason I wrote this book is to share this knowledge, so each of us does not have to conduct independent research about TSS in order to make decisions about our own bodies. There is much pressure to believe that the technoscientific is the future, but "new" is not always better, and, in this case, the unintended consequence of "new" can be death.

A Definition of Toxic Shock Syndrome

In order to understand the historical origins of tampon-related TSS, it is useful to begin with the clinical case definition of TSS put forth in

February 1980 and established by the CDC. According to the CDC, a clinical case of TSS included a fever of 102 degrees or more, rash, desquamation (flaking, peeling skin), and hypotension (drop in blood pressure, dizziness). It also included the broad category of "multisystem involvement," which encompasses three or more of the following: gastrointestinal distress (vomiting, diarrhea), muscular pain (creatine phosphokinase levels twice that of normal), mucous membrane issues (enlarged blood vessels within the eye, throat, or vagina), renal dysfunction (blood urea nitrogen or creatinine twice that of the normal level, without the presence of a urinary tract infection), liver dysfunction (serums twice that of normal), blood abnormalities (platelets less than 100,000/mm³), and central nervous system issues (disorientation). Lastly, tests for diseases such as measles and Rocky Mountain spotted fever had to be negative, and also negative throat, blood and cerebrospinal fluid cultures were necessary to eliminate other diseases with similar symptoms. The CDC also indicated that a TSS diagnosis of "probable" included five of the six categories, while "confirmed" included six of the six categories.[4]

This clinical definition fails to capture the materiality, suffering, and long-term effects for those who contracted it. Almost all cases start out with what appears to be the flu, with a fever, severe diarrhea, and vomiting. Most assume that they need rest and can sleep it off, only to find that they feel worse in the two to three days that follow. Personal blogs of women who contracted TSS describe a partner or close relative who insisted on taking them to the hospital, for at least a round of IV fluids. While there, the women, admitted as patients, were usually found to have very low blood pressure in the range of 70/40 and a high fever of 103 or 104 Fahrenheit. Molly, a blogger who contracted TSS in 2006 as a senior in high school, recalled horrible vomiting all day long and being so dizzy that she collapsed in the bathroom. She hallucinated and was unable to vocalize her need for help; after her mother took her to the physician, she was rushed to the hospital where she was diagnosed with TSS and treated with antibiotics, saline, and a plasma infusion. After being discharged, her hands and feet peeled like they had been sunburned.[5] Michelle (age unknown) experienced TSS in 2007, and she recounted falling into a coma, needing kidney dialysis, and requiring a breathing tube. She bled from her eyes, and her feet and hands

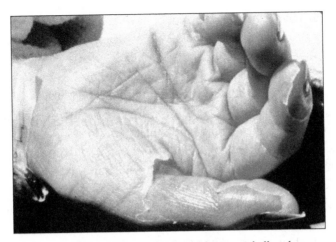

Figure I.1. Peeling skin on the hands and feet is one hallmark symptom of TSS. Source: Public Health Image Library, ID #5119. Courtesy of the Centers for Disease Control.

turned black and swollen as her organs shut down and limited circulation throughout her body. She emerged from the coma after a week and remained in the hospital, relearning how to do simple things such as getting dressed, feeding herself, and walking with a cane, which was a severe blow to her as a dancer. She also lost most of her hair, which grew back after about nine months. She returned to teach dance after a year, building up her strength to finally leap once again.[6]

These accounts are not meant to be voyeuristic or macabre, but to describe TSS in a more relatable manner. Though these are examples from two different women, TSS has been identified across the population, and it is somewhat of a misnomer to think of it as a specifically female ailment. It can present itself in children, men, and women who are not menstruating. Its etiology took a unique course when the overwhelming majority of cases at the outset were linked to tampon-using women. The toxin, a protein produced by the particular strain of *Staphylococcus aureus* responsible for tampon-related TSS, is specifically referred to as toxic shock syndrome toxin-1 (TSST-1). To further complicate things, there is also group A streptococcal TSS, though it is not associated with tampons. Throughout this book, I refer solely to tampon-related TSS, linked to *Staphylococcus aureus*.

Though TSS seemed to come out of nowhere, the bacterium *S. aureus* has many strains and is responsible for a variety of diseases, and about 20 percent of the general population carries *S. aureus* on the skin and in the nose. Named in 1884 for its yellow hued clusters, *S. aureus* produces a variety of ailments, including rashes, pimples, and boils.[7] *S. aureus* has different relatives, some of which produce enterotoxins, harmful and toxic proteins specific to cells in the intestine and responsible for more serious bouts of food poisoning. Others create exotoxins, toxic materials secreted and released by the bacteria, which may travel throughout a person's body. More recently methicillin-resistant *Staphylococcus aureus* (MRSA), currently known as the "super bug" contracted in hospital-like settings, has gained notoriety. *S. aureus* and its many bacterial derivatives can pack quite a punch in the realm of human diseases.

Tampon-related TSS is not contagious and is not an infection. It relies on multiple factors that come into play for a very small set of women. It is a complex process, difficult to understand, and impossible to condense into a sound bite or a quick public health announcement, though many scientists and public health advocates have attempted to do so over the years. Many scientists and research groups have examined TSS and TSST-1 and published results in academic journals that detail various elements of its etiology and microbiology, some of which conflict. It is not the goal of this book to list all of the scientists who have researched *S. aureus* or TSS and adjudicate their scientific accuracy, but rather I wish to shed light on how the vagaries and incongruities of scientific thinking influenced policy decisions that ultimately affected women. Significantly, the multiple variables related to the illness's occurrence and a lack of definitive evidence detailing its exact pathway intensified the health crisis. There was no scientifically agreed-on understanding about how tampons specifically triggered TSS, though the most promising research was presented in the proceedings *Toxic Shock Syndrome* by the Institute of Medicine in 1982.[8] Tampon-related TSS challenged essentialist notions of women's bodies; not all women were the same and vaginal flora differed from woman to woman. Though menstrual periods and tampons were involved, a simple formula of "mix both and stir" was implausible to re-create TSS because it simply was not a reality that every menstruating woman using a tampon contracted TSS. It also challenged essentialist notions of technology as inert; tampons broke down, sloughed, and caused change within the vaginal ecosystem, becoming a variable in and of themselves. Scientific assumptions had to shift. Women were not monolithic and neither were the tampons that they used.

Overview

This book draws on many interdisciplinary fields and is primarily situated within studies of gender and technology, histories of women's health and women's health activism, and also related literature about the history of menstrual hygiene, which is more currently referred to as menstrual hygiene management or menstrual management.[9] It intersects studies of technology and disease that examine relationships of medical practice to medical instruments and medical devices. It contributes to studies about technology and risk, and it looks at the relationship of injury to law.[10] In addition, it relates to concepts of biological technologies—not necessarily in the sense of biotechnology and genetic engineering but that of technology interacting with biological systems.[11] Policy studies of technology also address the relationships of scientific practice to government regulations, and how implementation of policy affects users and communities.[12] All of these threads interlace to inform my interpretation of the techno-bacteriological health crisis of TSS, that is, an illness resulting from a biological and technological interface, and one not easily quelled through the usual medical courses of action. Though there are scientific discussions about TSS, and passing references to it in women's health literature and self-help sources from the 1980s, *Toxic Shock* explores TSS from gendered, political, and science and technology studies perspectives in order to understand the history of this health crisis and its influence on the world in which we live.[13]

Calling tampon-related TSS a "health crisis" is purposeful, especially because it did not become a full-blown epidemic, and it centered on a formerly trusted, presumably benign technology. It generated surprise and a swift response. Christopher Foreman, a fellow at the Brookings Institution, describes the fear generated by potential public health harms as an "infectious disease or dangerous product that victimizes quickly and perhaps in ways unfamiliar to the general public." Characteristic of "emergent public health hazards" is speed, dissipation, and novelty that contribute to the fear. Fear is further heightened by the understanding that one chance encounter, versus long-term exposure, can bring serious illness or injury.[14] TSS captured these elements. A chance encounter with a formerly trusted tampon could bring on a new illness within twenty-four hours, difficult to diagnose in the initial stages because it acted like the common cold. In addition, once the element of fear took hold, it had its own set of consequences, with audiences unable to "hear" and comprehend experts' observations and conclusions.[15] Though many diseases and outbreaks had been publicized by news outlets, what made this one different to report on was the combination of a consumer technology, linked with the socially indecorous bodily process of menstruation, together producing a seemingly new illness.

The grounding assumptions and conceptualizations of bacteria and gendered technology are the focus of chapter 1. In order to think through this relationship of bacterium and technology as active co-agents, I develop the term "biocatalytic technology." The tampon, conceptualized as an inert plug to stop up the fluids of a mechanical body, instead served as a catalyst, prompting a bacterium that was at best in stasis to begin producing toxins. Individually both the tampon and bacterium were neutral, but due to ecological circumstances they triggered a harmful consequence. Constituent bacteria, menstruating bodies, and a reactive rather than inert technology converged to create the ideal environment for the S. aureus bacterium to live and flourish in some women. Opportunistic, the bacterium became the unintended user of the tampon technology. The inability to recognize the agency of these microbial entities within the larger scope of women's bodies—historically constructed as "problematic"—has profound effects on everyday health. Tampon-related TSS is an unintended consequence of technological innovation engaging with vaginal microbes, resulting in an emergent illness. Accounting for microbial constituents and the ecological landscape of gendered bodies would help imagine and mitigate deleterious outcomes. The term "biocatalytic technology" highlights the interactive rather than inert capacity of tampons, and it helps to explain the potential consequences of bacteria as technological users on women's health.

Chapter 2 addresses the medical facets of TSS and how a set of symptoms was stabilized into a defined illness with correlative healthcare practices. The illness challenged a medical assumption that tampons did not cause illness because they were an inert medical device. As such, scientific evidence was all the more crucial, and counterintuitive, to create a convincing case for tampon-related TSS. Medical professionals, including family physicians, pediatricians, nephrologists, and specialized epidemiologists at the state and national levels, encountered ill girls and women, and they puzzled over the quick decline of otherwise healthy individuals. Important to physicians in identifying this illness were their robust social networks, in which they described symptoms to each other, shared case studies, and suggested treatments while "in the field." These networks influenced national-level conversations to establish a definition for the syndrome, and a comprehensive system of monitoring was developed for current and emergent cases. TSS arrived at a transitional time for the CDC, as the failed flu vaccine of 1978 created bad publicity about the effectiveness and necessity of the organization. AIDS also came on the heels of TSS. In retrospect, TSS was but a blip compared to the now global spread of HIV/AIDS, but by comparison TSS came to be viewed sympathetically, as an illness killing cherished mothers and daughters. Public health advocates' work was also called into question by corporate researchers who represented tampon manufacturers who were none too keen on this illness threatening projected tampon sales and profits. They argued that the epidemiologic methodology was circumscribed as well as skewed toward finding fault with synthetic tampons. This resulted in conflicting hypotheses about the mechanism and role of the tampon in TSS, with many competing studies sponsored by corporate grants.

Following the medical identification of tampon-related TSS, there was an urgent need to alert the hundreds of thousands of women using tampons that they were potentially dangerous and deadly. Disseminating a message of risk challenged status quo journalistic practices, and chapter 3 examines the media coverage of a health crisis centered on women's reproductive health and menstrual management practices. The press had to figure out a way to talk about TSS in overly simplistic terms, in an era when the Federal Communication Commission (FCC) had only recently allowed feminine hygiene sprays, and then sanitary napkins and pads, to be advertised on television. Despite the loosened policy, the words "tampon," "menstruation," and "period" were considered socially inappropriate for general audiences, and arguments about maintaining propriety versus informing women led to newsroom fights. As the CDC released findings from its studies linking superabsorbent tampons to TSS, the media's squeamishness transformed into paternalism, with safety messages cast on a perceived audience of needy women. By September of 1980, the Food and Drug Administration (FDA) threatened P&G with a product recall, causing P&G to voluntarily withdraw Rely from store shelves, and it also required the company to alert women to stop using the product. Journalistic reports of TSS helped to shape women's reception of the recall, both instilling fear and caution but also providing gentle assurances about the safety of tampons. This contributed to a sense that the problem had been solved, when only the issue of Rely tampons had been eliminated. Other biocatalytic tampons remained on the market.

Though the majority of women did not suffer from TSS, others experienced a flu-like illness, hospitalization, and even death from using Rely and other superabsorbent tampons. Lawyers filed lawsuits against all the major companies for selling a faulty product and failing to adequately disclose risk. Chapter 4 explores the 1982 federal court case *Kehm v. Procter & Gamble* in which the plaintiff's argument sought to prove that tampons were not inert, thereby exposing that corporate presumption as well as announcing it to the broader public. The lawsuit also provides a window into the emotional suffering of the Kehm family, who lost a mother, wife, sister, and daughter with Patricia Kehm's death as a result of using Rely during the fall of 1980. Much of the trial strategically deployed scientific witnesses from both sides to sway the jury. Corporate managers and scientists cast tampons and their components as inert, women's bodies as interchangeable lab instruments, and vaginal microflora as unimportant, all of which were positions challenged and ultimately undermined by the plaintiff's experts. Though P&G researchers tested individual components to ensure that they did not cause birth defects or cancers, and were neither poisonous nor prone to cause irritations, the trial revealed that, due to their assumptions, corporate-generated data did not predict the emergence of tampon-related TSS. In part, the ritual of safety testing proved to be a reassuring yet futile exercise that did not generate data indicative of true risk. Leaders at P&G insisted that TSS was an industrywide issue, tampons had a long record of safety, and Rely was singled out unfairly, despite the results garnered by the CDC indicating otherwise. Some of their points were credible, yet the lawsuit highlighted the need for better testing and product labeling in order to avert more TSS-related injuries and lawsuits.

Since the threat of TSS subsided but remained, how to manage it became a politically contested issue. Chapter 5 addresses the political stakes of science-based policy used to warn women about the risk of tampon-related TSS. Different stakeholders, including the federal government, corporations, and women's health activists, exerted pressure to control the terms of policy, product labeling, and the language of warnings printed on tampon boxes. Damage to women's bodies did not end with the removal of Rely from store shelves. The solution entailed corporations calling on women to practice autosurveillance and self-police their bodies for symptoms of TSS, in essence exonerating manufacturers and outsourcing responsibility to women themselves by urging them to use the least absorbent tampon possible. But, without accurate labeling, this advice rang hollow. How to educate women and protect them from contracting TSS became a contentious labeling issue because corporations were not forthcoming with material ingredients, product absorbency, or a clear warning about TSS. To help women make informed decisions, feminist health advocates sought to provide science-based information about tampon absorbency rates, implement federal standards for descriptions such as "regular" and "super," and also lobby for legislation demanding that tampon material contents be labeled on the box. In particular, Esther Rome of the Boston Women's Health Book Collective (BWHBC) imparted feminist-minded standards challenging androcentric methods and models of the lab that determined these absorbencies, exemplifying why science and scientists must be accountable to communities and not just corporate data production.

The book concludes by examining the results and consequences of the bacteriological, technological, medical, journalistic, legal, and political influences on current-day understandings of TSS in the contemporary United States. Most are aware of controversies of hormonal birth control or the questionable safety of breast implants. However, the history of federal regulation of personal hygiene products, and activists' efforts to improve safety, arguably touched more women than these other more familiar stories. Significantly, the actions of labeling tampon boxes, providing information about material and chemical content, and offering more understandable warnings about TSS remain incomplete. Congresswoman Carolyn Maloney (D-NY) first introduced the Tampon Safety and Research Act in 1997, reintroducing it again in 2003, 2005, 2008, and 2011, to no avail. On May 28, 2014, Menstrual Hygiene Day, she again proposed it as the renamed Robin Danielson Act regarding tampon safety, in recognition of Danielson's death due to TSS in 1998 at age forty-four. The bill seeks further research into the chemical composition of tampons, additives, and their relationship to TSS since potential health hazards are not well researched or understood. This book supports the rationale for federal regulation and the need for transparent content labeling.

Contemporary Scientific Explanations

Current understandings about TSS are contested and evolving; moreover, succinct recommendations are difficult to crystallize. One hypothesis is that tampons alter the vaginal environment. Michael Osterholm, a Regents Professor at the University of Minnesota, who worked as an epidemiologist at the Minnesota Department of Health during the late 1970s and 1980s, specifically studied different brands of tampons and the relationship of absorbency to TSS. His studies identified higher absorbency tampons and their ability to hold oxygen within the otherwise anaerobic vagina as the key element in promoting toxin production.[16] For Osterholm, the oxygenation made all the difference in providing an ideal environment for the *S. aureus* bacterium to grow. In my interview with him he recalled that many news reports stated that TSS was related to poor hygiene, and therefore the advice was to change tampons frequently. This, he said was wrong. The fresh tampons simply brought in more air, thus fueling the toxin production once it got rolling. His research pointed to all superabsorbent tampons, in which Rely was only one example, boosting the risk for TSS from three-fold to nearly ten-fold as absorptive capacity increased.[17]

Where Osterholm saw gradients in tampon absorbency as significant, others focused on the material composition of superabsorbent tampons, especially the all-synthetic design of the Rely tampon. Philip Tierno, a microbiologist, contends in his 2004 book *The Secret Life of Germs* that there were three major factors promoting TSS in women who used noncotton tampons and, in particular, Rely. First were the synthetic components of Rely, consisting of foam cubes and the gelling agent carboxymethylcellulose encased in a polyester pouch. Tierno suggests that the gelled carboxymethylcellulose in essence acted like agar in a petri dish, providing a viscous medium on which the bacterium could flourish. Along with this, the foam cubes offered increased surface area for rapid growth. Second was the changing pH of the vagina during menstruation, to about 7.4. The optimal pH for *S. aureus* to trigger TSS is 7, or neutral. The relatively acidic, nonmenstrual vagina measures a pH of about 4.2, which keeps *S. aureus* well in check. Tierno also supported Osterholm's claim that a tampon introduces air into the usually anaerobic vagina, changing the environmental conditions. Finally, the pyrogenic toxins produced by *S. aureus* induced fever in humans. This fever of about 102 degrees proved to be the perfect temperature for *S. aureus* to reproduce and thus create further deadly toxins.[18] An additional factor was a woman's age; many adults had built up immunity to *S. aureus* and possessed the toxin antibody, while young women and teenagers were more susceptible without a developed immune response. As a result, TSS had a range of presentations from mild flu-like symptoms to literal septic shock.

Even in a recent 2016 interview in *People* magazine, JoAnn Pinkerson, a professor of obstetrics and gynecology and director of the Midlife Health Center, University of Virginia Health System, discussed how TSS can develop, but not its relationship to tampons. She deconstructed a four-step process of the illness in an attempt to simplify the explanation. The first step "is vaginal colonization with a strain of *S. aureus*, which can make the toxin," and not all *S. aureus* strains do. The bacterium then produces the toxin, and enough must be produced to penetrate "across the vaginal epithelium." Once this toxin leaves the confines of the vagina and enters the bloodstream, the illness requires "a lack of adequate titers of the neutralizing antibody to the toxin."[19] Though this description helps to explain the mechanism, it does not address the important variable of a tampon used to absorb menstrual fluid and its place within the chain of events leading to TSS. Furthermore, this is still not well comprehended by most women.

Patrick Schlievert, a microbiologist and head of the Microbiology department at the University of Iowa who studied *S. aureus* and TSS from the very beginning, argues that the particular strain that produced TSST-1 happened to gain traction about the same time that superabsorbents were marketed to women, so that the illness was coincidental.[20] This strain made the difference in the presentation of illness, and not necessarily the components of the tampon. In an email conversation with him, he described *S. aureus* as tremendously adaptive, as a "facultative bacterium." A facultative bacterium is quite resilient and able to assess changing environmental conditions. He explained, "It has oxidative metabolism for aerobic growth and fermentation for anaerobic growth," meaning it can still produce its own energy in either aerobic or anaerobic environments. *S. aureus* can potentially grow in both, but it really flourishes when oxygen is present, introduced in this case by a tampon. In addition, the normally fluctuating pH of the vaginal ecosystem affects bacterial inhabitants, and *S. aureus* thrives in the less acidic menstrual medium and the newly oxygenated environment provided by a tampon. To add more variables, he explained that different bacteria such as a healthy population of lactobacilli interact with the body and affect vaginal pH levels as well, possibly holding *S. aureus* at bay during the nonbleeding weeks of the menstrual cycle, or prompting flare-ups during menstruation.[21] The last element adding to the virulence of TSS is the powerful toxin, TSST-1, characterized as a protein and superantigen that disrupts and overactivates the immune system.[22]

In light of such a multifactored process with a menstrual management technology, and scientists' differing explanations of it even now, it is no wonder confusion and justifiable fear reigned in the late 1970s and throughout the 1980s. Manufacturers currently recommend that women use the least absorbent tampons possible and change them often. This seems sound, yet tampons do not directly cause TSS per se, and limited use will not necessarily prevent the illness. And it is the toxin, not even the presence of the bacterium, that ultimately generates the symptoms. The only way to really prevent TSST-1 production is to avoid *S. aureus* altogether, which is impossible.

In addition, women are not usually tested to see if they have the antibody to the TSS toxin, which would indicate immunity. Without this antibody, a previous and recovered encounter with TSS indicates increased risk for its virulent expression the second time around, possibly leading to autoimmune issues for some women. Testing for the antibody may help point both to women who are more resilient to the toxin and to those who would need to steer clear of tampons.[23] Instead, manufacturers rely on informed women knowing the signs and symptoms of TSS, which are deceptively similar to the common cold and difficult to discern as life threatening. This explains not only my generalized concern as a young teenager about contracting TSS, but also the daily pleas for help posted to social media outlets by young menstruating women, beseeching anyone for advice about whether or not they are experiencing TSS. The fears run deeper still, with researchers unsettled by the possibility of the TSST-1 strain and MRSA variant exchanging genes, which could create a very frightening "super bug" primed to affect tampon-using women.[24]

Gendered Approaches

A cornerstone of gender studies has been to question biological determinism and the fixity of binary meanings, such as man/woman, male/female, masculine/feminine. Women's studies, gender studies, feminist theory, and queer studies have pressed hard against the notion of a universal male and androcentric conception of the world, with a growing awareness for more intersectional understandings of humans. Feminist theory has a large swath of scholarship addressing the body, its social construction, and how meaning is derived from embodiment. Elizabeth Wilson, a scholar of women's and gender studies, argues that as important as this work is to the very identity and contours of feminist theory, it tends to be "antibiological." She adds, "There is a powerful paradox in play: antibiologism both places significant conceptual limitations on feminist theory *and* has been one of the means by which feminist theory has prospered."[25] I have found my research in this paradox that Wilson describes. The material reality of menstrual fluid, the repeated cyclical nature of menstruation, and the illness of TSS are indeed visceral and biological, felt in real time by humans existing in day-to-day activities. I have also read my fair share of scientific journal articles for this research, trying to both understand TSS at the cellular level while also being mindful of the culture in which the science is situated, analyzing it with a feminist eye. While at the University of Illinois, my colleague Cris Mayo joked that I was the only person left in the department studying actual women's bodies, the field had so moved into other areas. It is in this tension that research on biology about menstruation and the engineering of menstrual management technologies fall. It is the case of "both/and." TSS is both technobiological and socially constructed, and it must be read back and forth and across.

Discussions about menstruation on the whole need more thoughtful attention to meanings and their implications. There has been an unquestioning link between menstruation and identities of womanhood, which falls back on an essentialist understanding of "woman," and that conveniently sustains the man/woman binary. This reified notion, however, does not capture the whole picture of women or men or of the interplay of gender. The growing attention to transgender individuals has made it clear that biological body parts and processes do not define a woman. Yet menstruation has most definitely been a sign of being a woman, and as the feminist philosopher Denise Riley comments in *Am I That Name?*, menstruation summons a woman back to her body, often read as inferior to men, despite all the ways she may try to transcend prejudice with her mind, actions, and efforts.[26] Thus menstruation has been a fraught subject of study, and in my book *Under Wraps* I traced how pro-woman physicians worked to break menstrual stigmas and conceptualize menstruation as normal rather than a sign of weakness and infirmity.

Menstruation remains a strong signifier of woman, yet this is not entirely accurate. When I refer to "women" and "woman" in this book, I fall into the trap of signifying those humans who menstruate, did menstruate, or could menstruate. Yet this is shortsighted, for there are many kinds of women among us who do not menstruate. Though this list is not exhaustive, menopause, hysterectomy, pharmaceuticals, pregnancy, lactation, endocrine issues, excessive exercise, and other causes, as well as being transgender, are all reasons why women might not menstruate. I used the term "menstruant" and referred to women using menstrual hygiene technologies who temporarily pass as "nonmenstruants" in *Under Wraps*, but perhaps it would be better to refer not to women, but to "menstruators" as Chris Bobel explores in her book *New Blood: Third-Wave Feminism and the Politics of Menstruation*, since all women, however that category is understood, do not menstruate.[27] This would also allow space for those transgender men, along the various spectrum of transitioning, who do have periods. They are menstruators, too. It is not the intention of the book to write a queer history of menstruation, but one needs to be written, and I want to acknowledge the shortcomings of terms in writing about women and menstruation. Because I cannot escape the trap of language, in the book I employ the more historically bound usage of "women," in large part because that is what the archival sources mean and what stakeholders understood within contemporary popular debates. In an effort to disaggregate essentialist terms, "menstruator" is far more accurate and I also utilize that term throughout the book.

* * *

"[W]hat if you died from toxic shock syndrome and they put that in your obituary letting everyone know you died from a tampon[?]"[28] This question from a Twitter feed captures the common knowledge that tampons cause TSS, and that death from a tampon would be embarrassing and shameful. It also implies it would be a stupid way to die, in that such a death is both unnecessary and preventable. This sentiment—that it should not happen and it is avoidable—haunts those who contract TSS, and it circulates as an urban/suburban myth, blaming women for their tragic illness. If only they followed the warning signs. This is quite unfair and displaces responsibility. Corporations must be more forthcoming with ingredient labeling, and medicine can and should offer preventative tests.

For menstruators who have used and do use tampons, the nagging warning about TSS is pervasive. I untangle the history of tampon-related TSS by examining scientific discovery and lack thereof, policy and lack thereof, as well as women's reactions and the ways that many women paid the ultimate price by contracting a horrible illness and even dying due to the biocatalytic reaction that the tampon set into motion. Only extreme conditions prompted actions about tampon-related TSS, and this should be heeded as a warning for other similar kinds of unexpected and unintended techno-bacteriological illnesses. How tampon-related TSS was understood, reported on, and managed affects us to this very day and reveals the tensions inherent to relationships among feminism, medical science, technological developments, and bacterial agents of the human body.

1

Unexpected Consequences

A tampon is a thing. A bacterium is a life form. These assertions, however, are shortsighted. As it turns out, and as toxic shock syndrome (TSS) came to attest, both are quite more dynamic together than anyone ever imagined. This was difficult to envision because of the overwhelming assumption that tampons were inert, disposable objects. They sometimes caused irritation, an allergic reaction from embedded perfumes, or lacerations from an applicator, but they were not conceptualized as dynamic. That a bacterium typically associated with food poisoning or boils might possibly develop into a strain that could produce septic shock seemed like a stretch, but it became accepted knowledge. Agreeing on a new ailment of TSS and further specifying it as tampon-related TSS became part of a repertoire of illnesses predominantly affecting women.

What is not well conceptualized, and an idea that I propose here, is that during this process a bacterium became the overlooked and unintended user of tampons, thus changing the relationship of user/technology. The bacterium advantageously capitalized on the technological innovation to reproduce and multiply. Though tampons were intended for menstruating women to be the dominant users of the technology, it is constructive to think of bacteria as users, too. This changes subject/object orientation, thus shifting the conditions of agency. It is here that the relational activity of technology and bacterium must be far better conceptualized and understood as co-agents of unintended illness.

This chapter focuses on this relational activity. There are many conceptual underpinnings that need to be addressed to better understand this techno-bacteriological relationship. First, tampons are a technology, with a history of design and development during the twentieth century. Second, they share in common the ability to cause gendered injury, like many other technologies used to manage and regulate women's reproductive bodies. As such, and third, they fall into a loosely woven safety net of the Medical Device Amendments (MDA), which in theory provide a process by which therapeutic technology undergoes testing to assess its compatibility with the human body and its proclivity to do harm. Fourth, what these tests do not predict is how other organisms in and of the human body will interact with medical devices, because technology is not neutral or inert. This has a direct effect on the next important concept: that bacteria possess the ability to become technological users, and, as users, create unintended consequences for humans with which they share an ecological space. Finally, this techno-bacteriological interface has been poorly anticipated in terms of design and risk, so that resultant injury appears unexpectedly, as a surprise. The indecorous subject of tampons and menstruation made it difficult for many to willingly concede the game-changing scope of this technobiological illness.[1]

Tampons as Technologies

Tampons were neither regulated nor particularly trusted technologies when they first commercially appeared in the form of Tampax in 1936. They required a good degree of domestication as emergent technologies, accompanied by educational advertising teaching women about the benefits of the technology.[2] Because tampons were phallic-like in shape and a perceived threat to the virginal hymen, some educators, nurses, and parents felt convinced to leave well enough alone. They promoted the use of disposable sanitary napkins instead for adolescent girls.[3] Yet, by the 1940s, many young women were early adopters, because they recognized how tampons relieved them of the physical encumbrance of elastic belts, long tabs, and uncomfortably thick pads worn between the thighs.[4] Advertising, menstrual hygiene education films, and word of mouth shifted many women's opinions about tampons from dubious to acceptable; under certain circumstances such as dancing, swimming, or working long shifts, many embraced them as a useful tool of physical liberation.[5] Still, there was much cloaking, double entendre, and indirect language about how and when to use a tampon. To the uninitiated, the cryptic language of advertising made tampons seem like magic in a box; I have anecdotally heard more than once that a thoughtful but unknowing young boy would gift a girl in first or second grade this special box because she could do all kinds of amazing things with it, like ride horses or bikes, and do gymnastics.

By the 1960s, through skillful advertising campaigns, companies successfully associated bodily freedom and women's liberation with the use of tampon technologies.[6] Once women accepted tampons, they entered into a tacit agreement with the corporation, assuming that this commodity was safe. There were some complaints of abrasions, strings breaking, products leaking, and contact dermatitis related to deodorants and perfumes embedded in tampon materials. Other complaints regarded problems of disposal and clogged plumbing when they were flushed down the toilet. Yet, overall, cotton tampons enjoyed a solid reputation. They may not have worked well for all women, but they could be viewed similar to a bandage: a medical dressing to absorb blood.

Though we often think of tampons as static objects, designers, chemists, and inventors, working on behalf of large corporations, filed many patents to transform the plain old cotton tampon into something they thought would be significantly better and thus gain a larger share of the market. Though Tampax may have been the first cotton tampon to be successfully commercialized in 1936, others with different designs soon followed. Wix, a competitor of Tampax in the 1930s, incorporated a cellophane sheath, which, according to the inventor Frederick Richardson, was "to hold the body of the absorbent material in its proper desired shape, and in part, to enable the plug to be easily inserted into working position."[7] He suggested that deodorants such as phenol, peppermint, or wintergreen could be added easily to the cotton. At the Personal Products Corporation—a Johnson & Johnson subsidiary—George C. Graham developed a patent for a flexible tampon composed of "cotton, rayon, paper, hemp or wool" in 1957.[8] Simultaneously, he applied for a patent for a tampon composed of absorptive salts, including sodium carboxyethylcellulose or sodium carboxymethylcellulose.[9] He also received a patent in 1960 for a "tow tampon." This tampon would have longer rather than shorter filaments for better absorption of fluids by creating capillaries. This patent made claim on a particular manufacturing process and design, but imagined a variety of materials to satisfy the end product of a tampon.

Patenting as broadly as possible was common practice, and materials included "Dacron" polymeric polyester, nylon, viscose rayon, vinyl fibers, acrylic fibers, "saran" polymeric vinyl chloride, polyethylene, glass fibers, protein fibers, and silk.[10] Polyester emerged as a synthetic fiber in the 1950s, and the reference in the patent to Dacron reflected the proprietary name given to it by DuPont. Also by 1960, scientists at Kimberly-Clark Corporation, the maker of Kotex sanitary napkins, had received patents for tampons composed of 60 percent cotton and 40 percent "crimped viscose rayon staple fibers."[11] The variety of materials indicated that inventors were thinking beyond cotton grown on the farm, to fibers and substances easily created in the lab.

Viscose rayon emerged as a popular addition to tampons, proving to be both absorbent and cheap to procure. Derived from wood cellulose, it is processed with other chemicals, dried, and spun to form fibers. Unlike cotton or silk, which retain their properties and characteristics, chemical processes transform cellulose into a semi-synthetic fiber. Most of the popular brands of tampons—Tampax, Playtex, o.b., Kotex—have incorporated rayon, but because the labeling of ingredients is not mandated, that information is not readily available.[12] By 1996, researchers felt that there were only two all-cotton tampons available to test; all the rest contained rayon.[13] In part, Tambrands introduced "Tampax Naturals" that same year, calling the product line "the first U.S.-made all-cotton tampon"—despite that same composition of the original Tampax—in response to some women's desires for a natural tampon. However, rayon continues to be used as a core component of tampons. Even the employees of the Good Shepherd Food-Bank in Maine, on a goodwill tour of the neighboring Tambrands manufacturing plant in 2012, waxed eloquent about the machinery as it produced Tampax Pearl tampons, made out of both cotton and rayon, the fibers "spun into a solid mat."[14]

Inventors continued to develop new fibers and materials during the 1960s and 1970s. The scientists Billy Harper, Robert Bashaw, and Bobby Atkins developed sodium polyacrylate for Dow Chemical Company, filing a patent for the chemical in 1966.[15] Due to its polymer structure containing sodium ions, sodium polyacrylate absorbs anywhere from 200 to 1,000 times its own weight in water. The material forms into a gel, which in essence holds fluids. In 1978, Russell L. Johnson for the Kimberly-Clark Corporation devised a digital tampon meant to be inserted with a finger. It used a cotton-rayon fiber base, and capitalized on the newly developed "super absorbent fibers," including polyacrylate, cross-linked polyurethane, or polyester foam.[16] Currently, sodium polyacrylate is a common absorbent in disposable baby diapers.[17] Of course, bodily fluids from urine to menstrual fluid are not pure water, thus the polyacrylate is not as effective with salts and proteins, so it must be paired with other materials to produce an absorbent tampon or diaper less likely to leak.

By the mid-1970s, the leading tampon manufacturers landed patents for tampons that included some derivative of carboxymethylcellulose (CMC) as one of its absorbent components. CMC, derived from the more familiar plant material of cellulose, when synthesized by a reaction with chloroacetic acid, becomes a viscose thickening agent, shifting from powder to gel when introduced to liquids. It is used as a food additive to stabilize emulsions, such as ice cream, but also to help with gelling texture in toothpaste, detergents, or paints. It is considered nontoxic and hypoallergenic, and by all appearances, it is a dream material with which to work due to its relative stability. International Playtex, Inc., filed a patent for "preparation of water-insoluble carboxymethyl cellulose absorbents" in 1978, the purpose of which was for absorbency in a tampon.[18] Kimberly-Clark filed a patent in 1976 for a compressed tampon composed of absorbent fibers, including carboxymethylcellulose.[19]

By 1974 Procter & Gamble (P&G) already test-marketed its synthetic Rely, composed of a polyester sheath, compressed polyurethane (and later polyester) foam cubes, and carboxymethylcellulose, but continued to hone its own version of a CMC tampon, as evidenced by its patent encompassing many "absorbent devices" filed in 1981.[20] Incorporating CLD-2—the trade name for cross-linked CMC manufactured by Buckeye Cellulose Corporation, a subsidiary of P&G—this iteration of the tampon also included Pluronic L-92, a nonionic surfactant manufactured by BASF, helping the fibers to be more hydrophilic, and referred to as "mensesphilic" in the patent.[21] The significance of this surfactant would not be discovered until the early 1990s, when researchers found that Pluronic L-92 increased production of the TSST-1 toxin.[22] It is unfair to characterize this lack of oversight as purposeful, yet the zeal for superabsorbents overrode their downside.

In effect, the chemistry of absorbent materials had so flourished that the term "superabsorbents" defined this new category. A 1979 article title in *Chemical Week* proclaimed "Superabsorbents Seek Markets That Are Super," indicating the turn from plain old cotton or rayon to highly processed and synthesized components in search of applications for customer purchase.[23] The writer noted that personal care products and

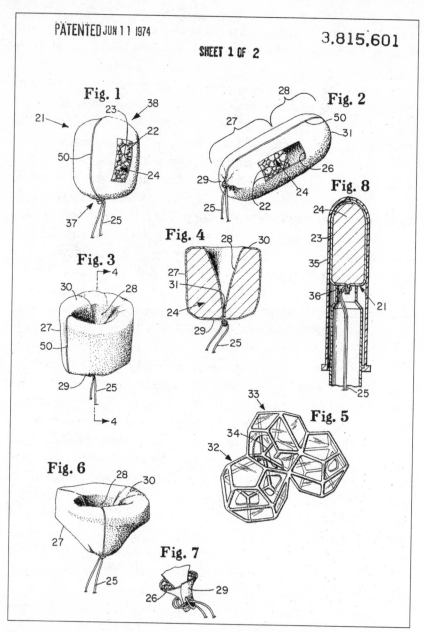

Figure 1.1. Patent for Rely Tampons, 1974. This patent displays Rely's novel features, including the shape, sheath, inserter, and polyurethane cells, later replaced with polyester foam. Source: Jean Schaefer, inventor; Procter & Gamble Company, assignee. Catamenial Aggregate Absorbent Body, US Patent 3,815,601, filed May 9, 1973 and assigned June 11, 1974.

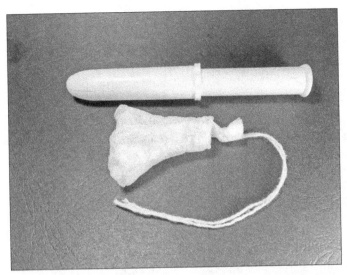

Figure 1.2. Rely Tampon and applicator (side view). The plastic applicator houses and inserts the tampon. The unique composition of the tampon is quite light and airy compared to a compressed cotton tampon. Photo by Sharra Vostral.

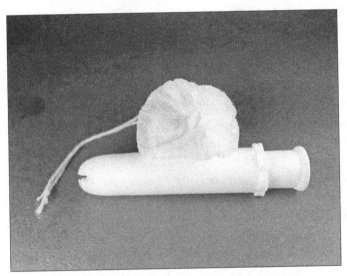

Figure 1.3. Rely Tampon and applicator (front view). The polyester casing is visible here, showing the cuplike shape as it expands, referred to as a "rosette." Within the case are small polyester foam cubes and the thickening agent carboxymethylcellulose. This tampon came from an unused sample box. Photo by Sharra Vostral.

diapers were prime areas for applying these new polymers, since superabsorbents could soak up 50 to 1,500 times their weight in water. Yet the weekly urged that "consumer education must be undertaken to promote other uses for the materials and to dispel the notion that absorbent means bulky." Because traditional materials required more volume rather than less to absorb an equivalent amount, this common wisdom needed to be dispelled to show that "new-and-improved" translated into a sleeker, smaller product.

Problematic Female-Specific Technologies

That tampons should be artifacts worth "modernizing" fits into the ideological scope of progressive science and technological determinism offered during the 1960s and 1970s. NASA experienced great success with the space program, inspiring a new generation of scientists to dream big in spite of the risks. Faster, nonhuman mainframe computers crunched mathematical formulas at blistering speeds. Insecticides and herbicides applied to crops yielded greater harvests, with abundance to share. And petrochemicals and plastics could be manufactured more efficiently and more cheaply than just about any material that they replaced. Scientists, it seemed, held the keys to nature itself and could not only solve the world's problems but also do it better than ever imagined. Though we now recognize there are costs for all this "progress" that were oftentimes conveniently ignored, nonetheless these huge scientific and technological gains created the impression that no problem was beyond the scope of technoscientific solutions.

The science of medicine developed further as well, with women's bodies and health needs receiving renewed attention. With the wild success of the birth control pill, corporations could no longer ignore women's desires to manage their own fertility and experience better pregnancies. Thus, progressive science and scientific medicine heeded the cultural message and began delivering more options to women, ranging from disposable baby bottles, to New Freedom sanitary pads, and, more ominously, products that caused injury as well.

One such pharmaceutical was thalidomide, a sedative prescribed to pregnant women to treat morning sickness and nausea. Widely available throughout Europe, Australia, and Canada during the 1950s and 1960s, thousands of women took the medication, unknowingly exposing their fetuses to toxins that caused birth defects, most notably the absence of limbs. Interestingly, it was a female physician hired in 1960 by the Food and Drug Administration (FDA) who stalled the drug's application in the United States, ultimately refusing its approval. Frances Kelsey, a pharmacologist who worked on a treatment for malaria among other projects, upended the erroneously held assumption that the placenta was impervious to chemicals by recognizing that its porous composition allowed pharmaceuticals to pass through it. Furthermore, pharmaceuticals affected adults, children, and fetuses quite differently. Her readings of British studies on thalidomide pointed to enough concerns that she requested further scientific testing rather than relying on more testimonials from the Richardson-Merrell pharmaceutical company. Kelsey held firm, despite pressure and bullying for the drug's approval, and demanded more proof of safety. By late 1961, German health authorities had linked thalidomide to birth defects, and they recalled the drug, which was available there over the counter. The March of Dimes estimated that more than 10,000 children were born with defects due to thalidomide, though only seventeen were connected to it in the United States, in no small part due to Kelsey.[24] It took until 2012 for the manufacturer Gruenenthal Group and its chief executive to apologize for the tragedy unleashed by the drug.

In a similar example, the Dalkon Shield, an intrauterine device (IUD) intended to prevent pregnancy, by all accounts seemed to be a promising method of birth control yet it also delivered unintended injuries. Though IUDs were not new, the design of the Dalkon Shield was unique—a plastic horseshoe crablike insert with fins, that when installed in the uterus encouraged white blood cell activity that in turn attacked sperm when present. With national marketing beginning in January 1971, over 2.5 million women used the Dalkon Shield, manufactured by A. H. Robins Company, until it was voluntarily withdrawn from the market in 1974.[25] At that time, the FDA did not require stringent testing of medical devices, and the agency's only recourse was to issue a recall after a sufficient number of physicians and patients reported problems.[26]

The undoing of the Dalkon Shield was its multifilament tail string covered in a nylon sheath that remained attached to the device after insertion so that it could be removed at a later date. It turned out that this string was prone to knotting and perforating, thus creating a perfect wicking agent, drawing bacteria from the vagina into the usually sterile uterus. For many women, pelvic inflammatory disease resulted, including infection, scarring of the fallopian tubes, and, in the worst cases, damage leading to a hysterectomy. For some women, the plastic fins on the device embedded into the uterus. For others, the device did not prevent conception and instead led to "septic spontaneous abortion" in which bacteria that wicked from the IUD infected the placenta and then the woman; this resulted in not only unwanted pregnancies and illness, but also eighteen deaths.[27] Compounding the grief brought on by a birth control device that caused permanent infertility was the revelation that A. H. Robins had previous knowledge of its defects. When A. H. Robins purchased the IUD from Dalkon Corporation, confidential memoranda noted the device's proclivity to wick.[28] More than 300,000 parties sued A. H. Robins in product liability cases, which continued well into the 1980s and ultimately led to the downfall of the company.

Medicines and devices related to women's reproductive health that caused far worse problems than the ones they promised to solve understandably created fear and anger. It was unwelcomed and unwanted news that novel solutions to maternal health and birth control led to damaging consequences in this era of "progressive" technoscience. There was also something particularly troubling about the damage caused to women's reproductive health when some scientists, physicians, and business representatives chose to ignore problems and instead narrow the frame of vision to exclude glaring errors. It is not a large leap to apply Langdon Winner's provocative thesis that politics are embedded into objects and technological artifacts to understand how these devices embodied societal ignorance and sexism.[29]

Yet, in the same era, women's liberation gained traction and feminism provided tools to critique medical "progress" and generate dissent.[30] In part, the women's health movement, begun in the late 1960s, called for woman-friendly, woman-centered approaches to women's life-course health needs, epitomized by information distributed in *Our Bodies, Ourselves*, edited by the Boston Women's Health Book Collective.[31] When the universal male stood in for all things human, and an androcentric approach devalued women's health concerns, the women's health movement insisted on the normalcy of women's reproductive life cycles, as well as the need for woman-friendly health advice. The force of women's health advocates was abundantly clear at the congressional hearing on the pill in 1970, with protesters bringing a halt to the all-male proceedings. Feminist health advocates could now mark side effects and ill health associated with medical "progress" as a significant cost rather than mere inconveniences to be endured.[32] They pressured public health officials and regulators to be accountable, and this marked an important shift in medicine to recognize patients' rights.[33]

Medical Device Amendments of 1976

The way that medical devices were viewed changed as well in the 1970s as a result of new regulatory policies brought forth by the 1976 Medical Device Amendments (MDA) to the Federal Food, Drug and Cosmetic Act (FFDCA). The FFDCA currently provides definitions for food (including chewing gum), food additives such as food coloring, dietary supplements, and even tobacco. In 1938, the FFDCA gave the FDA authority to oversee not only food and drugs, but cosmetics as well, in part to quell the cases of misleading labeling, egregious health claims, and outright dangerous additives to comestibles and medicines. However, there was no formalized review process specifically for devices, ranging from instruments to diagnose diseases to apparatuses worn on or implanted into the body, and the products required no official approval. Items such as sanitary pads and tampons, however, were classified as cosmetics (an odd fit rationalized because they touched the skin) and received minimal regulatory attention.

Passage of the MDA of 1976 gained traction in Congress, with Senator Edward Kennedy its prime advocate. Serious, undisclosed defects in technologies such as pacemakers, IUDs, and intraocular lenses caused harm and injury to patients, leaving a trail of product liability lawsuits in their wake. To address this regulatory deficiency, the amendment also created the Bureau of Medical Devices within the FDA specifically to monitor applications for approval.[34] According to the amendments, a medical device covers a broad range of instruments, diagnostic tools, and mechanical interventions to mitigate human health; it does not cover "chemical action," which is generally under the purview of drugs in the FDA.[35] The amendment also set parameters for three classes of medical devices according to their perceived risk. Class I requires the least regulatory control, including items such as dental floss, bed pans, or examination gloves. Class II calls for further assurances of safety, labeling, and monitoring to assess harm and prevent injury to patients. Powered wheelchairs, hearing aids, and tampons fall into this category. Class III represents those technologies, such as artificial hearts, that are novel and sustain human life but may cause harm due to their experimental nature.

Complicating the 1976 classification system was the treatment of devices considered to have a long-standing record of safety. According to David Kessler, who would later become the commissioner of the FDA in 1990,

> Pre-amendment devices are assigned to the least-regulated class that is sufficient to provide reasonable assurance of safety and effectiveness. Post-amendment devices that are deemed "substantially equivalent" to pre-amendment devices are assigned to the same class as their comparable pre-amendment devices and may be marketed after the manufacturer provides the FDA with premarketing notification.[36]

Thus, "if a manufacturer can establish substantial equivalence," it need only provide the FDA with a premarket notification. If not, the device must go through premarket approval. And, according to Kessler, since the "substantial equivalence" clause encompasses far less testing, cost, and time, it benefits a company to have its device ushered through the regulatory process with premarket notification.

In general, most tampons on the market before 1976 were "grandfathered" in to the new classification system, whereby manufacturers established "substantial equivalence."[37] Furthermore, tampons were categorized as Class II medical devices, a significant definitional shift from cosmetics. Despite the intentions to protect users, the system missed many new technological changes due to the language of "substantial equivalence." Thus, tampons marketed before 1976 fell into the least regulated class. This is significant to the TSS story and Rely tampons. Rely was first test-marketed in Fort Wayne, Indiana, in 1974 and P&G was not bound by federal law to produce new evidence of safety because it was technically a "pre-amendment device."[38] Thus, even though Rely tampons were relatively new in terms of composition, they were a Class II medical device previously distributed and did not require extra testing or scrutiny.

One of the shortcomings of the MDA is the way it renders medical technologies inert. Artifacts such as joint replacements, cochlear implants, and even wound dressings are technologies that affect biological systems, and they are increasingly intended for internal bodily use. Nelly Oudshoorn, who studies technology dynamics and healthcare, suggests that there are different harms associated with invisible technologies of the body, or those technologies not "seen" but found internally. She asks, "What forms of vulnerability emerge when technology moves under the skin?" Her research examines implantable cardioverter defibrillators (ICDs), more generally referred to as pacemakers. These ICDs regularize the beats of a heart but also tend to send out rogue shocks that come on without warning and are uncomfortable to endure. She argues that "vulnerabilities faced by . . . ICD users introduce other ways of coping with harm than the vulnerabilities caused by technologies external to bodies." Some of these coping mechanisms include keeping large magnets nearby to neutralize the shock, or alternatively feeling despondent about not only heart disease but also the painful treatment.[39] Because the technologies cannot be removed, and managing the underlying medical condition holds prominence over all other concerns, there is no respite from the detrimental "side effects" of the therapeutic technology with which the patient must comply.

Bacterium and Agential Power

These kinds of medical harms are not a surprise when viewed through Bruno Latour's provocative notion of technological agency, which offers a means to include objects, as nonhuman actors, on par with humans in considering relationships, outcomes, and events.[40] Latour's actor-network theory has been well discussed, and it is not my aim to enter into that debate. However, it, along with Stephen J. Collier and Aihwa Ong's development of "global assemblages," brings to bear the "new material, collective, and discursive relationships" of objects and things.[41] The political theorist Jane Bennett in *Vibrant Matter* expounds on this notion of material agency and the recalcitrance of things. She explores the vitality and capacity of things "not only to impede or block the will and designs of humans but also to act as quasi agents or forces with trajectories, propensities, or tendencies of their own."[42] This approach challenges the knee-jerk reaction to dismiss things, nonhumans, and technologies as just "stuff" and instead encounter them on their own accord and on their own terms. It is exactly this lack, and the correlating construction of tampons as inert, that fails to imagine them as energetic things with capacity to enact change.

If I replace the word "objects" with "bacteria" in the previous paragraph, this also changes the perspective about their agency in relation to humans. This should not be unforeseen, given the growing recognition of the deep relationship of bacteria to human life. The Human Microbiome Project sponsored by the National Institutes of Health (NIH) has revealed only a small fraction of the ways in which human bodies are intertwined with microbial entities.[43] According to Lita Procter of the NIH, who leads the Human Microbiome Project, "The definition of a human microbiome is all the microbial microbes [sic] that live in and on our bodies but also all the genes—all the metabolic capabilities they bring to supporting human health." Approximately only one in ten cells are "human," and the rest belong to everything else.[44] Furthermore, the mycobiome more specifically focuses on viruses and fungi, and this must also be incorporated to help counter the predominant attention given to bacteria in the microbiome.[45]

Despite the Western belief in rationality and individualism, we can hardly make the claim of personal sovereignty once we account for the flora and fauna that each of us supports, as well as support us, in our own ecosystems. The microbiome project, for my purposes here, helps to challenge the primacy of the human as the sole life force of the body. From this perspective, it makes sense that bacteria should be considered as agents, with the ability to act and influence outcomes. As Karen Barad, a feminist theorist, explains, "Agency is not held, it is not a property of persons or things; rather, agency is an enactment, a matter of possibilities for reconfiguring entanglements." Furthermore, if agency is enactment, which is not necessarily human centered, it helps take into account "entanglements of intra-acting human and non-human practices."[46] Thus, *Staphylococcus aureus* and tampons configured a new illness entanglement that crested in the early 1980s.

Generally, it has not been understood that bacteria intra-act, entangle, or configure. These are neutral conceptualizations, without judgment of outcome. Instead, bacteria are usually categorized by relational characteristics that indicate their increasing capacity to do harm to humans. "Symbiotic" is the least threatening, with organisms living and interacting together.[47] More specifically a relationship to bacteria may be mutual (benefiting both organisms), commensal (benefiting one but not harming the other), and parasitic (living at the expense of the other). Microbes on and in the human body are often described as "microbial inhabitants" or "microbial communities."[48] Some are even "residential microbial communities," which offers the bacteria a degree of legitimacy, as if they live in an appropriate suburban setting. Though these terms gesture to greater relational structures, it still seems that the bacteria are a community unto themselves. Michael Wilson, a microbiologist, acknowledges the dependency that humans have on them, and he describes a "human-microbe symbiosis," going so far as to refer to each of us as having a "microbial self."[49] Though this affords greater recognition of the work of bacteria, it still leaves the human self as the dominant life form.

As Linda Nash, a scholar of environmental history, points out, the modern conceptualization of the body relies on a bacteriological notion of disease as existing outside an otherwise healthful person, and this model applies to pollution, too. Although her concern is to highlight the deleterious effects of environmental toxins by reclaiming the ecological body—one more porous and situated within a landscape and polluted environment—this model is useful as one looking inward to the landscapes of the microbiome as well.[50] The body as a dynamic ecological space, a metaphorical rain forest, helps to recognize it beyond that of the human sentient being. Stefan Helmreich, an anthropologist who studies science, suggests that a reconceptualized nomenclature for humans, *Homo microbis*, may better reflect the makeup of human beings and the "microscopic companion species" laced throughout our bodies that are intrinsic to who we think we are as humans. Heather Paxson, an anthropologist who studies food, offers "microbiopolitics" to frame the ways in which "microscopic biologic agents" configure not just our microbiome, but also politics in public health and food safety, and how humans arrange structures of power.[51] Furthermore, Helmreich describes "symbiopolitics" as a term to refer to "the densely political relations among many entangled living things—not just microbial—at many scales."[52] I build on symbio- and microbiopolitics and argue that we must also engage these organisms as users with technologies in and of the body.

Instead of referring to bacteria as residents or inhabitants as they are also sometimes called, claiming bacteria as constituents acknowledges their greater agential power. For instance, constituents in political districts allow elected officials to represent their interests; the will of individuals is not always followed, but nonetheless inherent to the structure is the assumption that constituents should have a voice in larger political dynamics. Bacteria should not be afforded something akin to citizenship rights; however, keeping bacterial agency in the frame of larger health systems would serve humans well. By thinking about bacteria as constituents of the human body, a more robust, complex, and all-encompassing understanding of human-bacterial relationships emerges. Labeling bacteria as constituents avoids the problematic constructions of the "host" body in which a universal male bears the burden of feeding the greedy invaders. Never mind that the body is not a feminine hostess (also problematic in other ways), in which the body simply becomes the site for ungrateful and usually unwelcome guests. The more accurate description is that some bacteria are simply part and parcel of being human—*Homo microbis*—and considering them as constituents affords them a bit of recognition in the larger body politic.

Bacteria, and, for that matter, any unwanted organism that threatens to do harm, accumulate meanings of "the other" by the language used about them. For example, my father, an agronomist, often described a weed as a "plant out of place." As a child, I was comforted that the weed was still a plant that might do well somewhere else, just not alongside a corn crop. My critical reading now recognizes the power of labeling a plant a "weed," which disparages one plant while simultaneously naturalizing the legitimacy of another. This construction of a species "out of place" is prominent to descriptions of many ecosystems. Banu Subramanium, a scholar of race, gender, and science, discusses the political costs of describing these out-of-place organisms in racialized terms, and the prejudices laced into tropes such as "invasive species" versus "native species." This proclivity of naming conveys information about systems and structures of power.[53] How bacteria have been labeled and described in reference to colonization is a political description as well. Reading bacteria through postcolonial and indigenous studies changes the frame of reference. The colonizers (in this case human bodies) take on the assumption that they are the colonized and translate indigeneity onto themselves.[54] The (formerly) indigenous bacteria assert their sovereignty, form colonies and rebel, taking on the pejorative role of an invader. In this model, the body is not a holistic ecosystem, but an empire that has claimed its primacy and indigeneity, and thereby exerts dominance, power, and control to eliminate its unwanted subjects. Even language to reduce MRSA in hospital intensive-care units refers to "universal decolonization strategies."[55] Language paints an antagonistic picture of bacteria, an enemy that science and medicine must thwart.

Moving away from this a bit, and assuming that microflora are contingent communities with agency, one way to rethink the relationship of bacteria and bodies is with a feminist analysis. Feminism provides a means to examine nontraditional communities and those excluded or devalued by dominant power structures, and it reveals biases that tend to privilege one group while simultaneously dismissing another. A feminist-studies reading of TSS focusing on *S. aureus* as a marginalized community of the body demonstrates not only how bacteria are overlooked, but also the detrimental consequences of doing so. This framework provides a more inclusive reading of the body, not only as a microbiome, but also as one with constituent communities that may be affected in different ways by technological interventions. As one commenter about the microbiome project on the NPR Shots health blog noted, "What if the microbes stage a revolution? Or go on strike? Would they vote Dem[ocratic] or Rep[ublican]? What effect do the TSA scanners have on them?"[56] Though these comments are meant to be humorous, the writer captures the sentiment that we do not control our microbes, and we need to think more comprehensively about how technologies affect them and, in turn, how these interactions may affect us.

In fact, these technological encounters with the microbiome can have reactive and unexpected consequences. I contribute the term "biocatalytic technology" to better interpret, analyze, and understand technobiological interfaces. Biocatalytic technologies are those technologies that are not primarily dangerous to humans, but have the potential to catalyze microbial activity that may result in harm because of their use. For example, the microbial activity may precipitate an infection located at cellular interfaces and crevices of hip replacements, or it could produce toxins deadly to human organ systems. The dual analysis requires one of technological agency and microbiopolitics. This means looking at bacteria as constituents of the human body, with the potential to interact with technologies and become biocatalytic agents. The term "biocatalytic technology" offers a way to understand the actualization of reactive tampon technology with constituent bacteria. The term also provides language to interrogate those technologies that seem safe, yet still may precipitate other forms of harm because of their use.

Not only is it possible for technologies to catalyze change, but the bacteria can also interact with them as unanticipated technological users. This is an important conceptual departure because only humans are presumed to be technological users. There is much hand-wringing by engineers and designers about non-users, who tend to be characterized as stubborn and unwilling to accept progress or change. Sally Wyatt, who studies digital technologies, has argued for more robust understandings of non-use. She identifies four types of non-users: (1) resisters, who do not want to use a technology; (2) rejecters, who have voluntarily stopped using a technology; (3) the excluded, those for whom the technology was not initially intended; and (4) the expelled, who have stopped using the technology involuntarily.[57] These categories are extremely helpful in understanding why technologies are not adopted, and they move beyond blaming the non-users for their misguided ways. The flip side is to imagine an unwanted or unintended user. For example, a whale as a "technological bystander" becomes an unintended nonhuman user of low-frequency sonar, which is harmful to its existence.[58] In the case of TSS, the *S. aureus* bacterium became a nonhuman unintended user of tampons, able to exploit the technology. The superabsorbent tampons served its interests, and the bacterium capitalized on them to grow and flourish. As biocatalytic agents, bacteria become the reimagined users of technology.

It is important that scientists, engineers, and designers move beyond a mechanical understanding of the body to envision it as a robust ecosystem with bacterial constituents that have the potential to become users. Researchers must ask how medical and bodily technologies will interact with bacterial constituents. This approach challenges the current embrace of nanotechnology and its applications for human health and welfare. Tinier in size than one-celled bacteria, these technologies may become objects to them. This is not a moot point; there is a new menstrual pad in development that incorporates nanofibers.[59] This new pad may be a wonderful innovation, but we are not asking about the nonhuman users and what they may do with the technology.

The technobiological illness of TSS engages the two nonhuman entities of tampon and bacterium as necessary and vital cofactors.[60] Furthermore, the powerful biocatalytic relationship between technology and bacterium was not just overlooked (since this would imply willful disregard) but, worse, it was unimagined as a possibility because the tampon was presumed to be inert. In addition, menstruation was dismissed as an insignificant fluid of a leaky mechanical body fixed with a menstrual plug. Even James Todd, who first identified and published results about TSS in 1978, lamented that "it should have been obvious that the group of young women with 'vaginitis' were of menstruating age and, in fact, three of our original patients, in retrospect, were menstruating at the onset of their illness, but we missed completely the possibility of any connection with tampon use."[61] In some ways, it was refreshing that Todd did not immediately fall into the essentialist trap of linking menstruation to illness in girls. Yet the relationship of the vaginal flora to technology was overlooked and dismissed as inconsequential. The historical legacy of minimizing women's health concerns came to bear, and scientists were unaccustomed to thinking about bacteria as acting independently of the menstruous human body in their interactions with seemingly inert technology.

Risk and Injury

Imagining technology to have biocatalytic potential will change and expand the scope of risk. Though stakeholders look to science as a means to provide measurable data about risk, managing risk turns out to be as much of an art as it is a science. What exactly is risk and who holds responsibility for it? The answer to this question has changed over the twentieth century in the United States, with culpability falling across the spectrum to the individual, government officials, and corporations and their scientists and engineers. In part, an ethic of paternalism and social engineering marked a shift in the early- to mid-twentieth century from blaming individuals who were simply accident-prone and apt to injury, to an ethos that incorporated safety precautions into the very design of factory equipment "to solve the problem of accidents."[62] While shouldering responsibility for better equipment and design, engineers also exposed themselves to blame when things went awry. Henry Petroski, a civil engineer, has enumerated technological disasters such as bridge failures that haunt many engineers, and he argues we must continue to learn from these mistakes in order to prevent their reoccurrence.[63] Arwen Mohun, a historian of technology, argues that publics in the first part of the twentieth century were painfully aware of work-related risks inherent to dangerous jobs, yet they were unwilling to relinquish risk altogether. Thus, they demanded the safe, circumscribed risk in their consumer consumption of roller coasters, for example, that engineers accommodated in the design process.[64]

What is truly a risk, and what is perceived as a risk, means something different to many individuals, and there are a number of means to gauge this perception.[65] Building a nuclear plant and driving cars both pose risk, but often it is the nuclear power plant and its imminent breach of radioactive materials that cause more fear than the possible car accident when driving to the grocery store. Alvin Weinberg, a nuclear physicist and a research director at Oak Ridge National Laboratory from 1955 to 1973, proposed the idea of "trans-science" in 1972 to think about risk. He argued that science has the ability to pose questions, but not always the means to answer them, noting "they transcend science."[66] Thus, scientists have difficulty providing "facts" about risk "when scientists can offer only trans-scientific answers to questions of public policy in situations in which laymen, politicians, civic leaders, etc., look to scientists to provide scientific answers."[67] Weinberg's concept of trans-science suggests that policy makers will never have the data that they really need to make informed decisions because the science to produce the data does not exist. The most we can ask for is good judgment, which by definition, is not science.

Many disciplines have taken up the study of risk: cognitive psychology, sociology, communication, and others. How experts and laypeople view risk variables is a concept many have tried to assess. Others have examined how both men and women express concerns about risk through their gendered identities.[68] Yet it is important to the story of tampon-related TSS that scientists' perceptions about gender have influenced assessments of risk for women users. Most of these scientists were men, and though it is problematic to assume that an essentialized woman scientist would make better judgments, as the story unfolds it was clear that the women who made decisions at crucial junctures shaped the trajectory of policy concerning tampons and TSS in ways that were influenced by their experiences as mothers, friends to other women, and as community members with women. From protesters to epidemiologists to lawyers to health advocates, women's understandings of menstruation and how it was managed through menstrual hygiene technologies mattered greatly. Their identities as women at that particular historical moment did influence views of the science and the risk posed by tampons.

The significance of this is that the risks perceived to be low resulted in great harm to some women and was particularly gendered because of the manner in which injury occurred. Superabsorbent tampons such as Rely did not fit the mold for usual measures of product injury. They differed because they possessed the potential to precipitate a reactive consequence, but not necessarily direct injury from the object per se. The uneven injuries were difficult to track both medically and from a legal, compensatory model as well.

S. Lochlann Jain, an anthropologist who studies design and law, has theorized the social and economic consequences from manufactured goods wounding humans. She argues that injury is not merely an unfortunate accident but is integral and assumed within consumption, and therefore capitalism itself. She suggests "injury law demonstrates the recursive way in which design issues also materialize and naturalize sets of injuries as visible and compensable or invisible and non-compensable."[69] Jain looks at examples such as the Ford Pinto, cigarettes, and keyboards, to name a few. In these types of cases, the relationship of technology to injury can be interpreted as causal.

The likes of lead poisoning, asbestosis and mesothelioma, and other environmental pollutants are constant reminders of damage caused by human-created products.[70] Gregg Mitman, a historian of the environment and ecology, in the introduction to *Landscapes of Exposure* writes, "The preponderance of toxic, over infectious, agents of illness . . . reflects a long-term 'epidemiological transition.'"[71] Usually, epidemiological transition refers to stages of improved health directly attributable to a higher-quality standard of living as well as access to medical care, with correlating improved longevity and decreasing birth rate. However, it may be that "a range of medico-environmental materials from those used in medical devices implanted in bodies to waste products discharged into the environment" are marking a new transition to degenerative health, and that transition is characterized by David Morris, a scholar of medical humanities, as both postmodern and biocultural.[72]

The resulting injury brought about by Rely was complicated to delineate because the causal model of disease or acute poisoning, for example, did not fully account for relational injury. In and of itself Rely was not defective. It was not composed of toxic materials producing direct harm or triggering cancerous growths. As a medical device it was presumed inert, and Rely did not directly cause TSS. The injury incurred was bio-catalytic. Once lodged in a vaginal canal, Rely held the strong potential to interact with bacteria that may be present as constituent communities within some women's bodies. Because makers considered tampons to be inert, the leap to the reactivity of the technology seemed far-fetched.

It is only recently that the idea of indirect harm has gained some traction, and this can be seen in new policies by the EPA to limit perchlorates in drinking water. According to Sanjay Gupta, a physician and CNN's chief medical correspondent, "It's the first time we've ever regulated a chemical not because of what it does directly to you, but because it has an impact on iodine uptake that might affect your child down the road."[73] Thus, the capabilities to cause indirect harm were not well appreciated in the case of TSS. Yet, despite the prevailing wisdom of direct harm and inert technology, the live bacterium and synthetic superabsorbent tampon energetically interacted and were cofactors in producing illness. As Jain points out, design flaws may materialize as visible, requiring compensation, or remain invisible, and go unrecognized.

What people "see" is crucial. Take, for example, "the invisible gorilla" perception studies conducted by Christopher Chabris and Daniel Simons, which find that when people are asked to focus on one specific thing on a video, they miss the big picture of the costumed gorilla sauntering across the screen. Another attention researcher, Trafton Drew, used this same idea to test a highly skilled and trained set of experts who read data on screens: radiologists. Presented with multiple X-rays, and then an image of the gorilla, 83 percent were so focused on their object of intent that they missed it. This "inattentional blindness" allows them to home in on important and specific data, but since they are not looking for a gorilla they do not see it.[74] This indicates that the framing of a data set is highly important regarding what a researcher can "see." Jennifer Croissant, who studies the sociology of science and technology, discusses a finer point of agnotology, that is, absences of knowledge, not just rejected knowledge or purposeful ignorance, but "absent knowledges as forms of non-knowledge."[75] As Kathy Ferguson, a political and feminist theorist, suggests, "The questions that we can ask about the world are enabled, and other questions disabled, by the frame that orders the questioning. When we are busy arguing about the questions that appear with a certain frame, the frame itself becomes invisible; we become *enframed* within it."[76] Thus, the shape of knowledge had to change to see tampon-related TSS and, moreover, to address the gendered technology and indirect injury manifesting in women's bodies.

In addition, injury from bacterial activity does not fit a traditional model of liability with financial compensation rewarded to victims, because bacteria cannot be sued. Bacteria are not persons in the sense of an individual, legal entity, or even a corporation, from whom monetary remuneration may be sought. There is no money in blaming bacteria—perhaps in human error in regard to medically unsterile practices, or the spread of *E. coli* with unsanitary farming methods—but not for generalized infections or bacterial toxins, especially from constituent bacteria residing on a person that suddenly goes rogue. Yet still, the injury of TSS in this particular case had the cofactor of the tampon to precipitate bacterial growth in some women, and manufacturers are responsible for tampon design and production.

Trusting Consumer Goods

Though my interest is in exploring tampons as technological artifacts, they also have an identity in the marketplace as a commodity, premised on producers and manufacturers delivering goods that consumers purchase for a price. Though debating the nuances of capitalism is not central to this book, it is worth noting that American consumers have come to an implicit agreement with manufacturers about commodities that they purchase. In the case of the sale of goods in the United States during the twentieth century, consumers submitted their health and well-being, and—importantly—money to corporations, in exchange for goods of reasonable quality and no danger. How deeply this understanding of safe commodities is naturalized in contemporary U.S. society can be seen in the outrage leveled against corporations, such as the case in China of melamine added to milk in 2009, responsible for the deaths of at least four babies and illnesses in 53,000 others.[77] Cloaked in nationalistic righteousness, some vowed to boycott all imported food from China, others lamented that industrialism was occurring at the expense of health, and still others complained that policies about pure food were not up to the standards set in the United States. Besides fueling fears about the interdependency of global economies, the "bad" milk revealed an important naturalized assumption: in the United States, it is simply common knowledge that "good" milk should be produced and sold, and we are dumbstruck when systems fail to guarantee a safe product, and incensed when it causes illness instead of health.

This confidence in milk in the United States is also narrowly defined. In his lecture "The Cow Tipping Point," David Ehrenfeld, a biologist, looks at the ways recombinant bovine growth hormone (rBGH) as a biotechnology is not well understood, sometimes purposefully, in terms of both direct and indirect injury and harm.[78] For lactating cows treated with rBGH, the injury is often similar to other regularly lactating cows, such as mastitis and sore knees, though rBGH-treated cows suffer more and more often. Peer-reviewed papers by both industry and independent scientists often contradict one another, muddying the differences between naturally occurring BGH and rBGH. Despite animal suffering and the economic impact on producers to replace milk cows that die prematurely, these costs are not part of the "science" of whether or not to use the growth hormone. Questions for human health that are not obvious in terms of direct injury include the cross-species genetic exchanges in bacteria that weaken antibiotics, and rBGH's role in that. Ehrenfeld concludes that, due to our faith in science, "we forget that technology is unable, both in theory and in practice, to resolve most of the practical problems that it itself creates."[79] Furthermore, technical or scientific facts will not produce a moral resolution, because their scope simply is too narrow.

This viewpoint paints a discouraging picture for the ability of regulating bodies to provide intervention concerning risk and injury, especially in relation to indirect harm. Government intervention, testing, and regulation have also been tempered through politics and legislation over the course of the twentieth century, with many arguing that neoliberalism has put us all at risk by reducing oversight and asking corporations to regulate themselves.[80] Risk, limited safety, and tolerance for injury continue to be built into consumer goods, and tampons are caught in the crosshairs of these assumptions and ideologies. The complexity of tampon-related TSS is that the tampon causes indirect harm to some and not all menstruators, and the science supporting these claims has been very difficult to unpack because it is produced by both corporate-sponsored and independent scientists.

Technology's Double Edge

DuPont's now-famous slogan, "Better Things for Better Living . . . through Chemistry," evokes the ethos of progressive technoscience in twentieth-century United States culture. Consumers have been well trained to expect more from their purchasing power and for corporations to deliver scientifically managed products, including food. In her book *Empty Pleasures: The Story of Artificial Sweeteners from Saccharin to Splenda* (2010), Carolyn Thomas, an American studies scholar, notes that many women in particular came to rely on saccharin as a low-calorie sugar substitute, and in light of health warnings and recommendations to possibly discontinue it, women rallied to the support of saccharin, despite its risks. The links to cancer were insignificant to people following reduced-sugar diets, to people with diabetes, and to others who simply liked the pleasure of being able to eat sweet treats. Women flooded the FDA with handwritten letters and notes, begging for saccharin to remain on the market as a sugar substitute. Modern chemistry had delivered a miracle sweetener, and many chose to trust their taste buds rather than scientists' data pointing to saccharin's danger. In fact, the *New York Times* reporting on the recall of Rely in 1980 referred to the similarities between the two. An unnamed advertising executive noted to a reporter that "the reaction could be like saccharin. There's such a strong preference for tampons that it might outweigh the degree of risk."[81] There was some truth in this since the risk was low for most women. This attitude, however, pushed the burden of the illness onto women, citing their "preference" and choice to use tampons knowing that they were dangerous, rather than holding the companies responsible for the manufacture, design, and distribution of synthetic superabsorbent tampons.

There were plenty of mixed feelings and mixed messages about tampons. Before the recall during the 1970s, tampons, including Rely, enjoyed widespread support. For many women tampons were their only choice, and there was no going back to sanitary pads with cellulose wadding and elastic belts. For most young women who suffered through pads chafing the inner thighs, the discomfort of a bulky pad worn between their legs, and the awkward gait of walking around a pad, wearing a tampon, whatever its composition, eliminated these problems. In light of the superabsorbents that were readily available to manufacturers, and consumers' willingness to try more technologically sophisticated products, it is no wonder that more and more tampons incorporated synthetics and that women would like them.

In addition, tampon technology was particularly linked with women's liberation. Advertisers equated bodily freedom to political freedom, a claim that was hard to contradict and was reinforced in advertisements with women in white outfits undertaking all sorts of desirable activities. After using tampons, most women had no intention of returning to pads. Many women incorporated tampon technology into their daily lives, and this object became an important item in what I refer to as the "feminist toolbox." Like other tools such as birth control, trousers, and the right to enter a contract, tampons offered a unique vehicle to support personal independence and agency, and to absorb bodily fluid while remaining unencumbered. Because of this very personal and intimate relationship of the tampon to women's sense of freedom and well-being, the emergence of TSS seemed both impossible and particularly destabilizing. How could this object, so normalized and domesticated, suddenly become deadly? Some women, like the saccharin users, refused to believe that products might cause harm and continued on as before, their faith in Rely clouding facts and adding to denial. Others acquiesced to warnings and limited their tampon usage or switched back to pads. Others got angry and boycotted, and some sued manufacturers for product liability.

Many scientists continue to be divided about what exactly triggered the outbreak; with a strong history of scientific method and inconclusive results, it was and continues to be difficult to make scientifically informed recommendations in the face of contradictory evidence. Even in 2012, researchers publishing in the *Australasian Journal of Dermatology* asked as part of their article title "Is Menstrual Toxic Shock Syndrome Really Caused by Tampons?," raising the same decades-old and misleading question that researchers in the early 1980s did.[82] The title indicates doubt about the role of tampons due to the assumption that they are inert. If, as Langdon Winner argues, artifacts have politics, and if, as Bruno Latour and Jane Bennett suggest, things exert agency, then it is high time to recognize the social and political meanings of menstrual hygiene technologies as well as the multiple outcomes related to their technological use. Because tampon technology has historically been disparaged, is hidden from sight, is worn internally within the body, and is primarily used by women, this changes the scope of injury compared to a faulty automobile airbag or a dresser drawer that tips over onto a person. No contemporary woman in the United States has benefited from unearned privileges derived from purposely or accidentally exposing menstrual fluid for others to see. Tampons powerfully conceal a disparaged bodily fluid, and thus the social disregard for menstruation casts a shadow on related illnesses such as TSS. Because of these social roadblocks, the imagination must be stretched to consider bacterium that reside on bodies and in vaginal spaces as technological users of tampons, even though they were not the primary target audience. By examining TSS as the result of a biocatalytic technology, we can gain a better understanding of how we need to think very carefully and deeply about technologies for biological use, not just for humans but for nonhumans as well.

2

Mystery

People get sick all the time. It is easy enough to minimize symptoms such as fever, chills, or sweats. Imagine then, that a person's fever keeps rising, diarrhea and vomiting are unremittent, and fatigue and muscle weakness make it a Herculean effort to get out of bed. Deciding to seek professional, allopathic medical help carries an economic cost in the United States, so the decision to stay home and wait for the symptoms to subside is not unusual. In the late 1970s when a woman possessing these symptoms finally decided it was time to see her doctor, or a family member insisted she needed more immediate care at an emergency room, she would likely get an IV drip to replenish fluids and electrolytes, with further orders to rest at home. The sudden illness might take a turn for the worse, with her getting rushed into acute care and then suffering the onset of kidney failure. Still no one knew what was wrong. This all seemed very unusual for a healthy, young person, and it was likely that the attending physician would diagnose a severe viral infection.

Toxic shock syndrome (TSS) became this mystery illness in the late 1970s. What made it unique was that it challenged traditional forms of knowledge production about sickness. A direct causal model was insufficient to identify TSS. A paradigmatic shift to include a medical device as a cofactor was necessary for scientists and researchers to effectively associate tampons with TSS. Without a biocatalytic model as part of the usual scope of medical inquiry, recognizing this alternative pathway was not obvious. The politics of whether or not this should be "obvious" falls within the context of long-standing and systematic practices dismissing women's reproductive health. However, with numbers on the rise, the life-and-death emergency-room cases could not so easily be ignored because the sufferers were mostly white teenagers and young mothers. This unknown malady needed to be framed in new ways, recognizing tampon technology in the illness process and challenging the long-held view that tampons were inert. It also required public health officials to argue for an unusual etiology, and one that manufacturers of tampons initially disputed.

This chapter examines how TSS gained traction as an illness and also how medical practitioners and epidemiologists further associated it with superabsorbent tampons. Within the milieu of the time period, it was neither intuitive nor "common sense" and took a good deal of research, contested at multiple levels, to conclude that TSS was a real illness with the potential of becoming an epidemiological event. In addition, the Centers for Disease Control (CDC) was under a good deal of pressure after some less-than-ideal outcomes with the 1976 swine flu pandemic that never arrived, and Legionnaires' disease, which took nearly a year to analyze and identify. It could not afford to be the agency responsible for the deaths of thousands of young, mostly white, women, so it mobilized to thwart this emerging illness before it could unleash untold damage.

As researchers pondered what this set of symptoms might indicate, some possibilities emerged as potential culprits. Christian Schrock, an infectious disease specialist writing in the *Journal of the American Medical Association (JAMA)* in 1980 wondered whether it was a manifestation of herpes.[1] Bruce Dan, an epidemiologist at the CDC, hypothesized it may be a variant of scarlet fever.[2] Though it is the job of the epidemiologist to track outbreaks, both known and unknown, positively identifying an emergent and novel illness carries implications. Though sometimes medical-device technologies carry the risk of injury, postoperative infection, or even simply wearing out, they had not been assumed to catalyze illness in healthy individuals via bacteriological toxins. The very assumption of the safety of all tampons was called into question, which held both serious financial costs for corporations and also major adjustments to daily menstrual management practices for millions of women. How to identify an unknown syndrome, and the methodology used to do so, carried political consequences for federal agencies, corporate scientists, and women users, with ramifications still resonating today. In order to understand the scope of research and the marshaling of resources to contain the TSS outbreak in the late 1970s and early 1980s, it is useful to trace how this epidemiological event unfurled in the United States, looking at the relationship of state systems of public health with the national CDC, while acknowledging tensions not just between the public good and an individual's health, but also between an individual's health and corporate interests.

TSS: Background Facts

Though the exact numbers do not tell the story of TSS, from 1970 to 1980 the CDC counted 941 confirmed cases, 928 in women, and 905 at the onset of the menstrual period. The majority of women were white, but there were also seven black women, three Asian women, three Hispanic women, and two American Indian women.[3] In total, seventy-three women died during that time period. A 1983 summary in the CDC's *Morbidity and Mortality Weekly Report* (*MMWR*) outlined 2,204 cases of TSS, of which 96 percent were women, 90 percent occurred at the onset

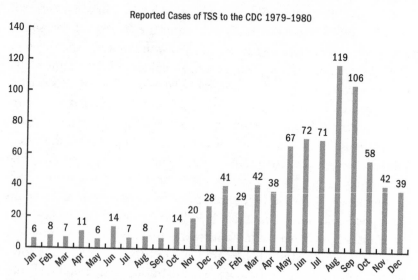

Figure 2.1. This bar graph regarding TSS represents the cases reported to the CDC, with 135 cases and 13 deaths in 1979, and 725 cases and 45 deaths in 1980. The number of reported cases reflected a steep rise leading up to 1980 and a sharp decline after Rely tampons were withdrawn from the market, according to CDC data. Source: U.S. Department of Health and Human Services, "Toxic Shock Syndrome—United States, 1970–1980," *Morbidity and Mortality Weekly Report* 30.3 (January 30, 1981): 25–36.

of menses, and 99 percent were tampon users.[4] A bar graph entitled "Reported Cases of Toxic-Shock Syndrome, by Date of Onset" in the same report represented the rising numbers of cases, as well as the general decline, over the ten-year period from 1970 to 1980. Though there were many reasons for the decline of TSS in the latter half of 1980, ranging from better treatment to the successful message about risk associated with tampons, the correlation of the Rely tampon recall on September 22, 1980, with waning occurrences is hard to dismiss.

Many have argued that thousands more were sickened but were not ill enough to have all the symptoms meeting the strict criteria of TSS (as defined in the introduction). Even those who likely died as a result of the toxin produced by *Staphylococcus aureus* did not always present all the symptoms associated with the clinical definition. There is not a mechanism to count these cases that fell outside what was reported to the CDC, and cases were collected with a "passive" system in which health providers contacted the CDC and not the other way around, so the numbers are presumably low. In comparison, 3,652 individuals died from influenza in the United States in 1980, for instance, and in the third week of January 1981, there were 21,125 reported civilian cases of gonorrhea.[5] By now it is clear that HIV/AIDS is endemic to every stratum of society and was not contained at that time. In relative terms, the scope of TSS was far less than other communicable diseases, yet its legacy can be found on every tampon box purchased today.

The narrative constructed about TSS was critical to its reception as an illness worth fighting. In a 1981 report by Arthur Reingold from the CDC, he noted that 99 percent of the women studied were white, and 97 percent of 1,020 cases were women in middle-class families with incomes from $15,000 to $25,000.[6] These young, white women were not constructed as derelict drug users; elderly, ill veterans; or irresponsible, gay men. They were future mothers and wives. No doubt the invisible hand of white privilege played a dominant role in constructing them as people worth saving. Additionally, an old trope of paternalism to rescue young women is evident as well. This is not to dismiss the good intentions of the researchers and agencies, or their ability to fulfill the mission of protecting public health. But, as a social practice, disease narratives carry meaning and consequences, and TSS initially benefited from its association with white women. However, TSS also suffered the stigma of being related to the disparaged female-specific bodily process of menstruation and the stigmatized tampon used to contain menstrual flow.

Identifying Illness

Recognizing, naming, and then treating a new disease is no small feat, and there should be a high bar for collectively agreeing that a set of symptoms and biological markers amount to an illness with social meaning. Recognizing the biological sense of disease is one thing, but socially responding to it is quite another. According to Charles Rosenberg, a historian of medicine, "it is fair to say that in our culture a disease does not exist as a social phenomenon until we agree that it does—until it is named."[7] Rosenberg identifies five major areas when "framing" a disease: (1) cognitive and disciplinary elements; (2) institutional and policy responses; (3) adjustments that individuals and families undertake; (4) relationships between doctors and patients; and (5) societal attitudes, values, and their rationalizations associated with the disease. In the case of TSS, these elements that frame disease are also at play. Medical experts identify a phenomenon of illness and name it; state and national health institutions weigh in to alert women; doctors, nurses, and healthcare providers must be educated to recognize symptoms; broader society reacts to the illness; patients incorporate the experience of illness into their personal identities. However, the unique elements in the framing of tampon-related TSS are both its association with technology and the biocatalytic quality of superabsorbent tampons. That is to say, the relationship of TSS to tampons muddied more traditional ways of identifying disease, raising difficult questions about causation, correlation, and association of technology with illness. It did not fit a typical pattern.

Furthermore, it is a bit inaccurate to call TSS a disease. It is neither communicable like the flu nor degenerative like arthritis. According to James Todd, the pediatrician who coined the name, a syndrome more accurately describes this illness. As he explained it, "A syndrome is a group of signs and symptoms and laboratory findings which seem to occur together and describe a single disease entity. But as it exists only that far, that is a syndrome." The illness moves to the category of disease when researchers "know the cause of those signs and symptoms" with laboratory findings to corroborate the diagnosis. When clinicians "can prove this cause," he affirmed, "then that's a disease."[8] This distinction of a syndrome is quite important, because it is a way to acknowledge the unknown elements while still recognizing and legitimizing an illness with its associative social components.

Agreeing on the elements of an illness is one thing, but the social system to keep tabs on it, as well as to determine its threat to large segments of the population, is a different set of skills addressed by epidemiology. According to Mark Pendergrast, an independent scholar, "epidemiology is a science of probability, not proof."[9] This succinct description captures the inherent tensions about methods used by Epidemic Intelligence Service (EIS) officers at the CDC in determining normal disease patterns or novel, unusual, or increased incidents of illness. The goals of epidemiologists are different from basic research scientists. The outcomes of halting an outbreak or stemming the spread of a disease call on different methods and reliance on correlation, and optimally direct proof, as basis for policy.

In many ways, the identification of TSS followed similar patterns characteristic of other epidemics. Mark Dworkin, an epidemiologist by training, outlines fourteen steps of an outbreak investigation, though they may overlap or happen in a different order. The first step is to verify an outbreak by examining what is referred to as surveillance data. This, of course, assumes known infections rather than those illnesses of unknown origins. After analyzing the data, a diagnosis must be confirmed, which again relies on known tests and lab practices. Beyond this, more severe outbreaks require an investigative team with a leader to delegate tasks and set agendas for more complex situations, and even create a case definition. The team counts cases and conducts "epidemiologic analysis," such as identifying variables, demographics, and patterns, for instance. This allows the team to develop a hypothesis about what may be going on and then determine control measures. Depending on the nature of the outbreak, more studies may be necessary, followed by analysis and additional control measures of individuals, treatments, or follow-up regimes. Epidemiologists use the language of "compliance" to describe how infected individuals, patients, or publics follow and conform to the recommended protocol. The last steps include communicating about the findings, establishing measures to prevent future outbreaks, and collecting surveillance data about the disease progression and its hopeful reduction through the outlined interventions.[10] Though this provides a distinct process of how ideal organizational operations would unfold within the CDC or a state department of health when confronted with an outbreak, a theoretical epidemic does not always account for real-life unknowns, the messy work of detection, and its relationship to the social world.

Epidemiology is part science and part social detective work, and it is this component that is problematic to other fields of science, and under scrutiny in light of evidence-based medicine. Epidemiologists must gather pieces of evidence, which become factors, and judge whether or not correlation is significant to causation. Researchers readily rely on inklings, hunches, and past experiences, and they depend on both creative problem solving and stringent methods to identify known and unknown outbreaks. However effective this approach may be, its weakness lies in its inability to eliminate sufficient variables, or even provide significant proof. Lack of an occurrence can constitute evidence, which also becomes questionable methodologically in other scientific settings. Epidemiology is also reactive and thus does not have the luxury of long-term clinical studies to lean on for legitimacy.[11]

This is important because at issue is whether or not the recommendations set forth by the CDC should be believed. Steven Epstein, a sociologist of health and medicine, discusses how trustworthiness is at stake with methods and procedures, and he suggests "knowledge emerges out of credibility struggles."[12] Scientists' claims must be believable in order to elicit support, shape arguments, and garner recognition. Yet the very thing that propels some of these research aims is characterized by differences in fastidious science and pragmatic science, as pointed out by Epstein, and defined by Alvan Feinstein, an authority on clinical trials at the Yale University School of Medicine.[13] Fastidious science relies on "clean" data and "elegant" research designs, and it is likely carried out by academically trained researchers, promoting an ideology of purity leading to truth. This method seeks ways to reduce ambiguity and bias, and produce clear findings. By contrast, the pragmatic approach accepts messiness, ordinary variables in field and clinical settings, as well as occasionally ambiguous results. These differences are linked to power struggles between science-based academic researchers and clinic-based physicians, but the tensions are inherent to epidemiology as well. Epidemiology embodies this conflict, with both its need for scientific rigor and also its requirement to act quickly on behalf of the public good, in the messy theater of human life, when there is no time to wait for "clean" results from a well-designed study. It is here where politics and health collide.

New Diseases, New Difficulties

By the 1970s, the Center for Disease Control, renamed the plural Centers for Disease Control in 1981 (changed to Centers for Disease Control and Prevention in 1992), was no longer just another governmental agency but one receiving national attention. The period of the 1970s benefited from the progressive technoscience innovations after World War II that ushered in mass antibiotics, vaccinations, and increased food production to curb world hunger. Many scientists, including those at the CDC, basked in what seemed like enviable and inevitable successes. However, this hubris ran into many troubling and systemic health hazards that challenged this narrative of success: cancers resulting from long-term smoking, illnesses stemming from toxins and pollutants in waterways, and degenerative diseases such as diabetes and heart disease linked to American diets. Furthermore, the role of experts in driving decisions about public health for the good of the whole ran counter to a reassertion of individual rights.[14] Disease entities were getting harder to identify, and publics expected perfection as well as interventions that caused no harm. More realistically, these high expectations ran into the fallibility of scientists who had promised more than they could deliver. It is within this milieu that the CDC engaged TSS as a potential public health threat.

During the 1970s and early 1980s there were significant epidemiological challenges. The swine flu campaign of 1976, promoted by President Ford, swallowed $135 million in public funds, seemingly wasted since this flu strain failed to spread as an epidemic after all. The new technology of the compressed air vaccination gun used during the public health campaign, presumably safer and more efficient because it could be used multiple times, frightened thousands of school children and came to symbolize everything that was wrong with public health interventions.

Referred to as "the gun" in my elementary school, we dreaded it. I distinctly remember a friend returning to class, her face red and puffy and streaked with tears after her shot, and my absolute relief that my mother did not provide consent for me to receive the vaccine at school. She was not alone in questioning the approach. By the end of 1976, only 33 percent of Americans had received the immunization. The vaccination air gun symbolized an efficiency model in vaccinating en masse, without regard to the deep bruises or debilitation experienced by individuals. Distrust for the whole thing increased after the media reported about the elderly dying from the vaccine (which was later disproven), and the appearance of the neuromuscular disorder Guillain-Barré syndrome as a "side effect," which seemed to be a pretty high cost. The CDC canceled the campaign in December.[15]

Also in 1976, Legionnaires' disease flummoxed epidemiologists at the CDC. During the month of July, the Pennsylvania Department of Health received hundreds of reports of acute pneumonia illnesses and deaths in a population of American Legionnaires who had attended a conference in Philadelphia and stayed in hotels there. In part, the usual lab practices to eliminate pathogens and identify whether or not it was a viral, bacterial, or fungal entity were yielding nothing. Tried-and-true practices such as culturing a sample in the lab and inoculating it in mice failed. The tests developed to identify a "known," by definition, would not work for an unknown, and the CDC succumbed to this quandary. It took until January of 1977 to finally confirm it was a bacterium, and the CDC identified and named it *Legionella*. This strain preferred pond-scum-like conditions, and "dark, nutrient-rich, almost anoxic environments" that happened to be found in the air-conditioning cooling towers at the Bellevue-Stratford Hotel. Once aerosolized, the mist floated from the towers into windows, the lobby, and onto the street, where the bacterium was easily inhaled.[16] Though air-conditioning standards changed to require more stringent cleaning, Legionnaires' has not been eliminated as a disease threat.

The identification of HIV/AIDS also proved to be a difficult challenge for CDC officials during this time span. First reported by the *MMWR* on June 5, 1981, it had not yet been named as a disease entity but was noted as an emergent phenomenon based on a cluster of symptoms in gay men, notably presenting a very specific kind of pneumonia that usually affects "severely immunosuppressed" individuals. Sometimes referred to as GRID (gay-related immunodeficiency disease), it was identified in mostly young, homosexual men by the end of 1981. According to the *MMWR* for the week of September 24, 1982, "between June 1, 1981, and September 15, 1982, CDC received reports of 593 cases of acquired immune deficiency syndrome (AIDS) [Formerly referred to as Kaposi's sarcoma and opportunistic infections in previously healthy persons]. Death occurred in 243 cases (41%)" with 75 percent of cases identified in homosexual or bisexual men.[17] By July of 1982 the syndrome was officially named AIDS (acquired immunodeficiency syndrome), and though also associated with intravenous drug users and hemophiliacs, the predominant message was that it sickened gay men.[18]

Priscilla Wald, whose work focuses on U.S. literature and culture, describes the importance of narrative in the process of the early identification of HIV/AIDS. Epidemiological narratives, she argues, "rely on conventions that facilitate the identification of an outbreak, but can also obscure relevant information." Significantly "those narratives can reproduce cultural conventions that influence scientific hypotheses."[19] This "outbreak narrative," constructed by media outlets, researchers, and epidemiologists, weaves elements of hope through science and warnings of human infallibility into a story. These stories explain diseases and epidemics, but also have the potential to obscure alternative paths of knowledge. Thus, the framing of GRID with gay people relied on a constricted definition of homosexual males as a stable category, which by most accounts is problematic and inaccurate. Also within this framing was a construction of the noncompliant, oversexed, gay man with multiple partners, whose insatiable sexual appetite fueled the spread of the illness. Narrating the disease in terms of promiscuous gay men additionally exempted numerous other presentations of it in humans who were not categorized in this way.

Though creating patterns, linking similarities, and tracing data points into a narrative is part of the identification of a new illness, the process is not neutral. If disease processes were neutral, they would not be stigmatized, villainized, or conversely accepted as normal or even corporatized as with breast cancer. Using Wald's notion of an "outbreak narrative," HIV/AIDS had all the hallmarks of an epidemiological story except, she argues, that "it could not be contained" as with the happier ending to polio, for instance. HIV/AIDS spread around the globe, no doubt the narrative of it being limited to gay men derailing other possibilities. The "othering" of that group and the burden of social discrimination against gay people all worked to misunderstand the disease.

TSS, though, predated and foreshadowed the HIV/AIDS crisis. It broke ground in discussing a taboo subject in public news media, as will be discussed more fully in chapter 3. It challenged the success narrative of immunization and destabilized the myth of technoscientific progress saving the world. A clear answer outlining the disease path never emerged, and no "cure" came about once the toxins of TSS took hold. Both women and gay men were left to patrol their own bodies, circumscribing their activity and relying on themselves to remain healthy in the face of a viral infection or a tampon-induced syndrome. The shift from public health to individual responsibility came to characterize the period in which both diseases emerged and were managed during the end of the Carter and beginning of the Reagan presidential administrations.

Origin Story

Though Wald suggests that every outbreak needs a narrative and has one constructed for it, I would also add that the named illness requires an origin story. However, this is not necessarily a story for public consumption, but for the researchers. The origin story builds credibility and enhances the reputations of the researchers. This is important, because the storytelling and correlative citations buoy careers, reinforce expert status, and simultaneously bring notoriety to academic institutions and collaborators. In addition, the origin story is retold in multiple academic journals, as well as retrospective accounts written by physicians, epidemiologists, and specialists in infectious diseases.[20] It is foundational to the storytelling in a literature review about the nature of a disease. TSS's origin story is important because of its meaning, but also because of how it functions factually, rhetorically, and symbolically in scientific discourse.

The origin story also operates by what remains unsaid. The stories often "disappear" the deep social networks of the physicians and researchers, and how these networks are absolutely vital to identifying an outbreak and creating a critical mass of evidence to present it as a case. Individuals' efforts and their discoveries are significant, but how the individuals in the network draw knowledge together to form conclusions is overlooked in the narrative of the heroic and masculine doctors and epidemiological detectives who seem to work as independent agents. On the contrary, practitioners forge deep connections through training programs, residencies, university clinics, and laboratories in federal and state departments of public health. In an era when the landline phone, paper mail, and printed weekly updates from the *MMWR* were the fastest means to distribute information, these social connections were crucial to knowledge sharing. And they had to make time to foster these connections as well, often traveling and visiting each other in the field.

The origin story of TSS is traced to 1978 when it was called "the toxic shock syndrome." It was named by James Todd and Mark Fishaut, pediatricians working in the Department of Pediatrics at the Children's Hospital of Denver and University School of Medicine, along with their colleagues Frank Kapral in the Department of Medical Microbiology at Ohio State University, and Thomas Welsh in the Department of Pediatrics, Herkimer Memorial Hospital in New York.[21] According to Todd and the other researchers, children were the primary group to be afflicted. As described in *The Lancet*, symptoms included high fever, rash, headache, vomiting, acute renal failure, and even severe shock in seven boys and girls between the ages of eight and seventeen during the years 1975–1977. The link that Todd, the principal investigator, was able to make between the children was that the infection derived from phage-group-I *Staphylococcus aureus*. He referred to this as "a unique new syndrome" affecting older children, different from scarlet fever or Rocky Mountain spotted fever, which share some similar traits.[22] It was also framed within the category of children's diseases such as Kawasaki's disease or Reye's syndrome. Such a small sampling was nowhere near an epidemic, more like a blip in infectious diseases seen in children.

When a new illness emerges, many ask whether it is something that is truly novel or something that has reemerged but was known by another name, or explained away through some other rationale. Bruce Dan, an epidemiologist at the CDC, remarked that TSS was not entirely new, and that the "disease had been reported as far back as 1972" with "four or five cases in the medical literature of diseases indistinguishable from toxic shock syndrome."[23] Philip Tierno, a microbiologist and immunologist, reports that the disease is older than that. He describes an incident occurring in 1928 in Queensland, Australia, in which contaminated inoculations for diphtheria sickened eighteen of twenty-one children, resulting in the deaths of twelve of them. Of the surviving children, many formed abscesses at the inoculation site and, when cultured, the fluid from the abscesses contained S. aureus. Links between illnesses resembling scarlet fever and the presence of S. aureus emerged in medical reports in 1908. Tierno also surmises that TSS may have been a factor in the flu epidemic spread through Athenian soldiers during the Peloponnesian War in 430 BCE.[24] The point here is that the entity causing these symptoms was not necessarily perceived as novel, yet Pat Schlievert, a microbiologist and assistant professor at the University of Minnesota during the 1980s, proposed that the bacterium in fact was a new, never-before-seen strain of S. aureus.[25] Whatever the case, medical experts linked the bacterium with a unique set of characteristics, named it, and wrote about it through recognized channels of academic journals, in ways that Rosenberg characterizes as "framing" disease.

Satisfying the markers of naming a new illness, Todd's article in *The Lancet* became the authoritative academic work on TSS because this was the only published piece to outline specific symptoms and name this staph-related infection as a syndrome. How this health crisis in children could be linked to tampon use took careful observation and training. However, a key component to this was the strong social and professional network that supported the research and fostered communication, as exemplified in Wisconsin.

Jeffrey Davis was the new state epidemiologist and the chief of the section of acute and communicable disease epidemiology at the Wisconsin Division of Health. He became familiar with TSS in 1978 while completing a pediatrics residency and fellowship in pediatric infectious diseases at Duke University, parallel in time to the publication of Todd's article. When his colleague Joan Chesney from the University of Wisconsin School of Medicine reached out to him in late 1979, describing three patients with symptoms like TSS, he was curious.[26] Chesney, the chief of pediatric infectious disease, was married to Russell Chesney, a nephrologist, also at the University of Wisconsin School of Medicine. They spoke to each other often about their patients and events occurring at the hospital.

On December 1, 1979, Russell described to Joan an unusual situation of treating an eighteen-year-old woman whose kidney failure came on briskly. Shock accompanied it, which was atypical. The patient also experienced aches, a rash, and became sick quite suddenly instead of in a more measured pace associated with kidney failure. Joan, keeping abreast of recent publications in pediatric medicine, recalled Todd's article in *The Lancet* that described TSS, and she thought that these symptoms sounded very similar. Just a few days later on December 5, she learned of a fifteen-year-old girl that came to the hospital with symptoms resembling TSS, who eerily experienced the same thing exactly one month before, in essence previewing the link to menstrual cycles. Joan Chesney also heard about a meeting with pediatrics and adult infectious diseases at Madison General Hospital occurring December 5. There, she found out about another unusual case of a twenty-five-year-old woman with sudden kidney failure that the doctors diagnosed as "kidney infection with shock."[27] Later she conveyed to a reporter, "It was like a déjà vu."[28] She linked the three together back to the Todd article, and she wondered whether an outbreak were occurring right in the heart of Madison. After talking with Davis, they concurred that this illness seemed like it may be TSS. Davis came to Madison to investigate.

He began by searching for commonalities among the women by asking questions about grocery purchases, which might have linked them through foodborne illness; travel and locale, pointing toward regional infections; and sex partners, suggesting sexually transmitted infections. Two more cases trickled into Madison in January 1980. One patient had a staph infection coming from an abscess on her heel, and the other was seemingly healthy except for the sudden onset of shock. A nurse or caretaker made note that this latter patient was menstruating. Davis, too, remembered from his medical training that often "menstrual history is overlooked."[29] He believed that it was "more than a coincidence" that each contracted her illness at the onset of the menstrual period. At about the same time, Dr. Andrew Dean of the Minnesota Department of Health called Davis, discussing five more possible cases. Davis anticipated Dean's description of this acute illness, and he recalled cutting him off while on the phone, saying, "Let me describe it to you."[30] Between the two of them, they counted twelve young women exhibiting TSS that seemed to be associated with their menstrual cycles.[31]

By early 1980, Davis's surveillance of four other Madison hospitals, along with his continued discussions with Dean in Minnesota, led him to contact the CDC. Davis also took the proactive step of mailing a report on January 31, 1980, to "3,500 internists, pediatricians and family practice physician licenses in Wisconsin" concerning the state of TSS, outlining surveillance procedures for the disease, and, importantly, establishing a protocol for specimen collection.[32] In essence, Davis positioned physicians in Wisconsin to be on the forefront of intervention concerning TSS outbreaks, wherever and however they might occur.

Well situated in the region's medical social network of university physicians and departments of health, Davis began receiving dispatches from the field: physicians informing him of their patients, laypeople self-reporting cases of TSS, practitioners confirming diagnoses, and reporters asking questions. Among these connections, Neil Rosenberg at the *Milwaukee Journal* got wind of the news of an ill teenager, and he reported about it on February 14, 1980.[33] The headline, "Fever, Signs of Shock, Puzzle Girl's Doctors," did not mention TSS, but it landed on the front page under the fold. This report supplied Davis's office phone number, and the newspaper proved to be an important way to reach a broad audience beyond healthcare workers. In part, it provided language to explain this array of symptoms, so it offered meaning to those who may be affected. Many folks in the Milwaukee area contacted Davis with symptoms; the surveillance system he coordinated was in full gear sorting probable TSS cases from other illnesses, and tracking this emergent outbreak, if it indeed was one.

Institutional Advocacy

As reports of cases spread beyond Wisconsin, the Midwestern epidemiologists were ahead of the curve and quickly emerged as leading voices on TSS. Andy Dean, from the Minnesota Department of Health, traveled to Atlanta in January 1980 to share with the CDC what the state epidemiologists had learned. During his visit, he met with Dave Fraser, the chief of the special pathogens division and the person who led the investigative team for Legionnaires'. Fraser called in his new EIS officer, Kathryn Shands, to gauge her interest and see whether it was a project she would like to take, to which she agreed. In my interview with her, she recalled later that afternoon she went out on a run with her colleague Bruce Dan, another EIS officer, and she described this new project, telling him that she was going to work on it. "That is such a dead end," he pronounced, advising, "You really don't want to do that." She laughed at how wrong this advice was, adding that "I wanted to do it, and I did."[34] Her role proved to be an influential one, and she also was notable as a female expert in a sea of male voices over the course of the year.

The quelling of Legionnaires' hung heavily on CDC epidemiologists. It had all the markers of a brewing epidemic, along with national news coverage and public attention. As Shands put it, it was "big" but it hit older people, who may have had underlying health issues. On the other hand, "TSS hit young, healthy people and BLAM! fast!" Shands emphasized. The speed and severity, along with young women as the cohort, drew attention. What the epidemiologists did not yet know was that during this same time Procter & Gamble (P&G) had embarked on a national

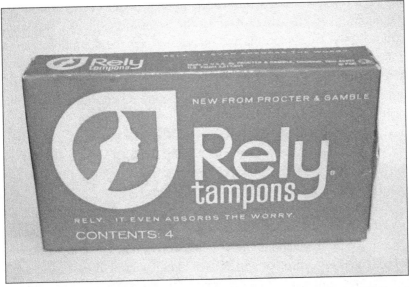

Figure 2.2. Sample boxes of four Rely tampons that arrived through the U.S. Postal Service into mailboxes across the country from the mid-1970s to 1980. The box encouraged women to try a "complimentary gift for you" from Procter & Gamble. The method worked well, with women converting to Rely from Tampax and other brands, increasing its market share. Photo by Sharra Vostral.

marketing campaign to distribute millions of free tampon samples, four to a box, through the postal service. The company's expertise in advertising and brand building systematically dropped its new superabsorbent tampon Rely into most homes. This formidable distribution system in effect sped up the rate by which women acquired the illness. Thus, the state epidemiologists and now the CDC felt the urgency that something was happening, but they needed evidence both to start tracing patterns and to understand whether or not TSS was emerging as an epidemic, defined as a widespread occurrence of an infection or illness at a specific time.

The first charge was to develop a case definition of TSS, based on the most obvious patients, so that epidemiologists could use it to seek out ill individuals and include them in studies. Shands requested input from various researchers and public health officials, including Jeff Davis from Wisconsin, James Todd (who had named TSS), Mike Osterholm of the Minnesota Department of Health, and Neil Halsey (also trained in pediatrics and an EIS officer from 1975 to 1977), to better define and agree on the criteria of TSS.[35] Naming and sanctioning a case definition, and then using that particular rubric to determine current and future presentations of TSS, circumscribed the terms of the illness. Though it outlined physical symptoms and manifestations, the definition carried political consequences because numerous infected women fell outside of the strict boundaries. Many physicians and women's health advocates have since argued that the less severe presentation of symptoms should be included within the terms of the definition, because it still resulted in the illness of TSS.[36] For clinicians, a diagnosis did not depend on a patient presenting all the elements, but for the CDC, it was important to rule out any cases that might not be TSS in order to improve a study's accuracy and reduce the margin of error.

As more cases were reported to the CDC, it became clear that TSS would require additional resources and coordinated attention. Shands became the point person of the TSS Task Force. When creating the team, John Bennett, the director of the division of bacterial diseases, included Dave Fraser from special pathogens and one researcher from each branch of the bacterial diseases division, including Debbie Blum from enteric diseases, George Schmid from zoonoses, and Bruce Dan from hospital infections. Dan, the original naysayer, became an important ally and researcher. While at the CDC, he questioned the transmission of TSS and its relationship to scarlet fever, and whether or not different kinds of bacteria might be producing a similar shock. He remembered a very vivid case published in the *Annals of Internal Medicine* in 1973, in which the physician and microbiologist Richard McCloskey injected himself with serum derived from an infected patient to prove that the infection was staphylococcal and not streptococcal.[37] This was important because by the 1970s staphylococcal infections were already penicillin-resistant. Thus, administering the proper antibiotic made a very timely difference in halting the manifestation of more dire symptoms. McCloskey became quite ill, achy, and feverish, and he experienced a severe drop in blood pressure. His assistant, William Jackson, took photos of the redness and rashlike quality to the skin, as well as the swelling on his arm at the site of the injection. He recovered with the quick administration of antibiotic injections, but that was enough to demonstrate the reality of staphylococcal bacteria to cause scarlet fever.

Lawrence Altman, a physician and reporter for the *New York Times*, describes a phone call years later from Bruce Dan to McCloskey, in which Dan suggested that McCloskey actually identified TSS, based on the reaction and lab cultures. Dan sought further samples from McCloskey's patient (there were none), but McCloskey did offer up his own blood sample, which had the antibody for the staphylococcal toxin, though it may have formed before his self-administered inoculation. Moreover, what was important to Dan was not just the bacterium, but also the toxin that caused the severe reaction. Dan wanted to test this hypothesis and use himself as the metaphorical "guinea pig." McCloskey did not want him to repeat it, and, moreover, one of Dan's supervisors at the CDC refused permission as well, according to McCloskey. Since Dan has passed away, I tried to corroborate this story with Shands who did not remember this incident, but she noted that "it would be characteristic of him to have made such a suggestion."[38] Forgoing a human subject, researchers at the CDC injected *S. aureus*, cultured from the vagina of a woman who had contracted TSS, into a primate. It did not go so well for the lab animal, and it died within twenty-four hours, indicating that there was something going on with *S. aureus*.[39]

With a specific set of criteria in mind, and TSS identified with both a bacterium and a toxin, researchers in different hubs began to track outbreaks and define patterns of infection. Through the *MMWR* of May

23, 1980, the CDC reported on this new illness and described the symptoms, as well as some of the preliminary findings from Davis in Wisconsin linking TSS to menstruating women.[40] There were a few prominent studies linked to state-level departments of health corroborating evidence, sharing results, and exchanging information. One was referred to as the Wisconsin Study, a case-control study emerging from Davis's original mailings, occurring during the winter and early spring of 1980. The results were formally published in the *New England Journal of Medicine* and Joan Chesney was one of the co-authors.[41]

During the spring and summer of 1980, the CDC also conducted its own studies, referred to as CDC-1 (June 27, 1980) and CDC-2 (September 19, 1980). The TSS Task Force monitored the daily reports from physicians, health departments, and allied health professionals about this new disease. With eight other states reporting incidents, in May 1980 the task force tabulated fifty-five cases of TSS occurring in the country. In June it launched a study, described by Dan, to examine "the critical factors involved in women during their menstrual period getting this severe illness."[42]

The first study, which came to be known as CDC-1, used the methodology of a "case-control study" to compare cases of infected individuals with those who were healthy, to discern whether or not tampons were a cofactor in the illness. This study concluded that indeed there was an association. The particular method is also known as a "retrospective study," in which researchers look back to find individuals who had the illness. This method is suited for tracking down infected individuals in order to understand a disease path as it manifests in the real world, not in a contrived laboratory setting. With this in mind, Dan recalled that the task force gathered fifty cases (though the *MMWR* reports fifty-two) of women experiencing TSS, and it compared them to "fifty other women who were matched obviously for sex, who were matched for the geographic area that they lived in, were within three years of age of the cases, and also were known friends of the cases," which assumed that they shared a similar socioeconomic status.[43] The task force asked questions of the women about their menstrual periods, use of different menstrual hygiene products, and medications as well.

The process was lengthy and methodical. Shands recalled it took quite a bit of time to craft the questions, and then to conduct interviews on the phone. Many of the study's participants were teenagers, and Shands described one fifteen- or sixteen-year-old girl, who, while on the phone with her, kept yelling to her mother for answers about when her last menstrual period started, as well as what product she used. When Shands asked her about her sexual activity, she said, "Wait a minute. Let me close the door."[44] This marked an important moment of women asking questions, rather than male researchers, and how the study's participants were more forthcoming with Shands than even with their own mothers. These personal and intimate inquiries were part of the questionnaire to confirm or eliminate behaviors that might foster and transmit the illness.

As she made final preparations for publication of the study's findings in the June 27 *MMWR*, Shands recalled her "panic when [she] realized that one more control using tampons and [the] study would not have been statistically significant."[45] This anxiety, and humbleness, about using good data to draw conclusions had real implications since she said "we [were] putting this out for the entire nation." She became concerned about the "matching scheme for the controls." Because it was a case-control study, the task force needed controls who were not tampon users, but it could not ask this directly during recruitment. Shands did not feel there was sufficient time to go to the schools and have teachers or school nurses help identify the participants, so the task force asked those who were already diagnosed with TSS to name someone in a peer group as a "match." Shands said most of them, as teenagers, provided a best friend's name. She reflected, if one was using tampons, the other one was likely to do so, too. A shortcoming was that they were overmatched. She began to wonder, what if one more of our controls had used tampons? They would not have been able to assert a statistically significant association of TSS with tampons; in essence, the groups would look the same.[46] She discussed her concern with Dave Fraser, urgently telling him "we are just one person into statistical significance!" He reassured her by saying, "That's why they are statistics. This is statistically significant." It was an important lesson in constructing studies, as well as the strengths and weakness of epidemiology (and is now used as an example in CDC training about the potential errors of overmatching).[47] As she put it, it is "not a hard science, it's actually a very powerful science."

What CDC-1 indicated was that tampons were associated with TSS, and for the epidemiologists, they needed to conduct further research.

The premise of the following study, CDC-2, was to refine it, and this time specifically ask about tampon brand. Conducted during the summer of 1980, CDC-2 examined methodology of "recall accuracy" and also the type and brand of tampon used. Though CDC-1 did not find significant differences between brands, CDC-2 did, and there was "an increased risk associated with the use of Rely tampons among TSS patients as compared with controls."[48] It is clear that Shands corrected the problem of "overmatching," and the report addressed what accounted for differences between the first and second report. One hindrance noted in the first was the small number of cases, and another was "the possibility that 'best friend' controls would be likely to use the same brands." Here, CDC-2 asked the women to "provide the names of 3 female friends or acquaintances within 3 years of their own age who lived within the same geographic area."[49] This broadened the circle and distributed the sampling method beyond just a tight-knit group of teenagers.

The report also clarified "risk associated with specific brands of tampons" including o.b., Kotex, Tampax, Playtex, and Rely (both super and regular). Among the women who used tampons and contracted TSS, 71 percent used Rely. The other brands fell quickly after that, with 19 percent attributed to Playtex, 5 percent to Tampax, 2 percent to Kotex, and 2 percent to o.b. Of the control group, and women who did not contract TSS, Rely users still represented the highest proportion at 26 percent. P&G had succeeded in wedging its way into the market and changing brand loyalty. With it, however, came unwanted publicity for the company, of which the litigation ramifications will be explored more directly in a later chapter. Corroborating evidence came from the Wisconsin Study and the Tri-State TSS study coming out of Minnesota, Iowa, and Wisconsin, which carefully examined cases, brands and absorbency as related to TSS after CDC-2 and its findings were reported in the September 19 *MMWR*. The researchers found that the absorbency of the tampon or the wearing of Rely "were the only variables that significantly increased the relative risk of TSS." Furthermore, the study directly implicated Rely, stating that "the rise associated with Rely was greater than that predicted by absorbency alone, suggesting that chemical composition of tampons was an important factor."[50] Thus, the science pointed to the fact that tampons, and especially Rely, were not inert.

Corporate Investigations

Public health officials were not the only ones interested in TSS. The tampon industry as a whole was apprised of growing concerns and preliminary findings by the CDC, and Shands had many phone conversations with managers, especially at P&G, during the spring of 1980. Questions came directly from customers, too, many of whom were dissatisfied by Rely's performance. The tampons efficiently absorbed not just menstrual fluid but all vaginal fluid, so some women reported difficulty removing the tampons when they got stuck. For some women, the tampon had so thoroughly dried out the vaginal canal, that pieces of skin adhered to it, and it also shed residual polyesters and foam, causing vaginitis and irritation. Others intuitively linked their flulike symptoms to the new tampon, and they called customer service to inquire about allergic reactions or possible contamination.[51]

As health concerns from its customer base grew, P&G marshaled its formidable resources to study TSS. The research arm at P&G, known as the Miami Valley Laboratories, functioned as an incubator and innovation center for research and development at the company, creating consumer items, pharmaceuticals, and chemical processes used in product development. As a separate branch of the company, it was free to take on special projects, as well as fund and sponsor external grants for academic scholarship.[52] The lab became preoccupied with TSS under the direction of James Stone Widder. An immunologist by training, he was appointed as the associate director of the special programs division at Miami Valley Laboratories specifically to study TSS. His research group comprised two chemical engineers, an enzymologist, a bacterial physiologist, a biochemist, an electron microscopist, a veterinary pathologist, and ten lab technicians. In addition, the special programs division funded seventeen external investigators or institutions to the tune of $2.65 million.[53] Within this infrastructure of corporate research, lab technicians were able to practice "fastidious science" with the ability to reproduce results. It is here within this very structured environment that more precise findings about TSS were explored, as well as where the seeds of doubt were planted about the "pragmatic" in-field findings gleaned from epidemiologists.

Widder contended that the link between *S. aureus* and TSS was just a hypothesis, and that the definitive cause was uncertain, which no doubt served the needs of P&G. The rationale he used to make this claim was based on his interpretation of Koch's postulates. Developed in 1884 during the genesis of bacteriology, the guidelines developed by Nobel Laureate Robert Koch and Friedrich Loeffler laid out characteristics by which a microorganism is responsible for the cause of a disease. Briefly, the microbe must (1) be abundantly represented throughout the body, and not in healthy organisms; (2) be grown outside the host and cultured; (3) manifest as illness in a healthy body, via the assayed culture; and (4) be identified in that newly infected and ill host, with a match to the original infecting agent.[54] There are some aspects and exceptions to this, such as asymptomatic carriers who do not present usual signs of infection and yet harbor the microbe (HIV, cholera, hepatitis C, typhoid) and the inability of scientists to culture all microorganisms.[55] Though Koch's postulates may serve as a strong guideline, and do work toward confirming infectious agents in most cases, the method is not foolproof. The postulates represent late nineteenth-century thinking, so that by the emergence of TSS there were nearly one hundred years of new science to shape and inform this practice.

Widder interpreted and deployed Koch's postulates to assert that no one had proven that *S. aureus* was causative of TSS.[56] He pointed out that scientists were able to identify *S. aureus* in infected bodies, but culturing it and inoculating lab mice did not produce TSS in mice. In fact, it was the toxins that produced TSS, and not necessarily the presence of the bacterium, since it often coexisted as a benign constituent in many individuals. This is why, for epidemiologists at the CDC, proving that serum drawn from an infected individual reproduced the symptoms of TSS in a rabbit or a human was very important in identifying causation. And Pat Schlievert, a microbiologist who began studying TSS during this time, was also able to isolate the serum and toxin, and re-create the symptoms in rabbits.[57] The scientists utilized Koch's postulates to turn it either way. TSS did not conform because it could not be reproduced through the bacterium. Or it did conform because it could be reproduced via the toxin created by the bacterium. For P&G, the disagreement was a means to raise doubt about the origins of causation, so that the correlation of tampons with TSS made by the CDC would be less authoritative.

As far as P&G was concerned, its scientists had conducted sound research, and there was no reason to question the integrity of the new product. In a memo from Gordon Hassing, a director of product safety, to Peter Morris in research and development on June 24, 1980, Hassing assured him that, "thus far, there is no direct evidence for the causal involvement of tampons in TSS. The etiology of TSS is unknown but is likely to involve an infectious agent." Though Hassing believed Rely was not an issue, he predicted that disfavor might come from the media. He continued: "The potential for adverse publicity for tampons as a product category remains high, particularly if the CDC data are made public irresponsibly. Strategically, we can only help to keep any publicity from being irresponsible." By positioning Rely as "part of the pack" as he called it, Hassing aimed to address the TSS-tampon link as just that: associated with a category as a whole and not a particular brand.[58] This tactic contradicted earlier marketing with its focus on the difference between Rely and other tampons. Grouping tampons together as similar was now crucial for the sale of Rely, and Hassing noted, "Keep this problem only theoretically associated with the category. This is extremely important because of the unique construction of Rely and its very high marketing profile." Hassing's concerns became more urgent after the CDC released its findings in the *MMWR* correlating TSS with tampons on June 27.[59] That same day, interdepartmental correspondence from area managers flatly ordered sales representatives to control their comments about TSS, stating, "You should not initiate discussion of this subject."[60]

Managers at P&G grew more concerned. The CDC had been keeping all the affected companies apprised of data and results coming from its studies. P&G, however, wanted to conduct its own research to verify the CDC report linking tampons and TSS. At first, researchers at the company requested to see the interviews and raw data sets from the CDC, including participants' names, but the CDC refused, citing patient confidentiality.[61] As a result, that summer P&G lawyers sought to subpoena records from the CDC in order to obtain the names of women interviewed during the CDC's investigations.[62] The CDC continued to make data available, but not the identities of survey participants. Team managers at P&G felt increasingly uneasy that conclusions were being based on self-reported cases to the CDC as well as retrospective studies.[63] In part, the dispute was about methodology and the pursuit of ill patients instead of a truly random sample, yet this ran counter to epidemiologic practices. The method threatened to undermine P&G's new product and create financial losses for the company.

In order to overcome this methodological impasse and challenge it with their own data, researchers at P&G exercised a new tactic: track down women who called the company complaining of sickness but later recovered, and talk to them more specifically about their health with an eye toward gaining access to their medical records, which presumably would more accurately reflect a diagnosis of TSS by a credentialed physician. According to Roscoe Owen Carter, the Ph.D. chemist in charge of paper products development and therefore Rely, the self-reporting of TSS to doctors and the CDC was dubious, with cases not meeting all of the criteria for the clinical definition. He believed "the only way that you could make a decision as to whether this might have been toxic shock syndrome was to get to the physician, talk with him, and then actually see the medical records, [and] go through these medical records."[64]

Company officials used this aggressive approach with Karen and her daughter, from a town in Indiana, who purchased Rely tampons from the local Kmart. She complained to P&G on July 25, 1980, that her teenage daughter was hospitalized with a staph infection and her doctor believed the cause of it was Rely. By July 31, Carter called her physician, who was quite forthcoming about the teen's symptoms, ranging from high fever and muscle pain to diarrhea. However, he withheld her name from P&G. This was of no concern to P&G, because members from Carter's division spoke to the Kmart store manager, who divulged the identity of both the physician and the patient. Under the guise of collecting medical evidence, strategists at P&G flagrantly violated patient confidentiality, abetted no less by the family physician and the Kmart store manager.[65] Strategists and managers at P&G wanted it both ways: to invoke the need for proper procedures by the CDC but violate customary patient/doctor confidentiality when it favored the company.

By September, P&G leaders recognized that public health officials were closing in on Rely. A memo from Thomas Laco, an executive vice president, to Edward Harness, the P&G Chairman of the Board, stated, "Our people believe that it's likely that the CDC and perhaps the FDA are headed toward concluding that tampons with super-absorbant [sic] components based on CMC may disproportionately cause TSS problems." This was based upon the CDC's own research, and the memo continued, "Our people consider the work extremely sketchy and nonconclusive." Laco reassured Harness that through their connections, "we have an opportunity to convince both the CDC and the FDA that they are barking up the wrong tree and that such a preliminary conclusion will prove to be wrong as additional data becomes available putting CDC into a very poor scientific light."[66] Though P&G may have hoped for the CDC science to be proven wrong, it is no wonder that due to the ongoing pressures P&G assembled what it called the "P&G Microbiological Task Force," whose duty was to "develop perspective on the the assumed role of tampons in the disease Toxic Shock Syndrome (TSS)." The task force summarized experiments and distilled the conclusions into a memo. The report indicated four findings: (1) "cross-linked CMC [carboxymethylcellulose] does not stimulate growth of S. aureus"; (2) "neither Rely foam material nor cotton stimulate growth of S. aureus"; (3) Playtex Plus and Tampax Super Plus, when using distilled water, seem to inhibit *S. aureus*; and (4) none of the tampons, using sheep blood, stimulated growth of *S. aureus*.[67] With all these tests coming back negative, one of the deep problems with which the scientists wrestled was that they had not identified a "causal relationship" between TSS and tampons. A literature review that they conducted on TSS, along with consultation with various government and university scientists, failed to produce a clear explanation for the association of tampons and TSS.[68]

In some ways, these various fact-finding missions were understandable. Things just were not adding up for the researchers at P&G, and scientists had wildly different ideas about what was happening. On one side, there were the state and federally funded epidemiologists who were documenting illness trends associating tampons with TSS. The exact mechanism of the illness was yet to be determined, but the epidemiologists' mission was to halt a potential epidemic, and that boiled down to a judgment call based on many pieces of evidence. Another camp wielded the mantra of inconclusive science, based on corporate scientists' as well as some academic researchers' assessments. This perspective viewed findings as a starting point, which raised more questions than they could answer.

Raising Doubt

In the book *Merchants of Doubt*, Naomi Oreskes and Erik Conway, historians of science, trace the ways that some scientists have not only abetted corporate interests, but also used the social capital of science to misdirect investigations about acid rain, ozone depletion, and cigarette smoke and their consequences for human and global health. Scientists protected institutional structures and financial arrangements by generating data that raised doubt about the extent of multiple damages caused by products and by-products of industry, thereby deflecting attention away from corporate culpability. In a similar manner, P&G also had a vested interest in raising doubt about the link between TSS and tampons, because the financial rewards from the tampon benefited corporate managers as well as stockholders. It should be noted here that P&G granted funding and monetarily supported some of the academic researchers, including James Todd and Jeff Davis, who were at the forefront of TSS research and later accepted this grant money.[69] The close financial ties between some scientists and many companies, including P&G, were not so apparent in 1980, but in hindsight the links raise questions and speculation about objectivity.

Such conflicts of interest rose to the surface with debates regarding what toxin produced and was responsible for TSS. Through a series of concessions and negotiations, Dan and Shands co-authored a piece with Schlievert identifying what they called exotoxin A.[70] By 1982, researchers discussed at least six different toxins, and by 1984 most agreed that *S. aureus* enterotoxin F, or SEF, caused the symptoms of TSS.[71] Currently, most refer to this toxin as TSST-1. During this same time, Merlin Bergdoll, a professor of food science and toxicology at the University of Wisconsin, had been researching foodborne illness and toxins, including that of *S. aureus*, which produces food poisoning. Lawyers, scientists, and health activists accused him of withholding data related to the particular type of toxin associated with TSS, and in 1984 *Science* reported on these allegations.[72] The *Science* article noted that from 1980 to 1984 Bergdoll accepted at least $150,000 from manufacturers, including $50,000 from P&G. As a result of his research, Bergdoll reported what he called "preliminary data" to P&G, which their in-house scientists were able to reproduce. These data indicated that Rely tampons encouraged the production of more toxins than any other brand of tampon tested. Rely was the only tampon to have the particular composition of synthetics including polyester and carboxymethylcellulose, though women would not have known this because these components were not indicated on the label. The retrospective position from 1984 questioned whether or not these "preliminary data" would have been useful in establishing a definitive link between TSS and Rely tampons. It also pointed to the active suppression of data that were unflattering and damaging to P&G.

Later, Bergdoll disclosed that not only did P&G support his research, but so did Personal Products, Tambrands, Inc., Kimberly-Clark Corporation, and International Playtex.[73] Joan Chesney, who had co-authored the Wisconsin TSS study with Jeff Davis, co-edited with Bergdoll a 1991 comprehensive volume simply entitled *Toxic Shock Syndrome* that amassed all the published research up to that point. The introduction noted, "It is difficult, sometimes impossible, to provide absolute proof that any particular compound is involved in disease, primarily because of the lack of a suitable test animal."[74] Bergdoll played both sides of the coin here. It is true that much of science points toward conclusions rather than asserting absolute facts, and that the shortcomings of methodology, such as the inability to infect animal test subjects with the bacteria to then run further experiments, is a serious limitation. Yet this is also the moment when publics expect more. When the CDC and other state departments of health had linked superabsorbent tampons to TSS, the cover of "absolute proof" raised by corporate and corporate-sponsored researchers was a cop-out, favoring their interests over women's health. Doubt raised is not always objective, and in this case it added to the already confusing cofactors existing around tampon-related TSS.

* * *

As the *MMWR* reports indicated, tampon-related TSS affected a small number of women. The attention it received from the epidemiologists was seemingly disproportionate to the few who contracted it. Yet the potential for more cases was drastic in light of P&G's outstanding distribution system and, importantly, the fact that women were using the tampons and actually liked them. Though this chapter has focused on the epidemiology related to superabsorbent tampons and Rely, the counterweight to these efforts was cultural: many women preferred the new Rely tampon because it did not leak and it absorbed heavy menstrual flow. P&G had successfully created loyal, repeat consumers.

Anecdotally, several women have shared with me a kind of wistfulness that they can no longer purchase and use Rely, because it was such a good tampon. I must admit, when I opened up one of my two sample boxes of Rely that I purchased from eBay, I marveled at their construction and how different they really were from compressed cotton tampons. The polyester was very light, and the cup design with the rosette expansion and closure offered an ingenious design. Rely tampons had a strong consumer base, which meant epidemiologists needed to be very respectful of them as users. In 1980, while Shands and Dan at the CDC investigated TSS, they spoke both to many women who they sought out as patients and also to those who voluntarily contacted the CDC. According to an article in the *Washington Post*, Dan fielded a phone call from the latter group. He recalled that this female caller suggested an explanation for the whole thing. "'I know why all this happened,' she said. 'They finally found a tampon that worked.'"[75] This caller did not look to science for answers, but she explained it through the common knowledge that menstruation is a curse, understood as the biblical burden shouldered by all women due to Eve's fall from grace. The modern-day punishment, in this rationalization, for "a tampon that worked" was TSS. In this version women were not allowed to experience a comfortable, leak-free period. This seemed like a cruel joke because the Rely tampon was actually very effective for many, many women. Yet the tampons were simultaneously a dangerous health threat, made more so because they did not fit a usual model of disease. The identification of tampon-related TSS challenged route paths of knowledge production and required a shift in thought to accept tampons as technological co-producers of illness. In light of prevailing attitudes about menstruation and the new kind of illness related to not-so-inert technologies, conveying a message of risk would not be so easy.

3

The Media Sounds the Alarm

According to the *Washington Post*, "In 1980, TSS was the third-leading news story in the nation, trailing only the Iranian hostage situation and the presidential election."[1] Republican Ronald Reagan ousted Democratic incumbent Jimmy Carter in a sound thumping during the fall, and the Iranian hostage crisis and botched rescue were tied to the election as well. Presidential politics and high-stakes international affairs were a sharp contrast to the emerging toxic shock syndrome (TSS) health crisis unfurling on women's menstrual habits and tampon choices. This turn of events was very jarring. In an era when the National Association of Broadcasters had only recently allowed sanitary napkins to be advertised on television in 1972, the shift to airing the words "tampon" and "menstruation" on nightly news was nearly unimaginable. That a "women's issue" ranked third behind two dominant national news stories spoke to both the significance of the illness and also the emergent politics of women's rights and women's health activism insisting on a woman's right to know. Conveying risk about tampon-related TSS challenged the status quo, forcing media outlets to articulate a woman-centered illness in which a supposedly benign tampon had taken a deadly turn.

The newsworthiness of tampons broke a cultural silence, and, moreover, generated a discussion that questioned tampons' very efficacy. The stakes of this national conversation were consequential for women users whose health might be affected, corporate leaders whose company profits were threatened, and federal health agencies whose trustworthy reputations were on the line. The ability to contextualize information held widespread political implications. How the message was articulated, and by whom, deliberately shaped the contours of this health crisis. Both the Centers for Disease Control (CDC) and the Food and Drug Administration (FDA) controlled the dominant narrative, but the media was a key intermediary delivering information from experts to consumers, and this chapter analyzes how information about TSS was translated and disseminated. The CDC's *Morbidity and Mortality Weekly Report* (*MMWR*) and press releases from the FDA explained the symptoms of TSS and warned women not to use Rely. Some news outlets interpreted these scientific reports, making them more accessible to a wider audience. Others conducted investigative journalism about TSS, drawing on first-person testimonials as evidence, while financial journals cast doubt on the illness and supported corporate missions.

Undoubtedly, news reports caught the public's attention because the illness seemed salacious; journalists could not easily write accurate articles without discussing women's bodies and reproductive processes, with vaginas implicated all around. Both judgmental skepticism and also prurient curiosity befell the coverage, raising the profile of TSS as a news item but also contributing to misunderstandings about it. Media coverage about TSS spiked again in September and October of 1980 when Procter & Gamble (P&G) engaged in reverse advertising to urge women to return unused tampons and not use its product, a first for a medical device. The message of risk became diluted after Rely's withdrawal and the health crisis seemed to wane, though TSS had not actually been cured. Without a singular tampon to blame, a more generalized warning transferred responsibility for the illness onto women and advised cautious use of tampons.

First Reports

Initial news reports about Rely tampons started even before they were associated with TSS. In 1975, the *Rochester Patriot*, an underground newspaper active from 1973 to 1982, ran a series of articles about the new Rely tampon and its assessment of them was unfavorable. Rochester, New York, and Fort Wayne, Indiana, were two cities chosen for the early test marketing of Rely. Residents received sample packets in the mail, with advertising on radio, on television, and in newspapers accompanying this rollout. The paper reported about the ingredients of Rely: carboxymethylcellulose and polyurethane, a carcinogen. P&G later changed polyurethane to polyester, but this ingredient remained in the early samples. The article claimed that "Rochester women are being made guinea pigs for a new product that P&G doesn't want to answer many questions about," and the reporters lamented that tampon composition "is not subject to review" by the FDA.[2] However, due to the paper's reporting and perceived trouble with the tampon in Rochester, P&G announced that it would remove the polyurethane. The story from the *Rochester Patriot* prompted other local radio stations as well as the larger mainstream Rochester newspaper, the *Democrat and Chronicle*, to carry reports about the tampon. Even the Monroe County Health Department conducted a survey of local women who used the Rely samples, and found that thirteen of thirty-nine reported problems, including itching, burning, and pain during removal, as well as the tampon falling apart. The department warned that "people just shouldn't use it (Rely) until they know that it is a different product."[3] These reports foreshadowed more trouble for P&G.

A few years later in 1979, both consumer services at P&G and Lillian Yin, the director of the Bureau of Medical Devices at the FDA, heard from M. C. of Los Osos, California. M. C. received and used free Rely samples, and wrote that not only was the tampon difficult to remove, but she needed Vaseline to do so because it stuck to her vaginal walls. Bleeding from the damaged skin occurred for two full days, and she felt the materials were simply not suitable for any tampon.[4]

While the *Milwaukee Journal* carried an article on February 14, 1980, concerning the "disorder" of TSS, it was not yet associated with tampons.[5] Only after the CDC released the May 23 *MMWR* report did more coverage follow. Dr. Bruce Dan, an Epidemic Intelligence Service (EIS) officer at the CDC working on the TSS Task Force, estimated that 100,000 medical practitioners, public health workers, nurses, and physicians, subscribed to the *MMWR*, yet as few as 25 percent of them may have been reached with that publication.[6] Many missed the May 23 report carrying a description of TSS, its symptoms, and its prevalence in younger women; thus more cases may have occurred but were unreported. The May 23 report noted, "Since October 1, 1979, 55 cases have been reported to CDC. Fifty-two of these (95%) have been in women" with seven deaths among that group. The report, however, had not yet linked TSS with use of tampons, though it did note that "of 40 patients in whom a menstrual history was obtained, 38 (95%) had onset of illness within the 5-day period following onset of menses." Two more experienced TSS within ten days of their period, and "13 patients have had recurrence of symptoms with a subsequent menstrual period."[7] The report confirmed the link to menstruation. This also made the illness all the more frightening, because it struck at the reproductive organs of every menstruator.

By May 30, a science reporter, Susan Okie at the *Washington Post*, picked up the *MMWR* announcement, and she interviewed Kathryn Shands, the principal investigator at the CDC on TSS, about this so-called new disease. Shands described one of the patients and noted that her "major impression was that this was an incredible disease to strike a completely healthy adolescent girl."[8] Shands labeled it as "scary," which was strong language coming from the nationally sponsored health agency. In my interview with Shands she recalled that the reporter "said something like 'this is really frightening,' and I said, 'Yeah, it's scary,' and this was the lead!" She added that afterward she got a lot of "grief" from her colleagues, reflecting that it was a "big mistake" to raise such a high alarm.[9] Though she learned from this incident how to be more measured as a spokesperson, there was good to come from this "mistake." Senator Edward Kennedy read this same article, according to Elizabeth Etheridge, who wrote a history of the CDC.[10] Kennedy was chair of the Subcommittee on Health and Scientific Research, Committee on Labor and Human Resources, and had called on William Foege, the director of the CDC, to testify about the health hazards of toxic dumps. Kennedy asked that he be prepared to address TSS while testifying. This testimony about TSS would then enter into the federal record and attract new attention to the illness.

On Friday, June 6, 1980, both Foege and Shands appeared in Washington, DC, for the hearing, along with Jewel Eastburn and Stephanie Haley, who both had recovered from TSS. In his opening remarks, Kennedy painted the grim scene of a "mystery disease, which strikes previously healthy people without warning, whose cause is unknown, whose treatment is uncertain, and which kills many of its victims." Furthermore, "It primarily affects young women of childbearing age, and of those cases reported to CDC as of May 23, 10 to 15 percent of the victims have died." Extrapolating from that, it was easy to imagine thousands of women dying, which was certainly cause for alarm. He pointed out that these "new disease mysteries" are usually solved, and that "the purpose of this hearing is to alert the American people, while the mystery still exists, to know what to look for, how to recognize the symptoms, when to seek help."[11] During the hearing, both Eastburn and Haley corroborated the symptoms from which they suffered, and, moreover, Eastburn attested that she dreaded its recurrence, which she had already experienced. Foege and Shands spoke about what they knew so far, and their prediction for upward of two thousand cases for the year, with a mortality rate of 10 to 15 percent. Shands attested that it was taking on national proportions, and she was in the process of working with other investigators to develop a case definition of TSS. Among current patients, she noted that 75 percent of the women had *Staphylococcus aureus* in their vaginas, and this "may or may not be of importance."[12]

Kennedy asked if it were "more or less complicated than Legionnaires' Disease," and Foege responded, "My guess at the moment would be that it would turn out to be less complicated to delineate what is involved with this syndrome."[13] This was optimistic but naive, for it is clear now that Legionnaires' is far better understood and treated compared to TSS, which is still a contemporary concern. Foege also asserted that this was likely not a new virus or disease. "In the 1970s," he added, "we discovered as many new viruses as we have discovered in any previous decade." He modified that with "I do not believe they are new viruses. On the other hand, I believe we sometimes see new diseases because of mutations or changes in organisms," such as penicillin-resistant gonorrhea. He expressed a tremendous amount of confidence with the current science of discovery, as well as some hubris that science must merely reveal what is out there; species already exist but for their discovery, not their emergence as a novel entity.

Kennedy's intent to publicize TSS worked. Later that night, Walter Cronkite, a broadcast journalist and anchor of the *CBS Evening News*, first reported that the Senate committee on hazardous waste had also discussed a new disease called TSS.[14] More coverage followed over the weekend in national and local papers. Headlines varied, with the *Bangor Daily News* announcing "Toxic-Shock Disease Probed"; the *Tuscaloosa News* asserted "New Disease Strikes Women, Report Claims"; the *Indianapolis Star* announced "New Mystery Disease Striking Women of Childbearing Age"; the *New York Times* led with the alarming "7 Are Dead of a Baffling, Newly Discovered Disease."[15] These headlines extinguished Foege's careful crafting that this was not a new, but instead a newly identified, disease. Headlines raised interest with words such as "baffle" and "mystery," while pointing to young, otherwise healthy women succumbing to a grisly demise.[16] Furthermore, harm to a presumptive universal white woman who was a mother or a potential mother added to the alarm.

In just three weeks, the *MMWR* announced the definitive link. It summarized three studies (CDC-1, the Wisconsin Study, and the Utah Study), the syndrome with its symptoms, and, significantly, TSS's association with tampons. While "no significant differences were found between the patients and the controls" in the CDC study, "50 of 50 cases with onset during menstruation (100%) used tampons, as compared to 43 of 50 controls (85%)." Furthermore, seventeen of the fifty-two women from the case-control study received vaginal cultures, revealing that sixteen of seventeen had *S. aureus* among their vaginal flora. The Wisconsin Study found similarly striking results, with "30 of 31 patients (97%) and 71 of 93 controls (76%)" using tampons during each menstrual period.[17] Among twenty-four of these cases, ten of them had experienced recurrence of TSS during a subsequent menstrual period. The Utah Study was significantly smaller with only twelve patients, but the trends were similar. Cases and controls showed predominant tampon use and association with the syndrome while ruling out person-to-person transmission, sexually transmitted infections, vaginal sprays, and douching.

More outlets picked up the findings from the *MMWR*, latching on to the connection of TSS with tampons. The *Washington Post* called it "a mysterious and sometimes fatal new disease" while the *New York Times* reported that "the use of tampons has been linked to a rare disease called toxic shock syndrome that primarily affects young women."[18] Both articles recounted the general findings from the *MMWR*, and both also concluded that there was no need to discontinue tampon use. The *New York Times* noted that "no particular brand of tampon has been associated with the disease," and it quoted Robert L. DeSanti, executive vice president of Tampax Incorporated. A long-standing tampon manufacturer with an estimated 40–50 percent of the market share at that time, it had every reason to downplay and contest the findings. DeSanti stated assuredly, "We have not encountered the illness at any time during more than 40 years of clinical testing of our product, so we have no direct knowledge of the illness." Here, he drew on the company's history as evidence to downplay and diffuse the *MMWR* announcement. In addition,

Friday's installment of the *CBS Evening News* with Dan Rather reported on the illness and its symptoms, treatment, and government recommendations. Shands spoke about TSS on the newscast and confirmed the connection with tampons saying, "It was a result that no one here wanted to find and in spite of that we found it."[19] She, too, was not keen on plucking tampons out of women's menstrual management toolbox.

By Monday, the *Wall Street Journal* chimed in, with a different tone to the whole story. While the mainstream news could be characterized as concerned, despite a bit of fearmongering related to the rather ill-defined risk factors, alerting the public to potential health problems was the general goal of the articles. The *Wall Street Journal*, however, took a decidedly business tone and began its article with the following: "Every consumer products company fears it: the government report that links its product to disease."[20] Echoing neoliberalism, the article reflected skepticism, a touch of disdain for federal regulation, and the dread of the impending public relations efforts to manage findings from a "government report." With sympathy toward corporate well-being and a more disparaging tone toward presumably hypochondriac women, the report continued, "Predictably, Tampax Inc. got phone calls from women all day last Friday." The report implied that the women's calls were overreactive and groundless, because "the CDC doesn't establish any causal link between toxic-shock syndrome and tampon use." Thus, with a sleight of hand the article dismissed both the actual report in which the CDC made a definitive link as well as the relevance of the callers' concerns. DeSanti, the Tampax vice president interviewed by the *New York Times* just days earlier, also replied to the *Wall Street Journal*, this time saying, "We have a lot of concern over the publicity given the report," acknowledging that "rumors have been circulating." Overall, the report seemed to concentrate on the bad publicity that might follow the announcement, and not on women's health due to tampon use. The article noted that, when judging stock prices as an indicator, damage from the CDC's report was limited. "Tampax, for one, was quoted at $31.75 a share bid, up 37 ½ cents in over-the counter-trading Friday." The article assured readers that "if consumers react like the stock market did, tampon makers haven't anything to worry about." This cocksure attitude dismissed the threat to women and instead reassured corporations. However, the stock market was not the best gauge of risk in a venue where traders and brokers were predominantly men, who did not have to be aware of the scope of tampon use or the personal consequences of TSS.

Controlling the Message

While the *Wall Street Journal* dismissed TSS as a temporary annoyance for the company, P&G executives felt less assuaged. Results from the second retrospective study conducted by the CDC were coming in (later named CDC-2), and this time the researchers asked specifically about tampon brands. Seventy-one percent of those who contracted TSS had used Rely.[21] The CDC alerted the FDA, which requested a meeting with P&G on September 16. In preparation, an FDA staffer ran to the drugstore and purchased a variety of tampons, and "the commissioner and deputy commissioner, the chief counsel (a woman), the head of regulatory affairs, the director of the Bureau of Medical devices and others" picked apart the tampons and noticed the "white specks" that were the minisponges in Rely.[22] Wayne Pines, the associate commissioner for public affairs at the FDA, admitted that he had "never touched a tampon before" this exercise, and the men's lack of familiarity with them was not lost on Chief Counsel Nancy Buc. She described the men as holding the tampons "like grenades," treating them as foreign and dangerous.[23] Of course, all but Buc were afforded the privilege of not knowing; now they needed a crash course in tampon design, reproductive health, and epidemiology to understand the scope of risk posed to tampon users.

The meeting was large: thirteen from P&G, twelve from the FDA, and three from the CDC.[24] Pines from the FDA recalled, "We were prepared to ask P&G to remove Rely from the market if it could not raise sufficient doubts about the validity of the CDC data."[25] P&G executives had prepared to offer a warning on the box to assuage the FDA, but Pines made it clear that it needed to do more than warn but also address the concerns raised by the CDC report. The counterargument P&G posed about the high association of Rely with TSS blamed women's problematic memories. Their theory was that women simply were not correctly remembering the brands that they used, an ironic consequence of the vast advertising campaign engaged by P&G to promote Rely. In effect, P&G argued that it was a casualty of its own success. The rationale followed that women mistakenly identified Rely even when they had used other tampons, which conveniently explained the discrepancy.[26] (After opening a Rely tampon, I do not know how anyone would confuse brands.) News coverage also supposedly swayed women's memories. This dismissive hypothesis gave women no credit for knowing their own purchasing patterns or even menstrual hygiene practices. The scapegoating of women to protect its investment pointed to the company's dawning recognition that it might need to relinquish its new product, which would therefore not return a profit.

This justification of erroneous remembering was conducive for the company, not for women users. Nancy Buc, the FDA's lawyer, remained dissatisfied with this and needed the company to either rule out Rely's association with TSS or offer a different explanation. With experience in consumer product safety, Buc contemplated terms of an official recall, now feasible due to the 1976 Medical Device Amendments (MDA). Tampons were Class II medical devices and, as such, were subject to this policy. The MDA offered an "imminent hazard provision" specifically known as section 518, which Buc could use to issue a formal product recall. This power had not yet been invoked for any medical device during its first four years by the FDA. Buc, however, used this as a negotiating lever. In my interview with her, she asserted that if P&G did not withdraw the product on its own, then she would take legal action, and thus allow them to "figure out what was going on" with its tampon before its reemergence on the market.[27] As Jere Goyan, the commissioner of the FDA at the time, explained it, "Section 518 provides for FDA to require companies to retrieve from the market certain products that may pose a health hazard, to notify consumers of the hazard, to refund the purchase price, and to reimburse wholesalers and retailers for returning hazardous products to the manufacturer, thus providing them an incentive to swiftly remove hazardous products from the market."[28]

Behind the scenes at the FDA, discussions of this looming tampon problem circulated within the offices of legal counsel and beyond. Nancy Buc worked for the FDA, and her counterpart for the Food and Drug Division of Health and Human Services (HHS) was Joan Z. (Jodie) Bernstein. As its general counsel, Bernstein reported to Patricia Harris, the U.S. secretary of HHS, who served as a cabinet member to President Jimmy Carter. This was a unique situation for three power-brokering women to be at the crux of policy making about tampons. In my interview with Buc, she recalled being absolutely enraged by the faulty tampons, and that TSS might result because of them seemed like "a special punishment for being a woman."[29] Bernstein had a teenage daughter at the time and was particularly concerned about the implications for tampon-wearing young women. Buc and Bernstein valued tampons as physically liberating and as a component of comfortable menstrual management, especially compared to sanitary pads. Buc recalled that Harris was less moved by tampons' attributes, suggesting that perhaps all tampons should be banned to curtail TSS entirely. Though Harris's intent was protective, Buc felt that this was an overstretch, as well as a disservice to women. Buc argued for a limited recall, and she stated that for this particular issue "it mattered that a woman held that job."[30] Harris deferred to Buc's judgment, and afterward she touted the strides made by HHS in hiring women during the 1970s, and the difference it made when women held decision-making powers as managers. "Throughout Health and Human Services," Harris boasted, "women manage programs, make policy and influence the direction of this department. This influence is apparent in the decisions we have made on such diverse issues as Title IX, toxic shock syndrome and welfare reform."[31] Thus, heading into the week's meetings with P&G, Buc had deep support and displayed some feminist swagger.

By September 17, the FDA released confirmation of the preliminary findings before the September 19 *MMWR* report, indicating "that the use of Rely tampons may increase the risk of toxic shock syndrome more than other brands."[32] The *ABC Evening News* ran an alert lasting twenty seconds, and other newspapers followed.[33] The *New York Times* also ominously reported that the P&G manufacturing plant in Cape Girardeau, Missouri, had halted production of the Rely tampon. In its press release P&G announced "we are temporarily suspending manufacturing operations until the question is resolved."[34] This indicated a severe shift in momentum for the brand, and one that required an emergency meeting by executives and scientific consultants. They needed to meet not at headquarters in Cincinnati, but somewhere central where advisors could easily catch a weekend flight for a Sunday meeting no less. The rendezvous point was Chicago's O'Hare Airport.[35]

In light of the CDC report, and the company's discussions with the FDA about a possible recall, P&G gathered its all-male "Scientific Advisory Group," referred to as SAG, at the Chicago O'Hare Hilton. They flew the advisors in on Saturday for preliminary discussions and to study reports and findings, and Gordon Hassing, an associate director at P&G responsible for product safety, called the meeting to order on Sunday, September 21, 1980. In testimony, Charles Fullgraf, the executive of the paper products division at P&G, recalled that there were ten to twelve scientists who convened on "an emergency basis."[36] They included Tommy Evans, a gynecologist from Wayne State University; James Todd of Denver, who named TSS; Patrick Schlievert, a microbiologist studying *S. aureus* and its toxins; and Mike Osterholm, an epidemiologist from the Minnesota Department of Health.[37] According to Tom Riley, a lawyer who would eventually try the first successful tampon liability case, the SAG found "that the data presented were fragmentary and inconclusive" but "they [P&G] could not refute the information with scientific facts in hand." From Riley's research preparing for his case against P&G, he also learned that the scientists did not endorse the pro forma statement provided by P&G on Sunday which read, "It is clearly the consensus of all investigators studying TSS that tampons are not the cause of TSS." Instead, he said that the scientists modified it slightly to "It is clearly the consensus of all investigators studying TSS that tampons are not the *sole* [emphasis added] cause of TSS."[38] The small addition of "sole" indicated a degree of complicity of tampons, largely due to the overwhelming evidence provided by the CDC data. Osterholm remembered Edward Harness, the P&G Chairman of the Board, asking whether Rely were involved in TSS, and the resounding answer from the scientists was "yes." Harness also asked, "Tomorrow, can I tell the women working at P&G it is safe to use Rely tampons, or tell the men that they are safe for their wives and daughters to use?" To that question, Osterholm answered "no."[39]

Due to this meeting, and the "de facto" recall already occurring in the press and with CDC-2, Harness concluded that the brand was sullied and damaged. Fullgraf had a similar reaction, and later testified that "even though there was not one shred of evidence that Rely—" which he then modified with the word "scientific" to say "there was not one shred of *scientific* [emphasis added] evidence that Rely was involved in toxic shock syndrome." This implied that there was other evidence that might not have been scientific, but Fullgraf dismissed all the data from the CDC. He continued by saying, "We concluded we could not risk the ongoing very bad publicity and we therefore concluded we should with-draw our product from the market."[40] Here, it was publicity that served as the rationale for a recall, not science, and not women's deaths.

On Monday, September 22, with no advance notice to the FDA, P&G announced it was taking Rely off the market in what it termed a "vol-untary suspension of sale," and that women should return any unused product for a refund. According to Pines, "This preemptory action was a PR coup. The company was able to recover the initiative by making its own announcement. P&G controlled its own story and took full credit for voluntarily withdrawing Rely from the market," a decision later lauded by the business press and held up as an example of crisis manage-ment and corporate ethics.[41] Yet this narrative of good business selec-tively forgets the foot-dragging beforehand, and the very careful crafting and implementation of the consent decree afterward. It also overlooks the fact that anything called "crisis management" would be unnecessary if the science conducted by the company was better and more compre-hensive by not assuming a monolithic woman or an inert tampon.

As Buc recalled it, she was prepared to go to court to seek an injunc-tion, and P&G was fully aware of her capabilities to do so. She had ex-perience with consumer product safety commissions, and both she and they knew the depth of her skill. There was a meeting previously sched-uled between P&G and the FDA for September 23, so instead of terms of recall, the parameters of the so-called voluntary withdrawal were ne-gotiated. There were different mind-sets toward these negotiations. One was to praise P&G, which Jere E. Goyan did when he said the company "acted on its own initiative," which from Buc's recounting was not ex-actly true because she had threatened legal action against it.[42] Conversely, some staffers working in the legal division of the FDA wanted P&G to admit liability and be punished, understanding full well that an admis-sion of fault would bring numerous lawsuits and monetary losses to the company. Buc recalled, "My staff was annoyed because negotiations really went very smoothly," with P&G complying with her demands.[43] Her staff instead wanted retribution. Whether or not it was a recall or a withdrawal, it was irrelevant to Buc, and she repeated to me the mantra "perfection is the enemy of the good." With this approach, she felt that negotiation would work far better to secure cooperation with the com-pany and remove the tampons once and for all.[44] She led discussions on the consent decree with Powell McHenry and Jim O'Reilly, P&G's legal counselors, and outlined the minutiae of what P&G was required to do. For Buc, simply ceasing sales and offering a refund were insufficient, and P&G stopped fighting and conceded to the consent decree without, however, admitting a defect or fault with the product.

The trick with the consent decree, as Buc recalled, was that P&G "didn't know what was causing [TSS], but neither were they [P&G] able to rule out that they had [ruled it out]."[45] And, without a clear understanding of the relevance of the tampon components to TSS, Buc could not just simply order the elimination of one or more parts from the production process to spare the brand. Furthermore, there were enough signals and indications from the CDC "that something [was] going on, but not necessarily what."[46] In terms of her job, the "what" was less relevant, because her charge was to protect consumers, and in this case the health of women. But she wanted them to keep their tampons, too.

Buc and Pines were deep in the woods of risk management, and what to do concerning a formerly benign yet suddenly deleterious medical device. P&G wanted more proof and more science, yet young, mostly white women were dying during and after their periods (even though TSS was not limited or exclusive to white people or women). According to Sheila Jasanoff, a scholar of science and technology law and policy, "Regulatory policy often has to strike a balance between the benefits of waiting for definite scientific proof and the costs of exposing the public to risk until such proofs are available."[47] The FDA waited until the CDC completed its study but issued a warning before the release of the *MMWR* report. And, as Jasanoff also notes, "decisions about risk are neither wholly scientific nor wholly political, and therefore demand novel collaborations between scientists, public officials, and private interest groups."[48] Here, the FDA relied on CDC science rather than on corporate pleas, and it utilized the new MDA but also limited its scope to Rely, though other superabsorbent tampons, including Playtex, Tampax, Kotex, and o.b., were implicated.[49] TSS would not be eliminated entirely, but the tampon creating the greatest risk for the illness would be, allowing the other tampon brands to remain on the market.

To use Jasanoff's language, the "novel collaboration" was the consent decree; a "triumph" according to Buc, it resulted from her experience in consumer safety, the new power wielded by the 1976 MDA, and

Buc's feminist mission to mitigate risk. She mentioned in my interview with her that "even Sid Wolfe," the long-standing consumer advocate and co-founder and director of the Public Citizen Health Research Group, "couldn't find anything wrong with it," which she took as a compliment. At the core of the consent decree was Buc's deep intent to communicate risk to women.

The twelve-page consent agreement was enacted on October 1, 1980, the highlights of which were summarized in a memo circulated to staffers. First, it established that the "FDA and CDC believe there is an association between TSS and the use of Rely." Though P&G "disputes this association and denies Rely is defective in any way," it agreed to the following:

a. Discontinue sale and distribution of Rely;
b. Make efforts to withdraw all advertising;
c. Conduct a broad based consumer notification program that reaches 95 percent of all women within four weeks;
d. Conduct a retrieval/refund program with periodic status reports on its effectiveness;
e. Make available to FDA all notification and retrieval documents; and
f. Not re-introduce Rely without prior written permission of the Director of the Bureau of Medical Devices.

Finally, the memo noted that the "FDA accepts the agreement but does not waive rights to future administrative or judicial enforcement. FDA will review all Procter & Gamble's actions and notify the company when the program has been concluded."[50]

The comprehensiveness of this plan was unprecedented, especially in its attention to reaching women through multiple media venues and hitting them repeatedly with the same message of risk. The unique part was that P&G, and not the FDA or CDC, was responsible for doing the communicating. Some of the specific details included targeting women in the eighteen- to thirty-four-year-old age group, who were the original recipients of the free samples. Each woman would optimally receive this message four times, through television, newspaper, and radio. The agreement required that "P&G shall run day network advertising because this element effectively reaches women of all demographic groups,

A message to users of Rely tampons from Procter & Gamble.

Women who use Rely® tampons should stop using them and return the unused product to Procter & Gamble for a refund.

Government studies show that tampons are associated with an increased risk of Toxic Shock Syndrome (TSS). This is a newly-discovered disease that affects mainly women who use tampons during their periods.

Toxic Shock Syndrome can be very serious and is believed to be responsible for a number of deaths. Almost all women who have had the disease have recovered.

Some recent studies indicate that Rely was apparently involved with Toxic Shock Syndrome to a greater extent than other tampon brands.

Toxic Shock Syndrome was first reported in November 1978. It is believed to be caused by a toxin produced by a bacterial infection (Staphylococcus aureus). In June 1980, the U.S. Center for Disease Control (CDC) first linked it to tampon use. No one yet knows how or why tampons are associated with this disease.

In June, based on research conducted up to that point, CDC said that tampon use alone was not sufficient to cause the disease. CDC also said that no particular brand of tampon was more involved than others.

But on September 15, CDC announced a new study. It compared women who had Toxic Shock Syndrome with women who did not. The study confirmed that Toxic Shock Syndrome was associated with tampon use. It also indicated that Rely was apparently involved with more cases than any other brand. Here are the key data available to date:

DEFINITE TSS CASES REPORTED TO CDC				
		Brands Used*		
	= Cases involved	Rely Brand	Other Identified Tampon Brands	Unidentified Brands
CDC Study #1 (completed June 20)	52	17	43	2
CDC Study #2 (completed September 12)	50	35	22	0
Other cases reported to CDC	140	24	19	100
Total CDC cases (through September 23)	242	76	84	102

*"Brands used" totals more than the number of cases reported because some women used more than one brand

On September 21, P&G convened a scientific advisory group to review all known data relating to TSS. The group concluded that the available data were still fragmentary, but advised that the results of the latest CDC study should not be ignored.

Therefore, on September 22, Procter & Gamble announced it was suspending sales of Rely and that it would refund money to consumers who had Rely in their homes.

The Food and Drug Administration offers this advice to consumers:

"The current evidence indicates that women should stop using Rely. Women who want to reduce their risk of toxic shock even further may want to consider not using any tampons at all, or using napkins part of the time during their periods.

"Women using tampons who develop a high fever and vomiting or diarrhea during their periods should stop using tampons and see their doctors right away."

The FDA and CDC have said they will continue studying Toxic Shock Syndrome to find out what causes it and why it is associated with tampons. Procter & Gamble will participate with the government in this important effort.

In the meantime, Procter & Gamble advises women not to use Rely tampons and to return unused Rely for a refund.

You should know these symptoms of Toxic Shock Syndrome:

- High Fever (102°) and
- Vomiting or diarrhea

If you have these symptoms during your menstrual period, discontinue use of tampons and see your doctor at once.

How to return Rely and obtain refund:

Send your unused Rely tampons with your name and address to:
Rely,
P.O. Box 8448,
Clinton, Iowa 52736.
And you will receive a refund including cost of mailing.

NOTE: You may see Rely advertisements in the November issues of various women's magazines. Unfortunately, these issues were already printed when the decision to suspend sales of Rely was made on September 22, 1980.

© 1980, The Procter & Gamble Company

Figure 3.1. Alert from Procter & Gamble. An example of a newspaper advertisement directing women to stop using Rely and alerting them about the symptoms of TSS, as outlined by the terms set forth by the FDA. Source: "A Message to Users of Rely Tampons from Procter & Gamble," *Hopewell News* (October 8, 1980): B-4.

but particularly young homemakers." According to the Bureau of Labor Statistics, in 1980 47.7 percent of women were employed, and about the same were categorized as "not in the labor force," which likely meant they were unpaid laborers taking care of small children. The decree presumed that they owned televisions (by 1980 about 98 percent of homes did) and were watching soap operas.[51] Advertisements were directed at "two hundred and three (203) television market areas in the United States covering virtually all households with televisions," with over six hundred television stations represented.[52] For radio, "P&G shall run an average of twenty radio messages in each radio market per week for 4 weeks." Specifications for newspapers included length and frequency, "one thousand lines in size" about half a page, in 1,200 newspapers, in the food section, because this "is where most women look for news and advertisements about items they purchase in retail outlets," despite the fact that many first heard of TSS in the news section.[53] The outlets, however, were the same spaces in which P&G advertised its product rollout less than two years earlier.

As Pines put it, "P&G agreed to conduct a campaign—comparable to what it might do to introduce a new product—to tell consumers not to use their product," which was an unusual turn of events. Yet it was the only way for P&G to regain a degree of trustworthiness in light of the bad publicity associated with its dangerous product; thus, it had self-serving ends. Where Buc created terms and policy through legal means, Pines worked the public relations angle by influencing the script for the television reverse-advertising campaigns. It ran as follows:

> If you use Rely tampons, here's an important message from Procter & Gamble. Women who use Rely tampons should stop using them and return any unused product to Procter & Gamble for a refund. Procter & Gamble has suspended the sale of Rely tampons. This action has been taken until more is known about a new disease called Toxic Shock Syndrome. Tampons have been associated with this disease. Tampons don't cause the disease but seem to contribute to its development. Some studies suggest that Rely tampons increase the risk more than other tampon brands. Look for Rely in new advertisements to learn how to get your money back from Rely tampons. In the meantime, we advise you to stop using Rely tampons.[54]

According to Pines "more than 90 percent of the women understood the basic message—a very high percentage for any commercial."[55] Women may have understood to stop using Rely, but this did not mean that they understood TSS, or that any of the agencies had solved the problem of tampon-related TSS.

Pines also observed "from September 17, when the first press release was issued on the CDC date, until the second week in October, when the ad campaign began, Rely was in the news consistently." And, with forty deaths, he felt "the publicity campaign was commensurate with the public health threat."[56] Many newspapers ran stories, and the television networks also broadcast news reports about the illness. Because of the hype and concern, there was also an urge to explain what was causing TSS, even when scientists did not entirely understand its origins. One theory, suggested in the *New York Times*, was that TSS thrived because tampons "could act as a stopper against the bacteria and create a benevolent environment for their growth or because tampons could cause small internal ulcerations or abrasions where the bacteria could multiply."[57] Another was that "women's menstrual blood, instead of being eliminated from the body, might be forced back up the vaginal canal, through the open Fallopian tubes and into the peritoneal cavity or lower abdomen, where the toxin could be readily absorbed."[58] These explanations were speculative and incorrect. P&G also maintained its voice in the aftermath. A report in the *Boston Globe* quoted Edward Harness, the P&G Chairman of the Board, explaining that sales were suspended "despite the fact that we know of no defect in the Rely tampon and despite evidence that the withdrawal of Rely will not eliminate the occurrence of TSS even if Rely's use is completely discontinued."[59] Although Harness was accurate in saying that TSS was not eliminated, he was misleading. Rely did not cause direct harm through usual means of measurement; it caused harm through its biocatalytic proclivities that the company did not imagine to test.

The multiple and mixed messages about TSS contributed to misunderstandings of the illness, as well as the fear factor surrounding it. James Todd, who identified the illness in 1978, lamented its overexposure in the media and the multiple incorrect theories put forth, including that the "'Rely tampon *causes* toxic shock syndrome,' 'toxic shock syndrome and Kawasaki syndrome are the same thing,' 'toxic shock syndrome is really scarlet fever,' 'tampons cause ulcerations which allow the organism to get into the bloodstream,' 'tampons force blood into the peritoneal cavity.'" He was perturbed that the theories were not vetted, "and each received national news coverage in the nightly news with no requirement for critical review or confirmation." His high profile and expert status caused a media rush at the Children's Hospital Colorado, according to Kyla Thompson, its public relations and media director, who dispatched queries and coordinated press conferences.[60] Todd observed that "the media hyped the controversy at the expense of lingering public confusion and hysteria," the speculations resulting in what Todd now dubbed "toxic schlock syndrome," a disparaging twist on his original term.[61]

While Todd protested misinformation, other media outlets struggled with delivering a message at all, in large part due to the mores of menstrual silence that many men enforced. Tom Brokaw, the longtime anchor for *NBC Nightly News* (1982–2004), mentioned this discomfort in uttering anything about menstruation in contemporary broadcast news reporting of toxic shock syndrome, despite the potential for an epidemic. He recalled that there were some men in the newsroom and one of his "older colleagues" who would not say "menstrual cycle" or "sanitary napkin" and who announced at a meeting, "I will not say 'tampon' on the air."[62] It was a lesson for Brokaw in advocacy, especially when women were 50 percent of the television audience but the newsroom did not reflect that. Staffers influenced him as well, and he listened to their concerns. "The women here who were still just researchers and clerks and so on said 'This is really important to us.'"[63] NBC was still slow in reporting. Judging from the newsreels available at the Vanderbilt Television News Archive, NBC was the last of the three major networks to even air the story, days after P&G recalled its product. It ran on Saturday, assigned to Jessica Savitch, the weekend anchor of *NBC Nightly News*, with the "women's story" left to the woman reporter; the recall happening earlier that week on a Monday.[64] Arguably, the news story was a women's issue about women's bodies that ultimately transgressed the menstrual etiquette of silence.[65] Yet the initial nonreporting amounted to sexism-in-action, contributing to, rather than preventing, an illness that disproportionately affected women.

With such silences and inconsistencies, there was an urgent "need to know." Fifty million American women used tampons.[66] Thus millions were using them every day; this was not like other outbreaks where one might steer clear of a hotel with a Legionnaires' outbreak or a restaurant implicated in food poisoning. Any woman could not just immediately step out of her body or stop her period in order to avoid menstrual hygiene products. She could use sanitary pads, but for the converted, the pads were miserable. Women wanted to know what to do, and Kathryn Shands from the TSS Task Force quickly became a "woman's voice" during this episode. She appeared on the PBS *McNeil-Lehrer Report*, ABC's *Nightline*, the three major networks' nightly newscasts, as well as within a two-page spread in *People* magazine (along with Dr. James Todd in a second article). In this article, she was pictured on her road bike, her mode of transportation to and from work in Atlanta, sporting plaid pants and cuffs rolled up to avoid the chain and chainring. Unable to change outfits before the interview, she remained in her street clothes, the reporter and photographer denying her a more professional and scientific pose in a lab coat similar to the representation afforded Todd.[67] Her presence as a healthy, active, young, female doctor studying this illness associated with tampons brought a degree of essentialist assurance that government entities were serving women's welfare by initiating the withdrawal. She directly stated: "Don't use Rely tampons. Other tampons should be changed at least every six hours and used only intermittently."[68]

Shands's voice, along with many other reports in national newspapers such as the *New York Times*, the *Washington Post*, the *Wall Street Journal*; regional papers such as the *Wilmington Morning Star* and the *Indianapolis Star*; African American newspapers such as the *Baltimore Afro-American* and the *Atlanta Daily World*; and international press such as Canada's *Globe and Mail*, all ran stories and alerts. Popular magazines such as *Good Housekeeping* and *Seventeen* ran articles in 1981, due to the time lag associated with publishing a periodical. The CDC estimated that tampon use among women fell from 70 percent to 55 percent by December of 1980.[69] All of these news outlets contributed to TSS being one of the top stories of the year, which was both a success for Nancy Buc at the FDA and a relief for Kathryn Shands at the CDC. The messages of risk sought to spare tampon users the fate already succumbed by others who were sickened by Rely. But prescriptive messages are not always heeded, and the testimonies of TSS sufferers often left a more lasting impression on consumers.

Women's Voices: Reactions and Responses

Articles appeared in newspapers about women's firsthand accounts of suffering from problems related to both Rely and TSS, and the *Chicago Tribune* ran a cover story in the spring of 1981.[70] Angela Nalbone participated in a study for P&G in 1975 about its new tampon in which she voiced concerns about this product. Nalbone was quoted in the paper saying, "Basically, I liked them, but I noticed that they pinched when I put them in. It really hurt. I could feel the plastic applicator open up when I was inserting the tampon. I thought, gosh, if that applicator was damaging me, how would I ever know it because I'm already bleeding." She continued: "I'm not that bad when it comes to pain, but putting the Rely in brought tears to my eyes."[71] Not only was Rely causing damage, but Nalbone, a medical secretary, heard stories from women about other brands, too. Playtex deodorant tampons gave one woman a rash and sores; other women came into the office after the tampon string broke off, needing a doctor to retrieve the tampon; other superabsorbents disintegrated, and Nalbone's daughter Lisa used Playtex deodorant tampons and she recalled, "I had chunks falling out of me about a week after my period stopped."[72]

Other women fared worse. "I'm angry and very bitter about the whole thing," Linda Imboden conveyed to a reporter from the *New York Times*. "If I had known the danger, I definitely would not have used tampons." Imboden suffered from lasting damage after contracting TSS; she lost the use of her hands, which were characterized as "claws" in the news story, and gangrene took away feeling in her fingers and toes. Things got worse when her hair fell out. Without the use of her hands, she lost her job as a nursing home aide. In light of the whole thing, she was among the first to sue P&G even before the official product withdrawal. Without a warning on the box, there was no way for women to recognize the danger, her lawyer attested, yet P&G knew the risks.[73]

In an anonymous, qualitative, online survey that I conducted, I asked women about their memories of this health crisis, how they learned about TSS, and whether or not they used Rely tampons.[74] When asked how they felt once they learned that tampons might make them ill, responses were strong, such as "it [the warning] didn't say it would make me ill; it said it might kill me. I felt rather alarmed and determined not to leave a tampon in too long ever again." This person heard the message of possible death and changed her habits. Another responded that it was "strange that something that was suppose [sic] to be safe was now not so safe," reflecting the sentiment that tampons had suddenly turned bad and protections presumably had failed. Others were only "a little worried" because they did not use Rely, and another woman said, "Having used Rely for some time without problems, I wasn't concerned," and she dismissed the warnings as irrelevant to her.

I asked when women stopped using Rely, with one saying she "only used the 4 free ones" and another replied "immediately after [since] I was convinced I would die if I did [use them]." Here, when informed of the risk, she chose another form of menstrual management. I also asked when they first learned about TSS, and many had heard about it on television nightly news. One woman knew a high school classmate who "was involved in a lawsuit against Kotex" due to TSS, and this was her first memory of it. One respondent noted quite frankly that she learned about TSS when "my doctor diagnosed me with it in 1979 after using Rely tampons." She added that she did not require hospitalization, but she knew "others who died, lost fingers and toes, [and] spent much time in ICU."

Another respondent had different memories related to Rely, because her "father worked at the plant where they were made. When I found out about TSS and its link to Rely, it felt like something was going to happen to my family. Two weeks later my dad announced he was being transferred to Cincinnati. This move was one of the most traumatic events of my young life." Here, the withdrawal of Rely affected the livelihood of her family in terms of her father's ability to earn a wage rather than the illness harming her directly. Though his job transfer affected her personally, there were many others sympathetic to P&G as an engine of job production. Punishing the company hurt workers, so that some saw it not as a woman's issue but ultimately as a threat to male breadwinners. These responses show the varied reaction to these news reports, how messages of risk and the consequences of TSS were heard differently, and the cost of TSS on women's bodies.

Another memory came from an oral history that I conducted with Chris, who was a college student at the time. At Allegheny College in Meadville, Pennsylvania, Chris arrived on campus to begin her freshman year in the early fall of 1980. She recalled trial-sized products in the "welcome box" she received when she moved into the dorm. Only one week after classes began, disturbing and shocking reports rippled through campus about TSS. In light of this health danger, officials at Allegheny College "deputized" brothers from the college fraternities, as Chris put it. No doubt this counted toward their public service requirement, because all sororities and fraternities include that as part of their membership duties. Armed with clipboards and lists of all the incoming freshmen women, the brothers set out door-to-door to procure and dispose of all the unused Rely tampons that were part of her welcome package. Rather than having a flirtatious interchange with "cute" guys, Chris said that she instead had an awkward conversation with them while she and her roommate rummaged around looking for Rely.[75] Though the college took the risk and danger seriously, it was a paternal as well as patriarchal reaction, in which women could not be trusted to dispose of the tampons themselves. Nearby at the University of Maryland, students also received free samples of Rely during freshmen orientation. After the recall, some women living in one of the dormitories threw the tampons out of a sixth-floor window. One student commented to a news reporter, "Those things are killing people."[76] Here, they took things into their own hands in an act of defiance to secure their health and even save their lives.

The woman who garnered the most notoriety about TSS had not contracted it through tampon use, though her message about the ravages of the illness was heard by many. A successful writer for the *New York Times*, Nan Robertson was postmenopausal and had no need to use superabsorbent tampons. In the September 19, 1982, edition of the *New York Times Magazine*, her article "Toxic Shock" appeared.[77] Her first-person testimonial was unusual for such a high-caliber journalist, made more unique due to the topic. She told her harrowing story of TSS, contracted in November 1981. She detailed her near-death experience, the sheer luck of one doctor diagnosing her correctly, and the damage from the quick progression of the toxins that left her with gangrene and required the amputation of the end joint on each of eight fingers. As a reporter dependent on a typewriter, this was devastating. Yet, through sheer willpower, multiple surgeries, and grueling physical therapy, she described the slow process back to using her hands and fingers for the most mundane tasks: opening a jar lid, picking up a coin, pulling a door handle. Her physician was floored by her stamina at age fifty-five, and her recovery convinced him of the importance of treating her with the correct antibiotic ("beta-lactamase-resistant antibiotics" because *S. aureus* had already developed resistance to penicillin). *People* magazine quickly picked up the story and interviewed her about her experience with TSS.[78] In 1983, she won the Pulitzer Prize for feature writing based on this article.

What is evident is that Robertson's very personal story resonated with readers. They sent her hundreds of letters, now housed at the Arthur and Elizabeth Schlesinger Library. They recounted how moved they were by the story; how they wished her well; how TSS affected a sister, daughter or friend; and how brave she was to move past the illness. She heard from Walter Annenberg, of the Annenberg Fund, who donated $5,000 to the Institute of Rehabilitation Medicine where she carried out her physical therapy sessions. In the letter to her doctor (which he sent to her as well), Annenberg wrote, "This is one of the most moving, tragic personal episodes that I have ever read. Reading this piece was actually an emotional experience for me and my respect for this lady is boundless, because of the calm manner in which she recounted the harrowing details."[79] Her position as a journalist with the *New York Times* no doubt brought her privilege, and people listened to her, perhaps more so as a seasoned woman than a teenager who had contracted the illness from a tampon. Yet she became a voice of the illness and an advocate for patients and their treatment.

Robertson received many heartfelt letters, like from "Betty," who believed that her daughter died more than fifteen years ago from undiagnosed TSS. She had been trying to learn more about the illness ever since. With Robertson's notoriety, she saw an opportunity for health activism. Betty believed that no one at the hospital asked her daughter whether or not she was using a tampon. Thus, if hospitals included that question of a person with a fever during admission procedures, she felt this would also tip them off to start thinking about TSS. She concluded, "PS I have little hope for the idea of warning labels on tampon packages—warning labels on cigarettes seemed not to have stopped smoking."[80] Robertson responded by assuring her that her piece had saved other lives and that "doctors have now been able to correctly diagnose for Toxic Shock." The outpouring of "mail has been astonishing both in quality and quantity, and that, of course, included your own letter," which she used to help Betty see that she was not alone. She addressed Betty's concerns about labeling by letting her know that "consumer groups are forming or have formed to bear down on irresponsible tampon manufacturers in cooperation with State health boards and the Federal Government."[81] This she likely knew after speaking with Judy Norsigian from the Boston Women's Health Book Collective during the summer of 1982, and from their efforts as consumer advocates to work with industry to create labeling standards for tampons (further discussed in chapter 5).[82] From Betty to Robertson to Norsigian, it was clear that the message of risk was disseminated and heard, but more needed to be done to provide information about both tampons and TSS so women could make better informed decisions.

Making and Managing Policy

In the aftermath of the withdrawal, two notable shifts occurred. One dealt with individual women's decisions about tampons and tampon pur-chases, and the other dealt with policy in light of tampon-related TSS. For one, many women heard the message loud and clear to stop using Rely. Many women had been persuaded to try the tampons because they conveniently arrived in mailboxes as samples. Though some of those women forsook their old tampons for the new, it took little convincing to switch brands or return to familiar staples after learning about the devastation of TSS. Some women simply swapped Rely superabsorbent for another brand's superabsorbent—Kotex or Playtex, for example— while others chose old standbys. Rely had done remarkably well in the superabsorbent category, with "70 percent of the market share of highly absorbent tampons."[83] Within the context of the Rely recall, however, Tampax experienced an unexpected boon. Thomas Moore, the execu-tive vice president of Tampax, Inc., reported that the overall market had lost 20 percent of sales since the summer of 1980, though he was quoted in the *Washington Post* saying that "it seems to have leveled off, and if anything is starting to increase . . . very slowly" (ellipsis in original).[84] He added that Tampax had not lost sales, due in part to women switch-ing back to this brand. According to *Fortune* magazine, "Dollar and unit sales were up sharply in the last quarter of 1980, and market shares hit 56.7%—a three-year high," attributable to women's purchasing reactions and switching among the brands. As a result of the shift, Tampax also returned to its roots by "reintroducing its 'original regular' tampon, larger than modern versions and filled with 'pure and simple' cotton rather than fibers treated for extra absorbency." It would be the only tampon on the market able to claim "all cotton" composition for the time being, a shrewd business maneuver since all superabsorbents contained synthetic elements, and most regular tampons were composed of cotton and rayon.[85] However, cotton alone could not claim the absorbent powers that the hybrid synthetics could.

This shift did not go unnoticed. Epidemiologists who actively worked on the original reporting of TSS during the summer of 1980 were adept and kept following and tracking the illness. The April 1982 volume of the *Journal of Infectious Diseases* published the final findings from four separate studies, but even beforehand public health officials spoke with the press during the spring and summer of 1981 about ongoing data.[86] Mike Osterholm, an epidemiologist at the Minnesota Department of Health, traced high-absorbency tampons to incidents of TSS before Rely was withdrawn from the market and also afterward, when it was no longer available after September 1980. In theory, if Rely were the predominant cofactor, its elimination as a variable should have reduced the number of tampon-related TSS illnesses. Indeed, he found that women were well aware of the link between Rely and TSS, and as a result they consciously chose to switch brands. However, the brands they switched to were also superabsorbents, and the rates of TSS did not decline in the state of Minnesota. According to the study, Osterholm and his co-author, Jan C. Forfang, sought out retrospective cases, such that sixty-one cases were identified as having occurred before 1980. From January 1980 to June 1981 "114 (83.8%) cases were tampon-associated" and during the eighteen-month window "there was no difference ($P > 0.2$) in the quarterly distribution of total or tampon-associated TSS cases." To put a finer point on it, there were "55 tampon-associated cases" while Rely was on the market, and "59 tampon-associated cases" following its removal.[87] He collated the data in a table (see table 3.1) depicting the brands and their association with TSS in Minnesota.

There were many reasons for this, including the grass-roots engagement of the health department, its active role in reaching out to physicians rather than employing a passive data collection system, and a

TABLE 3.1. Cases of tampon-associated TSS in Minnesota

Brand Use Exclusive*	No. of Cases (%)		P Value
	January–September 1980	October 1980–June 1981	
Kotex	3 (5.4)	8 (13.5)	>0.2
o.b.	2 (3.6)	1 (1.6)	>0.2
Playtex	11 (20.0)	18 (30.5)	>0.2
Pursettes	1 (1.8)	1 (1.6)	>0.2
Rely	25 (45.5)	1 (1.6)	<0.001
Tampax	7 (12.7)	27 (45.7)	<0.001
Other†	6 (10.9)	3 (5.0)	>0.2
Total	55 (100)	59 (100)	

The brand listed was the one that was used exclusively from the beginning of the menstrual period through the day of the onset of the illness. The manufacturers of the tampons reported are Kotex, Kimberly-Clark Corp (Neenah, Wisc.); o.b.*, Johnson and Johnson Products (New Brunswick, N.J.); Playtex*, International Playtex (Stamford, Conn.); Pursettes*, Campana Corp. (Batavia, Ill.); Rely*, Procter & Gamble (Cincinnati, Ohio); and Tampax*, Tampax (Palmer, Mass.).

†Other was defined as the use of more than one brand of tampon or brand unknown.

Table 3.1 Cases of tampon-associated TSS in Minnesota by tampon brand use with the onset during the nine months before or after removal of Rely tampons from the market. In this table, the cases of TSS attributed to Rely dropped significantly after it was pulled from the market. Yet brands such as Playtex and Tampax saw dramatic increases, in part because women switched to these superabsorbent tampons. Eliminating Rely—though a problematic tampon—did not eliminate TSS. Source: Table re-created from Michael T. Osterholm and Jan C. Forfang, "Toxic-Shock Syndrome in Minnesota: Results of an Active-Passive Surveillance System," *Journal of Infectious Diseases*, 145.4 (April 1982): 462. By permission of Oxford University Press.

waning but present media component. He also felt that a reason they got such good data had to do with the way they handled the interviews. He recalled, "In every interview we did we had a trained female investigator from the STD area who understood how to do interviews."[88] These were not conducted with parents accompanying their teenaged daughters into the room, or with a less personal tone over the phone, so he felt the results were more accurate. Thus, the sole removal of Rely did not protect women from contracting tampon-related TSS.

Not only did they do a better job of finding people with TSS, but they also looked at the way the tampon created an aerobic environment in the vagina. Based on his studies, he concluded that it was the oxygen brought into the usually anaerobic vagina that prompted *S. aureus* to multiply and produce toxins. Thus, he concluded that the higher the absorbency, the greater the volume of oxygen, and the greater the risk of TSS.[89] In addition, multiple tampons that were changed too frequently only guaranteed the bacterium a preferred aerobic environment, exacerbating the problem.

Discussions about more deliberate alerts and warnings about the illness continued, especially in light of emerging data and findings such as Osterholm's. That some form of label was needed was clear, even immediately after Rely was withdrawn. On October 20, 1980, the FDA issued a press release for proposed labeling, opening up a thirty-day comment period. It read:

> WARNING: Tampons have been associated with Toxic Shock Syndrome, a rare disease that can be fatal. You can almost entirely avoid the risk of getting this disease by not using tampons. You can reduce the risk by using tampons on and off during your period. If you have a fever of 102° or more, and vomit or get diarrhea during your period, remove the tampon at once and see a doctor right away.[90]

This wording was fairly specific, and it included the familiar "you" rather than a more formalized third-person voice. Though the FDA requested that manufacturers "voluntarily put warning labels on their products and conduct educational programs," nothing was required. The suggested warning was an important step in the regulatory process, but did little to ease confusion.

By the spring of 1981, there was a notable lack of conformity among manufacturers, with some affixing stickers on boxes, and others printing the warning on the outside of the box. Tampax was the sole outlier, adding only an insert. A Kimberly-Clark Corporation representative, speaking to a reporter from the *Washington Post*, commented, "'There's a little bit of confusion among the brands,' he said. 'Some packages have it displayed right on the outside . . . and some don't have anything' except a package insert'" (ellipsis in original). Thomas Moore, Tampax's vice president, said the company would insert a statement inside the box about TSS, with updated information based on current research and findings.[91] Of course, the insert was easy to edit and change, but also it was far better for the aesthetics of the branding and it hid the risk posed by tampons deep within the box. The comment period lingered, and by June 22, 1982, the FDA announced the guidelines. The comprehensive statement could be on the package or in the box, accompanied by a shorter alert, reading as follows: "Attention. Tampons are associated with toxic shock syndrome. TSS is a rare but serious disease that may cause death. Read and save the enclosed information."[92] This alert was far less specific than the one initially proposed, omitted any reference to symptoms, and diminished the threat rather than providing useful guidance, other than to "save" the insert. No doubt manufacturers pressed for more vague language, carefully crafted to communicate minimal risk, thus exonerating them from accusations of deliberately selling a misleading product, without offering details about context, tampon absorbency, or symptoms of TSS.

Keeping the Message Alive

Contiguous with the TSS health crisis was the political transition from the Carter to Reagan administration, with appointees, including Nancy Buc at the FDA, swept out of office and replaced by Reagan staffers more sympathetic to business and deregulation. The messages of risk about tampons coming from federal entities would no longer be the dominant way in which women would learn about tampon-related TSS. Neoliberalism characterized many of the decisions and actions undertaken by the Reagan administration, and delays in tampon labeling were one more example. Furthermore, the lack of labeling was deliberate, a consequence of the overreach of the Office of Management and Budget (OMB), which was charged to promote efficiency and reduce government paperwork. In essence, the OMB dictated whether or not the FDA could move forward on anything that created paperwork, including any policy about tampon labeling and informational inserts.

Many began questioning the effectiveness of the FDA in light of these delays and feared poor health consequences for the American public. How were messages about risk to be communicated when the very agency charged to do so was thwarted by other regulation, which was politically motivated? Al Gore, a congressional representative from Tennessee at the time, was part of the July 16, 1982, hearings before the Subcommittee on Oversight and Investigations about the implementation of the MDA by the FDA. He managed to bring the discussion of tampon safety and their risk as medical devices into this hearing. Although contact lenses were the main topic (with many urging the FDA to remove them from Class III and regulate them as Class II), at issue was the ability of the FDA to ensure safety and protect consumers' health with the implementation of the MDA. In part, companies were not required "to report to the FDA when there is a death or injury related to one of their products." Gore drew a parallel example for comparison. "If somebody sells a waffle iron that is defective and burns down a house, they are required by the Consumer Product Safety Commission to report the fact that they have knowledge that they have a defective waffle iron that has killed somebody." Furthermore, "If it is a pacemaker or a hip implant or some other medical device, they do not have to even tell FDA that their product has killed someone, even if it kills several people." The problem for Gore was that the OMB did not allow the FDA to "implement that section of the law, passed in November of 1980," before Reagan took office. Gore argued that, at the OMB's instruction, "the regulations were held in abeyance," favoring companies at the expense of patients and consumers.[93]

In a statement at the hearing by Sidney Wolfe, who represented Public Citizen Health Research Group, he provided figures that backed up this contention. He claimed that "there has been a drop-off in FDA enforcement activities during the first 2 years of the Reagan administration" with recalls diminishing 45 percent in 1981 compared to the years 1977–1980. During that same time, there were about 200 recalls per year, but by 1981 during the first half there were only forty-three. This did not include the voluntary withdrawal as with Rely. Wolfe argued that the FDA was not fulfilling its duty to follow the letter of the MDA or use its powers to enforce the law.[94] The *New York Times* summarized Gore's assessment during the hearings: "the companies' actions were evidence that the Reagan Administration's regulatory delays and preference for voluntary compliance were endangering consumers."[95]

During the hearing, the committee asked about other devices, specifically hair implants and tampons. John Dingell (D-MI) asked Arthur Hayes, the commissioner of the FDA, about the postponement of labeling tampons in regard to the risk of TSS. Hayes spoke about the unknowns of the disease, which made it difficult to label accurately, which in part was true. However, Dingell pressed about the rather lax compliance with voluntary labeling, made worse because there was no proposed mandatory standard for labeling or performance. During Gore's turn to question the commissioner, he pushed harder on the point in the following exchange with Hayes:

> GORE: On page 6 of your statement, you cite the experience of FDA with tampons, and the toxic shock syndrome as an example of how well voluntary cooperation by the industry works. But in fact, when the regulation was held up for 20 months, when it became clear to the industry and to this company [Playtex] that they were not going to have to do it, they took the warning that was already on the box and took it off the box. Now, how can you cite that as your premier example of how voluntary cooperation from the industry works to solve this problem?
>
> HAYES: Because less than 2 years ago, when the first associations were published between TSS and the tampons, and when there was not unanimity, nor even a consensus about the association, even less the cause, or what sorts of information a warning should be giving in fact, the manufacturers did voluntarily put information there.
>
> GORE: They thought you were going to require it. It wasn't until a little bit later that they found they didn't have to take FDA seriously on this point.
>
> HAYES: And they guessed wrong, didn't they?
>
> GORE: No.
>
> HAYES: Yes. We have just come out with a final rule.
>
> GORE: Do they have to put this warning on the outside of the box?
>
> HAYES: They do. They either have to put the comprehensive warning on the outside, or they must put an alert on the outside if there is not room for that and the comprehensive warning on the inside.
>
> GORE: So they don't have to put the warning on the outside?
>
> HAYES: Not the whole thing that you read, because in fact for some products it is not physically possible.[96]

The exchange pointed to the highly political nature of labeling. The inconsistent guidelines favored companies that wanted to downplay the risk of their product. However, it still benefited them to have information about TSS, because they would have deceived women that the product was safe and exposed themselves to future liability if they did not include the warning. It was a narrow line that the companies chose to walk. But, as Gore raised with his questioning, the either/or labeling on the inside of the box or the outside did not amount to an alert. It was confusing to him and to consumers, and it was insufficient in communicating risk.

The Power of Messaging

Despite the congressional hearings and the product withdrawal, P&G still fared very well as a company. In business circles, it gained credibility for withdrawing its product and also for taking control of its corporate message to minimize damage to the company as a whole. P&G enacted what is now referred to as "crisis management," playing out in newspapers, television reporting, and government press releases, with top officials heavily quoted throughout the ordeal. The principles of this management developed into the following elements: (1) designate a team to handle the crisis; (2) engage the media; (3) work with government entities; (4) employ the top company executive as a spokesperson; (5) and "above all, do the right thing."[97] P&G was at the forefront of this new business model, with other companies such as Johnson & Johnson following this method when someone laced cyanide within its Tylenol capsules in 1982, resulting in seven murders in the Chicago area. Ultimately, the P&G crisis-management method communicated directly with consumers through a coordinated and massive advertising campaign to *not* use its product, but the language and scope of saturation were heavily guided by the consent decree hammered out with the FDA.[98] This anticampaign generated a different sort of media attention, with P&G's public service commercials newsworthy, appearing on an episode of NBC's morning newscast the *Today Show*, for example.[99] In fact, to many business leaders the TSS crisis cemented the legacy of P&G, and even within the company itself, the decision to remove a product, take a hit to the stock price, and write off $75 million in losses all became touchstones of the company's success story. Bob McDonald, the CEO from 2010 to 2013, noted "that story becomes legend, lore, which creates the culture we want, around integrity and trust."[100] Thus, the media orchestration was very important to the representation that P&G cultivated during this time period.

Touting the success of crisis management does not equate to good public health policy, however. Without agreed-on language, and the FDA unable or unwilling to pressure companies more directly, industry offered warnings as it wished. Tampax inserts implied that TSS cases had dropped, which Arthur Reingold, a TSS specialist at the CDC, argued was not exactly correct since reported cases may have dropped, but not the actual cases.[101] Playtex removed its warning from the outside of the box entirely. Experts seemed to be delivering inconsistent advice and there was no clear labeling; business, too, felt the instability of the market. The *Wall Street Journal* led an article with a headline, "State of Alarm: Tampon Industry Is in the Throes of Change after Toxic Shock," calling the "absorbency race" among manufacturers "over," as well as observing problems associated with tampons—cuts, abrasions, and ulcers—as "a subject of zero research."[102] Indeed, due to this state of alarm manufacturers began decreasing the absorptive capacity of tampons.[103] Furthermore, feminist administrators interested in protecting women's health and regularizing warning labels once staffed the FDA and HHS, but they were no longer part of Reagan's government appointees. With Rely off the market and taking the fall for superabsorbent tampons, other companies were not going to poke around and draw more attention to tampons or TSS.

Medical Communication of Risk

The multiplicity of media attention—from congressional hearings, to television newscasts, to local newspapers—to TSS as an illness in the late twentieth century can be understood through the concept of "healthscapes." Adele Clarke, a sociologist of science, technology, and medicine, convincingly argues for the construct of biomedicalization to help make sense of the increasingly medicalized social transformation of society that began around 1985. She suggests the term "healthscapes" to get at the ways these understandings become infused in society. According to Clarke, "Healthscapes are ways of grasping, through words, images, and material cultural objects, patterned changes that have occurred in the many and varied sites where health and medicine are performed, who is involved, sciences and technologies in use, media coverage, political and economic elements, and changing ideological and cultural framings of health, illness, healthcare, and medicine."[104] Tampon-related TSS fell on the cusp of this transition from medicalization to biomedicalization, and in many ways it is a precursor of the elements that she outlines. Tampons absorb the fluid of a normal bodily process—that is, menstruation, heavily medicalized as an illness, constructed as abnormal and disease-producing from the inception of professionalized medicine during the nineteenth century—and were officially claimed by biomedicalization when classified as medical devices in 1976. The "biomedicalization healthscape" also usually flouted "technoscience, its interventions, and its promises for the future."[105] Here, the opposite occurred. Not only was a tampon technology at the center of the blame, they were now deadly, and the whole business of menstrual hygiene management was under scrutiny. One headline from the *New York Times* captured this sentiment: "Disease Calls an Industry into Question."[106] Indeed, TSS *became* the healthscape for which tampons would now be linked.

The healthscape of TSS was deeply intertwined with health communication. In general, health communication examines both the relationship of communication between healthcare providers and patients within a healthcare delivery system, and also how communication and media influence public health and health promotion.[107] An important factor in the narrative of tampon-related TSS was the ways in which information about a new illness and potentially dangerous tampon were not only communicated, but also crafted into a story. Different stakeholders shaped the story, from mainstream, underground, and business newspapers, to sanctioned medical journals and governmental alerts, to word-of-mouth concerns between family and friends. Mainstream media sensationalized headlines, but the outlets also seemed to want to provide information to women so they could protect themselves. This was paternalistic and also created a tone of individual responsibility in which women were duty-bound to scrutinize their tampons and were culpable for any illness incurred. Underground and feminist papers pushed back and faulted the products and manufacturers, understanding that lack of oversight was part of a larger dismissal of women's health concerns and the normalization of the "universal male." Scientists lamented the runaway news reports, which left no space for the slower and laborious peer-reviewed findings to arrive. Individual women commiserated and supported one another, dismayed and angered that tampons, a tool to hide their periods, were exposing them to lethal danger.

Another challenge to reporters was the very complicated scope of TSS, the lack of a clear cause-and-effect explanation, and the desire for oversimplification of scientific and medical topics. It often was reduced to tampons causing TSS, which is understandable but misleading. Marcia Angell discusses the media coverage about a similarly gendered issue, breast implants, and their potential for harm.[108] Although she discusses the potential for a weak risk with the implants, I would argue that they are another medical device possessing biocatalytic potential, but her point remains that though caveats are important to scientific theory and practice, they do not make for a good story in the newspaper.[109] In the case of TSS, it was not an issue of weak risk but caveats, which also happened to be the main component of the illness and were not well reported. Without a pragmatic way to screen or help women understand that they were not part of the risk pool, the reports were necessarily frightening and alarming, and they assumed it was every woman's duty to police her body for signs of illness, rather than push back on manufacturers to make better and safer tampons. In an effort to protect susceptible women, all menstruators got caught in the paternalistic drag net, and the true threat was very difficult to ascertain.

Despite the damage caused by tampon-related TSS, it was far better that it occurred when it did in the fall of 1980 than immediately afterward. It is not clear that actions would have been taken to force Rely's removal since well-positioned women's advocates and advisors were missing from the administration that took over in the 1980s. Though Rely needed to be taken off the market, it did not eliminate tampon-related TSS, and the long reach of the OMB impeded the FDA's power, even as it sought some semblance of an alert about TSS on tampon boxes. Without strong policy coming from the FDA, pressure would need to come from other quarters to compel companies to produce safer tampons and also to provide accurate labeling. As the following two chapters will discuss, litigation and feminist health advocacy proved to be effective ways to unveil corporate decision making and to force companies to clarify the message of risk.

4

Grounds for Liability

With Rely no longer on the market, there was time for reflection. The withdrawal of Rely created a false sense of security that the crisis was over, yet something had gone horribly wrong. Women were uninterested in dying quite unnecessarily from a tampon, and what followed were liability cases against all the major tampon producers that sought recompense for long-term illness and death. Tambrands, Kimberly-Clark, and Playtex together faced at least one hundred lawsuits from women or their families who sought legal recourse due to contracting tampon-related toxic shock syndrome (TSS). Procter & Gamble (P&G), though, had the most, with more than four hundred cases pending by 1982, still insisting that Rely was just another brand of tampon, and that it should not be singled out for causing TSS.[1] By 1989, the *Chicago Tribune* reported that there were "nearly 900 lawsuits and more than 200 other claims" against P&G, with six cases going to trial and reaching "settlements with virtually all the other 1,100." P&G set aside $75 million to cover litigation expenses, and "insurance companies reimbursed the firm for the 58.2 million it paid in settlement costs."[2]

One specific case, *Kehm v. Procter & Gamble*, was unique in the way it exposed commonly held and faulty corporate assumptions, shedding light on intrinsic attitudes about women's vexing bodies, tampons as inert technology, and industry scientists as infallible. This 1982 product liability case took place in the federal courthouse at Cedar Rapids, Iowa, in which the family of Patricia Kehm sued Procter & Gamble for punitive and compensatory damages. Patricia Kehm, twenty-five, a wife and mother of two small children, used and wore Rely tampons and passed away from TSS on September 6, 1980. Tom Riley, a former state representative and senator to the Iowa General Assembly, had just started up his law firm in 1980. He and his firm, including his daughter Sara who was in law school at the time, took up this product liability case against P&G, which shaped into a metaphorical "David versus Goliath" matchup. Importantly, the case laid open the ways that P&G division leaders dismissed and disregarded incriminating evidence and "explained away" findings that did not support its sales goals or profit expectations. In large part, the corporate culture was ill prepared to foresee tampon-related TSS because it relied on its own proprietary science, created lab tests that failed to account for the vaginal ecosystem, and used women test subjects to stand in as universal for all menstruators. Only after the Food and Drug Administration (FDA) threatened to issue a formal recall did the corporation publicly acknowledge an association of Rely with TSS, but not any wrongdoing. Through this lawsuit, Riley uncovered the corporation's internal dialogues and exposed the fallacy that tampons were inert. The case demonstrated how blind faith in corporate scientists, as well as unsuitable lab protocol, failed to imagine the biocatalytic risk associated with tampons and created grounds for liability.

The Test Case

The first case to garner national notoriety concerning tampons and TSS was *Lampshire v. Procter & Gamble* in March of 1982. Deletha Dawn Lampshire, a teenager living in Littleton, Colorado, was one of the first to sue and go to trial with P&G due to her experience with TSS. Her attorney, Jon Kidneigh, asserted that she contracted it from using Rely in May 1980. Thomas Calder, one of P&G's attorneys, argued she merely had the flu. Part of the plaintiff's case alleged that Lampshire experienced a personality change afterward. She went "from a happy-go-lucky 16-year old who wore frilly dresses and was elected class president to a temperamental and often-depressed college freshman who dressed in jeans and couldn't keep good grades."[3] This assessment was a highly gendered one in which her health was measured against normative "feminine" behavior. However, it is unusual in that it addressed psychological effects, rather than the ravages of physical debility or even death. She also testified that "I feel dirty, and I still do," further adding "[n]o man would want to marry me."[4] Thus, she perceived that TSS diminished her value in a world where her worth was linked to her status as a prospective wife.

In part, that she lived instead of died worked against a more favorable verdict. The jury deliberated for twenty hours and found "Procter

& Gamble was negligent in selling a defective product, but it also concluded that the young woman who brought the case did not deserve any money."[5] Despite a hospital stay due to classic symptoms of the illness, including "low blood pressure, high fever and peeling skin," the jury awarded nothing toward her $25 million lawsuit. The gender dynamics toward this teenager were unkind; her suffering was rationalized as part of adolescent angst, and P&G contended that Rely did not cause TSS.[6] In addition, her illness predated the Centers for Disease Control (CDC) studies published in the *Morbidity and Mortality Weekly Report* (*MMWR*), and she lived to tell about it. In essence, she did not suffer enough, and she was devalued as a female teenager and her experiences were readily dismissed. This case was an important precursor for the corporate lawyers as well as future claimants in tactical strategies for upcoming lawsuits.[7] Corporations learned techniques to raise doubt by enrolling scientists as expert witnesses, and claimants understood that suffering needed to be obvious and directly articulated to the jury.

Tampon Injury

Tom Riley was well known in Cedar Rapids and throughout Iowa during the 1970s as a representative to the Iowa House and Senate. After his failed run in 1976, he returned to law and established the Tom Riley Law Firm in 1980. He focused on injury cases, wrongful death, negligence, and injustices caused by others. Riley garnered a reputation of winning cases for regular folks who were disadvantaged by corporate wrongdoing. Thus, when Mike Kehm approached him about possibly suing P&G on behalf of his wife, Pat, who died from TSS after using Rely tampons, Riley recognized both the publicity it would provide his new firm and also an opportunity to seek justice for a wrongful death.[8]

Riley "filed suit on September 30, 1980, against P&G in federal district court in Cedar Rapids for $5 million in compensatory damages." Riley began preparing for a trial and learning about tampons and TSS, subjects he knew quite little about. Like other men thrown into the gender-segregated world of menstrual hygiene management, he sought out a box of Rely to see what they were like, though it was difficult to obtain since the withdrawal had already occurred on September 22. A local pharmacist had a few waiting to return to P&G, and he gave him a box. Riley recalled that "although there was nothing illegal about the transaction, both the pharmacist and I acted like there was," because the product felt like contraband. Riley added:

> At the office, I read the ironic slogan on the light blue box, "Rely, it even absorbs the worry." The choice of the brand name "Rely" reminded me of a law school course that dealt with fraud. One of the essential elements to make out a case for fraud was that the victim had to "rely" on misrepresentation. The reasoning behind the law was that the victim had to trust what he was being told because, if he did not, the misrepresentation didn't influence his decisions. P&G had picked for its tampon product a name that meant trust.[9]

Here, Riley identified the premise for his argument. The product was not trustworthy, and P&G had misrepresented its safety by failing to warn. As he gained access to corporate documents, he also learned about conversations that P&G had with the FDA, in which they worked to convince the agency that Rely was inert. The company also stressed that correlation with TSS did not prove causation.[10] He also discovered that P&G knew that tampons were associated with TSS by the end of June 1980, prior to Pat Kehm's death, and this became the backbone for the case.

The case came to trial in 1982, lasting from April 5 to April 20, with a total of thirty-one witnesses called to the stand. They ranged from family members, university scientists, epidemiologists, and even an actor reading from the deposition of recently deceased Earle Cleveland Haas, the inventor of Tampax tampons and its telescopic applicator. Media outlets, such as the *New York Times*, the *Wall Street Journal*, and *Time*, covered the trial as it unfolded, and the startup cable subscription news provider CNN also took note. It was a major national case on the heels of the recall, and it was important because it yet again publicized the dangers of tampons and called attention to the risk they still posed.

Challenging Science

The plaintiff, Michael Kehm, represented by Riley, sought compensatory damages for the loss of his wife and his children's mother, as well as punitive damages to punish the company for "reckless and wanton indifference."[11] On the other side, Timothy White and Steven Warbasse of Cedar Rapids, and Thomas Calder and Frank Woodside from Cincinnati, represented P&G. As the defendant, P&G set out to argue that Patricia Kehm had not contracted TSS, a position they argued since the admitting physician had neither diagnosed nor noted TSS as the cause of death in her medical record. Furthermore, she had not exhibited a rash, one of many symptoms related to the syndrome, which they claimed was necessary for the clinical definition. Thomas Calder argued that she did not even meet the criteria of TSS set by the CDC, stating that "the definition of toxic syndrome [sic] is very precise. You either meet it or you don't meet it. So we feel strongly if you don't meet it the complaint has no probative value."[12] P&G chose experts to reinforce this very strict definition, while Riley sought out experts who testified about the difference between clinical versus case definitions of TSS, which would encompass a much broader set of individuals who did not express all the major categories of the syndrome (these include fever, rash, peeling skin, hypotension, as well as multisystem involvement of three or more organ systems) required to be part of a CDC epidemiological case study.

Trials are by definition contentious, but this case had nasty elements from both sides. Riley complained that P&G had not made its list of expert witnesses available, and only because of a court order were the names released by the company.[13] Riley lamented he had insufficient time to prepare questions, witnesses, and cross-examination strategies, as well as secure additional witnesses in rebuttal due to this purposeful maneuver. At one point during the trial, Calder requested a mistrial after Riley appeared on the fledgling network CNN to discuss the case. Calder protested that Riley divulged more than just a reporter's accounting of the events of the day, and he handed over an incriminating VHS recording of the interview. The judge, however, refused to convert the VHS tape to Betamax (the only video-viewing technology in the courtroom), and he further determined that jurists had no access to cable television, so he overruled the request for a mistrial.[14]

A central component of Riley's argument was that P&G failed to warn the consumer. He argued that managers willfully ignored government reports and scientific findings about TSS. He contrasted this with the professionalism of scientists working on epidemiological studies at public health agencies and the researchers whose work appeared in journals such as the *New England Journal of Medicine* (*NEJM*). However, P&G was in the business of listening to its own scientists, and part of its contention was that the CDC produced methodologically questionable and bad science, and their in-house research had yielded nothing so grossly negligent as the plaintiff suggested. In actuality, both had valid, if not overstated, gripes. They also both deployed experts to raise doubt or endorse the very scientific studies on which the withdrawal of Rely was based.

Specifically, a point of contention was the use of published, scientific studies and whether or not they should be admitted into evidence. A crucial part of the Kehm case was to establish a timeline concerning when scientists could have reasonably known about the link between TSS and tampons in order to prove that P&G had previous knowledge but carried on with business anyway. The scientific studies established not only concrete dates, but also an assessment that superabsorbent tampons such as Rely were more likely to be involved in cases of TSS. For example, Riley intended to admit results reported in the *MMWR* of June 27, 1980, as evidence, which was unfavorable for all tampons since the CDC reported that they were associated with TSS.[15] Pretrial discussions between the lawyers and the judge foreshadowed the arguments to come. The court, trying to assess the character and content, asked whether the *MMWR* report was "a statistical analysis," in which Riley corrected the judge describing it as an "epidemiological study." Calder retorted and disparaged the data, defining the report in the *MMWR* as the "result of a survey" and furthermore "a method of showing statistical association." Neither was entirely accurate, but the rhetorical jockeying was part of the pretrial warmup. The court queried: "I assume you have experts that are going to have the pros and cons on this statistical—." Without missing a beat Riley replied, "Goes to the weight of the evidence."[16] This gamesmanship of the lawyers over scientific data as admissible evidence at the beginning of the trial continued throughout, with the judge and jurists left to determine the merits, veracity, and quality of various scientific and epidemiological studies.

The contention over the admissibility of published reports came into sharp focus with a witness, Dr. Bruce Dan, formerly an Epidemic Intelligence Service officer at the CDC and now testifying for the plaintiff. In order to prove the claim that Kehm was not only damaged by Rely but also died from its use, and, even worse, that P&G had prior knowledge about TSS, Riley needed the testimony of this heavyweight expert. Dan's extensive work at the CDC, where he served on the TSS Task Force, established his unique knowledge base and skills. In addition, his extensive publication record in highly esteemed journals, such as the *Journal of the American Medical Association* (*JAMA*) and the *NEJM*, also anchored his status as an expert witness.[17] Finally, his findings linking TSS to Rely in particular provided the data that the FDA needed to recommend its removal. As successful as Dan was (and continued to be later on as a healthcare journalist for the ABC television network), the defense counsel of P&G worked to contain his knowledge claims, and they questioned his ability to comment on studies in which he had no part as a primary investigator or team member.

At issue was the fact that the *MMWR* reported findings from the Tri-State study, which included results from state epidemiological studies in Minnesota, Wisconsin, and Iowa, for which Dan was neither an author nor a contributor. Frank Woodside, another lawyer for P&G who also happened to be trained as a physician, explained, "My objection is based upon the fact that the information that came from Utah, Minnesota and other states would be hearsay, and we would, therefore, object to the inclusion of that information in the exhibit which has just been marked and handed to Dr. Dan."[18] The labeling of this knowledge base as hearsay, though the tactic was ultimately unsuccessful, was an important argumentative angle. Woodside did the same thing when Riley requested to admit the actual Tri-State study as an exhibit, and Woodside objected that "no foundation has been laid to establish that Dr. Dan is familiar with the methodology, et cetera, that would have gone into the performance of those studies."[19] Thus, since he did not perform the studies or have a hand in the studies, his perspective about them, Woodside argued, was opinion. However, Sheila Jasanoff, a scholar of science and technology policy, makes clear that the role of experts in court is different from that of other witnesses:

> Persons may be recognized as experts in the courtroom by virtue of "knowledge, skill, experience, training, or education"; once they are so certified, they need not, like laypeople, limit their testimony solely to

matters known through direct, personal experience. Expertise, as conceived by the law, clearly encompasses the special sort of competence that we term "science," but it is a significantly broader concept.[20]

Thus, Woodside's attempts to utilize hearsay as a rationale to exclude Dan's testimony were ineffective exactly because Dan, as a scientist, encompassed that broader sense of competence.

In turn, Riley needed that very competence of Dan, through his former position at the CDC, to make clear to the jury the epidemiological model of testing, and the process by which infectious disease was identified to ensure public health. Significantly, epidemiology relies on retrospective, versus prospective, methods that define the very discipline. In essence, the hallmark of a prospective clinical trial is a wide sampling of individuals, ideally found at random, that create a representative sample by which results can be compared and aggregated. With a retrospective method, researchers seek out afflicted individuals and track potential outbreaks. The practice usually relies on subjects' recall of events. While this method is advantageous for speed, implicit to it is the fallibility of memory. In addition, the subjects are not randomized, so attention is necessarily focused on specific individuals. According to Dan, "At the CDC we cannot afford the time to spend years investigating certain diseases." Though he saw the value of doing long-term studies on degenerative diseases such as cancer or heart disease, he testified that "the CDC's main mission is to prevent unnecessary disease and death, which means very quickly, very expeditiously we must find out exactly what is causing illnesses and stop them." By identifying and examining people who were ill, and presumably contagious, a retrospective study provided a means to identify "the critical factor and hopefully eliminate that factor." He concluded that a prospective study would take years, and for the purposes of the CDC it was "unethical for the fact that people would be dying while you were trying to do the study."[21]

According to the lawyers at P&G, this type of study unfairly and unnecessarily singled out Rely tampons, so that bias was built into the very studies that aimed for "objective" results. P&G hired Alvan Feinstein, a leading epidemiologist at Yale University, to serve as a witness. Feinstein had a reputation of supporting corporate interests, and the tobacco industry found him to be an ally due to his studies that mollified the effects of smoking.[22] He and his colleagues Mary Harvey and Ralph Horwitz compiled a report that critiqued the series of studies on which the FDA decision to withdraw Rely was based. The article appeared in *JAMA* in August after the *Kehm v. Procter & Gamble* trial, but clearly the co-authors' work was contiguous with the trial that spring. In their article, "Toxic Shock and Tampons: Evaluation of the Epidemiologic Evidence," they chronicled the studies and also critiqued the structure and results.[23] Two areas in particular, diagnostic bias and reporting bias, muddied the results in their opinion. They noted that the "constellation of nonspecific manifestations" thwarted definitive diagnosis, and the publicity surrounding TSS likely compelled physicians to report cases in higher than usual numbers to state departments of health, even when TSS may not have been the correct diagnosis. They also questioned the accuracy of women's memories about past menstrual periods in the retrospective studies, much the same as corporate leaders did in the arguments with the FDA before Rely's withdrawal. Finally, they concluded that what the CDC provided was a "tampon hypothesis" that "obviously cannot account for the many cases of toxic shock that have no menstrual association or that have occurred in persons who did not use tampons. For menstrually associated TSS, the validity of the hypothesis was uncertain."[24] According to Riley in his memoir of the trial, he stated, "Their bottom-line conclusion, which they promised P&G they would testify to in court, was that the epidemiological studies by the CDC and the state public health departments were invalid."[25]

Feinstein testified that the epidemiologists of the CDC-1 study created leading questions due to its poor construction. He claimed that the survey singled out the Rely brand, a methodological faux pas, so that the way the survey questions were worded led respondents to "remember" that they used Rely. The language at issue was found in an evidence exhibit, which the P&G lawyer had him read aloud: "Have you ever used Rely tampons (which may have been sent to you as a sample)?"[26] This, according to Feinstein, was inappropriate and not at all objective. Riley in his cross-examination asked him if he got this information from a "secondhand source," to which Feinstein replied "from a colleague," who remained unnamed.

Feinstein's testimony is problematic. Riley tried to secure Kathryn Shands, the epidemiologist who directed the TSS Task Force, as a witness after she resigned from the CDC. In my interview with her, I asked about the opportunities to serve as an expert witness in lawsuits, and she said it was a path she was not interested in taking, in part because her career had shifted to psychiatry. I did, however, specifically ask her opinion about this point of contention in the trial concerning bias in CDC-1 and the wording of the questionnaire they used. She said that they did not ask about any particular brand or Rely in CDC-1.[27] The task force specifically constructed the follow-up study to pinpoint tampon use, and the CDC-2 survey asked, "If you used tampons, what brand(s) and absorbency(s) did you use?"[28] This documentary evidence contradicts Feinstein's testimony, reinforcing Riley's contention that Feinstein's job was to raise doubt.

Alternative Readings

Feinstein's testimony exemplified a problem for Riley. Who could he call on as witnesses who were not already somehow paid by P&G, or working on TSS research funded by P&G grants? The reach of P&G was so extensive that its funded scientists controlled the tone of the research conversations about TSS. Riley surmised: "Having positioned itself to control laboratory evidence of the Rely connection to TSS and having employed the best experts to deal with the only evidence available—the circumstantial proof of the epidemiological studies—P&G was now ready to go to court to take on the victims of TSS or their families who blamed Rely tampons for the injuries or deaths."[29] In this regard, Philip Tierno was an important expert witness for Riley. Tierno, a clinical microbiologist holding a Ph.D. who worked at the NYU Medical Center, weighed in particularly late in the controversy. Riley learned of Tierno's interest in TSS through the files and letters provided by P&G during trial preparation. In late October of 1980 after the recall, Tierno sent letters to the CDC, FDA, and research scientists at P&G, outlining what he saw were research leads about the chemical and microbiological causes leading to TSS. Tierno held that this was not a path of research that he intended to develop any further, but that it would provide a road map should any of the scientists pursue it.

Though the FDA politely thanked him for his interest, Dr. James Widder from P&G not only phoned him to discuss his findings, but also visited him in his New York lab and invited him to submit a proposal for a grant funded by P&G.[30] Though Tierno chose not to pursue this, he stayed close enough to TSS research to be considered an expert witness at trials. In short, Tierno theorized that the Rely tampon contained components that chemically degraded, thus raising the risk for TSS. After learning about Tierno's interests, Riley commented that he "recognized that it was not critical whether I understood or agreed with the Tierno theory—it was only important to have a scientific theory from an expert that the jury could hang its hat on if it wanted to compensate Mike Kehm and his two small daughters for the loss of a wife and mother."[31] For Riley, his credentials were right for the case and legitimized an alternative theory. It also forced P&G to engage his scenarios, rather than just disparage the CDC or raise doubt about correlation. Riley recalled a conversation with Jon Kidneigh and Steve Kaufman, lawyers who were working on behalf of Deletha Lampshire and her TSS case, stating as much. He commented to them, "The only way they [P&G lawyers] can prove Tierno's theory is wrong is by proving what is right and that will still be that Rely tampons cause TSS. Besides, we don't have any choice because P&G has got everybody else in their hip pocket."[32]

According to Tierno, he got curious about TSS after his wife asked him why she had not contracted TSS from wearing Rely tampons, and he conducted a side investigation on his own. First, he assayed her vaginal flora and determined that she did not carry *S. aureus*, the bacterium responsible for TSS. Though this answered why she personally did not contract TSS, Tierno probed a bit further. He collected all the stray Rely tampons he could find before they disappeared. He broke apart the tampon into its major components of the polyester shell, polyester foam cubes, and carboxymethylcellulose (CMC) chips. He began by studying the CMC chips, in part because they gelled when wet, but also because he knew that the cellulose structure could be broken down into glucose, in particular, by plenty of different bacteria naturally occurring in the vaginal canal. Tierno inferred that it was all but common knowledge that CMC would break down by bacterial action, and that this was cited in the scientific literature as early as the 1920s and well into the 1960s. As he expressed at the Kehm trial, "Well, I was surprised, because I considered that any product that is put in the vagina or any orifice which has normal flora would be inert or should be inert, and in fact, I discovered it was not inert but biodegradable or broken down."[33] He noted that the particular process included the enzyme beta-glucosidase, produced by bacteria, breaking the bonds of CMC to produce glucose, a simple sugar.

To describe the cumulative effect of multiple bacteria on CMC, Tierno explained it to the jury through analogy. "Let's say you needed a dollar or hundred pennies to complete an operation in enzyme activity. Some bacteria may have a nickel's worth. Some may have a penny's worth. Some may have a fraction of a penny's worth. And even toxic shock strains of S. Aureus possess beta-glucosidase activity."[34] All that different activity amounted to a 97 percent presence of the enzyme, but with quite varying and variable amounts in women. Tierno called it the "summation effect," that "it's no one single bacterium alone that acts, but the concert of many of the normal flora that can start the slow degradation of the product in a matter of hours."[35] Though he did not say it, this variability seemed to be a crucial scientific key. When, for instance, would the enzymatic threshold be reached, under what circumstances, and to what effect? If his hypothesis were true, it suggested that P&G was remiss in overlooking the vaginal bacterial activity in relation to the supposedly "inert" materials of the tampon.

Tierno relayed that the CMC in Rely tampons was different enough that he began referring to it as Rely CMC. This difference was due to the fact that in its production, chemists modified a powdered substance named CLD-2 to its chip form, a cross-linked carboxymethylcellulose supplied by the Buckeye Cellulose Company (a subsidiary of P&G). In the process, Tierno argued that something happened to change the bonds so that they were more easily broken by the enzymatic action of beta-glucosidase. He determined this by testing the CLD-2 powder, the Rely chips, and a non-crossed CMC produced by Sigma Chemical. Both the CMC from Sigma and the Rely chips supported similarly quick dissolution times. This also led him to conclude that the Rely CMC was no longer cross-linked because it was easily dissolved. He also tested another cross-linked CMC, CLD-2 named Acdisol, produced by the FMC Corporation to see how well it would support the growth of S. aureus, compared to the Rely CMC. As Tierno put it, he saw virtually no growth with the Acdisol, but a "two log" increase with Rely CMC, that is, a growth of a hundred million organisms from 10^5 to 10^7. He ran

a similar test with the Sigma CMC, with similar results in its support of
S. aureus growth.[36]

This attention to the variants of CMC raised doubts about which one
was in use and whether or not its properties were inert. Riley sought to
show the jurists proof of its reactivity by having Tierno demonstrate a bit
of chemistry. Riley requested permission from Judge Edward McManus
to begin a chemistry demonstration before Tierno's testimony, the premise being that the process would take about two hours. More important,
he wanted the culmination of the reaction to synchronize with the conclusion of his direct questioning, for a climactic finale. Riley described
how Tierno would mix the components, adding distilled water to the
Rely CMC chips, with the reagent of beta-glucosidase, derived not from
bacteria but from a purer form in almonds, and let the mixture warm
under a lamp, which would replicate body temperature. Though Tierno
could have warmed vials in his pocket, Riley worried that jurists might
be dubious of "the old switcheroo," as he put it, and he argued that the
lamp provided transparency during the chemical reaction. Before anything began, Woodside vehemently objected. First, he claimed, "it is not
to be performed under conditions which are similar or identical to those
which exist in the menstruating woman, for which reason the experiment or demonstration would not contain any relevant information."
Furthermore, "it's not significantly similar to those conditions under
which tampons and, in particular, Rely carboxymethylcellulose would
be used or exposed."[37] This protest was quite ironic. In fact, this was
exactly what P&G scientists did when testing materials outside women's
bodies or conducting absorbency tests without "relevant" information.

The demonstration proceeded nonetheless, though the judge denied
Riley's request for an early setup. He instead had to initiate Tierno's testimony with an explanation of the experiment, with it warming underneath the lamp in front of the jurists. Tierno's role was to show how the
Rely CMC would not just gel but liquefy, thus creating a tangible piece
of scientific evidence that the product was chemically at fault and reactive, rather than inert. In theory, this explained how it was broken down
into its component part of glucose. In a letter dated October 2, 1981, to
the editors of *The Lancet*, Tierno reported on the glucose theory, and
he later wrote about it in detail with his colleagues Bruce Hanna and
Megan Davies.[38] Whether or not the glucose theory is accurate from

contemporary standards is quite difficult to assess. In terms of the Kehm trial, however, it was enough to raise doubt. It was the performance deployed by an expert witness that gave credence to Riley's contention that the Rely tampon was not inert and that P&G possessed prior knowledge of this problem.

Skepticism about the courtroom lab demonstration seeped into the tone and questions posed during the defense lawyer's examination of Tierno, immediately putting him on the defensive. Recall that the beta-glucosidase demonstration sat in view of the jurists during this cross-examination. Woodside asked about the demonstration in a pejorative manner, with the egos of both men clashing, as reflected in the following exchange during the trial:

> WOODSIDE: Now, as a matter of fact, what you did with your little experiment is you just sort of—well, let me ask it a little differently. In your lab do you measure exactly how many chips you put in each one of those little test tubes?
> TIERNO: You know, I don't know if you are trying to antagonize me, but of course we measure.
> WOODSIDE: I consider that an insult, sir.
> TIERNO: Well, I consider your comment an insult, sir.[39]

Tierno later retorted, "We weigh it, we do better than counting."

The antagonism continued over the categorization of toxins associated with TSS. Here, the "facts" were less important than the techniques of shaming Tierno in order to make him appear to be an incompetent and inexpert witness. Woodside, for P&G, rebuked Tierno about providing speculation rather than facts in the following exchange about enterotoxins related to TSS, named A through F, some of which were identified by 1982, and others that had yet to be determined.

> WOODSIDE: Now, A and B . . . don't have anything in the world to do with toxic shock syndrome, do they, sir?
> TIERNO: That's not true. You don't know that for a fact. There may be a synergy which I have not commented on because it is speculation and—
> WOODSIDE: Well, sir, don't comment to me on speculation.

TIERNO: Well, you are asking me a question.

WOODSIDE: I didn't ask you to speculate. I want only facts.

TIERNO: Well, I have to give you that information in the answer.[40]

In this exchange, the tension between "facts" as determining evidence for a trial and "facts" as scientific knowns led to contrary ends, and they had different purposes for scientific discovery versus case-building outcomes.

Tierno also conveyed the difficulty in studying the ecosystem of the vagina and the number of variables at play in even trying to explain the bacterial processes related to TSS because women had such varying microflora. As Tierno put it, the vagina was "a very difficult thing to replicate." In the laboratory, he could only seek to control various aspects and parameters. The demonstration in the courtroom of gelling and liquefying the CMC reinforced this exact difficulty. Riley asked, "The work that you have done here in the courtroom today, you weren't attempting to duplicate what you would find in the vagina of a menstruating woman who used tampons, were you, sir?" Tierno replied, "I didn't see any vaginas here. I mean, I am working in tubes. I am working in tubes, not in a vagina."[41] He concluded: "That's why I said there are many factors that are involved. Not one particular factor should be weighed more than the other, but the summation of all these factors play a vital role as to why there is such an increased incidence of TSS using Rely products opposed to the other tampons."[42]

P&G attorneys called Peter Reilly, a professor of chemical engineering at Iowa State University, and an expert in the chemical composition of cellulose, as a witness to counter Tierno's contentions. Reilly testified that the whole beta-glucosidase experiment was entirely problematic due to the fact that the very enzyme that Tierno procured from the supply house was not in pure form, and, moreover, contaminants contributed to the breakdown of CMC, rather than the enzyme itself. Though not available at the trial, an article he published to the same effect in 1985 outlined the details of the experiment, further discrediting Tierno's hypothesis.[43] Reilly contended that the microbes did not degrade the CLD-2 component of the Rely tampons, so it could not provide nutrients to any bacteria, including *S. aureus*. His work, it should be noted, was supported by a grant from P&G. In terms of the trial, the point was to cast doubt on Riley's expert witnesses, not necessarily to prove definitively the mechanisms by which tampons served as biocatalytic technologies. Raising doubt was enough.

Woodside called another witness, Patrick Schlievert, a microbiologist and assistant professor at the University of Minnesota who studied TSS and its toxins. Schlievert asserted that it was the bacterium, and not Rely, that caused TSS, and furthermore, there simply was not enough evidence to implicate P&G in selling a faulty product.[44] Schlievert also happened to be one of the experts summoned to Atlanta to meet with folks at the CDC during the summer of 1980 to assess the state of TSS. He testified to the court that, while there, he heard no discussion about tampon manufacturers needing to warn consumers. Furthermore, he had begun testing the components of Rely, assuredly stating that they did not significantly increase toxin production. Most notable to his testimony was his proposition that the cause of TSS was a new strain of *S. aureus*, producing a different kind of toxin, pyrogenic exotoxin C. He also reported that it was resistant to the antibiotics ampicillin and penicillin, as well as to some heavy metals. For these reasons, and the fact that TSS could present itself in nonmenstrual cases, Schlievert testified that the tampons were not a factor. It was the new bacterial strain that caused TSS, which was merely coincidental with Rely; thus the technology was not causative. It only seemed correlative because of the timing.

Toward the end of the second week of the trial, the judge took more proactive steps to accelerate the pace. He called Riley and Calder to the bench, to ask them the intent of the expert witnesses, in particular concerning the issue of testing and how it related to the types of damages that the plaintiffs sought. The judge asked, "What I'm saying is, the testing goes to negligence, and we don't have that in this case, so what is the relevance of testing anymore?" Calder replied, "I think it has a great deal to do with showing the lack of likelihood that the product is defective, and it also surely goes to the punitive damage issue which Your Honor has permitted to be in the case." The judge suggested to them "we have been hearing an awful lot about testing," and furthermore that "testing properly, goes to the question of negligence, which we don't have in this case anymore. We're talking now about design and warning." Calder explained, "And to show the reason that a warning was not given, we show that the product was tested thoroughly and shown not to need a warning."[45] Though the judge's efforts were unsuccessful at moving things along, the conversation highlighted conflicts between corporate and publicly funded science, and how each were deployed for different ends.

Firsthand Witnesses

Despite the heft of the expert witnesses, with their multiple degrees and institutional affiliations, it may have been the more traditional testimony of direct witnesses that proved to be most effective in swaying jurists' opinions. The court transcript reveals how family members established the timing of Patricia Kehm's period and use of Rely, and also how lawyers from P&G worked to discredit the women's memories of Patricia's menstrual cycle, as well as dismiss her use of Rely at all. They aimed to show that Patricia Kehm did not use Rely and that she did not contract TSS. For the defense lawyers, this had merit because there was no "smoking gun" of a used tampon or any emptied tampon boxes, and furthermore the attending physician at the emergency room had not identified TSS as the cause of death. For the plaintiffs, the purpose of family testimony was to establish the dates and times of her menstrual cycle and to prove that she used Rely. Testimony from medical personnel at the hospital revealed the problem of encountering an unknown illness and how best to treat it.

In terms of use, Patricia Kehm's sister, Colleen Jones, testified that it was she who encouraged Patricia to switch from Playtex and try the Rely samples. Jones recalled telling her how absorbent they were, even while Kehm was pregnant, and "when it came time for her to start using tampons that she should try them." Kehm's daughter was born in June, and Jones again promoted the tampons in late July, six weeks after the delivery when Patricia's period began again. When pressed about why she could so accurately recall the timeline of her sister's period, Jones explained, "I stopped over to her house one day, and she told me she was—wasn't feeling good, and then on top of that she had her period, and I said, 'Oh, have you tried Rely yet?' She says, 'I'm using them now.'"[46] In addition, Kehm's mother, Jean Robinson, reported on her daughter's biorhythms as well as her purchasing patterns. She, too, had particularly detailed events that she associated with her daughter's period because it correlated with her granddaughter's baptism at St. Patrick's Church. It was August 24, 1980, and they had also stopped at the store for tampons, among other things. While there, she criticized Patricia and asked, "So you are going to try those dumb things?" (meaning Rely tampons).[47] Patricia's husband, Michael, also testified about her use of Rely, only made apparent to him after her immediate death. After her passing at the hospital, and after his return home, he stated, "Even though the doctors couldn't confirm that that happened to be it [TSS], I seen [sic] a box of Rely tampons, and I, in a moment of anger and disgust, I threw them in the wastebasket."[48]

Hospital workers, too, concurred about Kehm's period and tampon use. An emergency room nurse, Lois Sterenchuk, noted in Kehm's medical record "Tampax removed by L. Sterenchuk, RN," which provided P&G with an important piece of evidence.[49] However, she later explained that "I use the word 'Tampax' I guess as I might use the word 'Kleenex' in place of facial tissue. Something like that."[50] When asked to describe the appearance of the tampon, she called it a "mushroom shape," hardly an accurate accounting of Tampax that elongates when it absorbs fluids. She had no reason to save it, and plainly stated, "I took it out. Just like I have every tampon in my thirty years of nursing. I have never saved one yet. Held it up, looked at it and disposed of it."[51] Thus, the evidentiary tampon would not be produced, and had no reason to be for medical purposes.

Even as the defense pressed Dr. John Jacobs, the attending physician in the emergency room on September 6, 1980, when Kehm was admitted, he became sympathetic instead of an asset to the P&G case. Jacobs was unfamiliar with TSS, as were many physicians at that time, but he quickly learned. Prior knowledge would not have helped much, however, as Kehm's body succumbed to the toxins that thrust her into shock. No amount of medical effort at that point could have reversed the chain of events taking place in her body. The medical report did not identify TSS as a cause of death, though the coroner's report did. The defense homed in on this discrepancy, and the lawyer Timothy White asked Jacobs for the reason why tampons were excluded from the reports, asking him to read the medical record to the jury to confirm this omission. White asked, "Now, does that make any mention under diagnosis of tampons?" Jacobs quickly caught the error, and replied, "Well, of course, tampon is not a medical diagnosis."[52] Riley's perception was that the lawyers tried to depict Jacobs as negligent, but his sharp testimony made the defense lawyers look foolish instead.

The Limits of Testing

Scrutiny of P&G's research and development practices would not have come to light except for the need to ascribe blame to a faulty product. The larger issue in this case was not the testing that P&G dutifully performed. It was rather the interpretation of conflicting science claims, as well as the lack of testing; the tests unperformed left the unknowns unfound. This phenomenon of only being able to test for known outcomes plagued testing at P&G. Harry Collins and Trevor Pinch, science and technology studies scholars, describe this as "experimenter's regress": that is, the difficulty for "a test to have an unambiguous outcome because one can never be sure whether the test has been properly conducted until one knows what the correct outcome ought to be."[53] In many ways, the scientists had no means to predict, measure, and test for the outcome of TSS, precisely because it was unknowable during early testing, though it became an issue by 1980. Yet, by relying so completely on empirical models, which encompass the very definition of testing, scientists were tethered to the data, not to the conditions surrounding it. New materials, circumscribed testing, and women's bodies that were not quite cooperative as lab instruments foiled scientists' abilities to predict health hazards.

Scientists practiced a ritual form of data production, required not only for managers and CEOs but also for the FDA. The very act of producing data creates a sense of calm and assurance that the data will reveal potential risks. Whether or not those data are useful is altogether another question. A ritualistic practice of testing confirms known unknowns, and it generates information and trust. But when scientists formulate tests based on limited or shortsighted questions, and do not actually know the unknowns to look for, the data can be devoid of meaning because it misses the big picture; it fails to recognize the forest for the trees.

Corporate scientists did not shirk their responsibilities to test, but they garnered data in areas that were more readily testable. They ran tests with three main objectives: (1) to assure purity of the components; (2) to assess their toxicity and teratogenicity; and (3) to measure responses of women with in situ human trials. In fact, these tests were fairly comprehensive and by all accounts quite reasonable for what was expected of the company during that time period. The purity of the product, measured by testing individual components, required assessing ingredients against known qualities. This lab work proved to be fairly straightforward and rather routine. Toxicity of components as well as the proclivity to cause birth defects or cancer required the study of live animals, generally mice, and how they reacted to the ingestion of each ingredient, followed by an examination of offspring delivered by those same mice. Once the mouse trials established basic safety, human trials commenced. Groups of women, under the supervision of a gynecologist, wore Rely during their menstrual cycles, experienced a number of vaginal exams, and reported problems or issues along the way.

Herbert L. Ley, a former FDA commissioner, and hired by P&G as a consultant, testified on behalf of the company that it had actually exceeded testing in anticipation of changing requirements within the Medical Device Amendments (MDA). As an expert witness, he reviewed the application to conduct clinical trials with Rely tampons that the company submitted to the FDA, and he testified that it was more than adequate; the safety tests indicated that there was "no evidence at all of any problem of a safety nature." This included testing for mutagenicity and teratology, which was beyond the minimal requirements.[54] Ley disclosed that preclinical animal studies dealt with short- and long-term exposure of Rely's components, including "acute toxicity" with the duration lasting "a full week" and "long term toxicity, usually two years, to determine if there are carcinogenic effects." They also ran "vaginal irritation tests" in animals for the components to make sure they were not abrasive, inflammatory, or allergenic when introduced into the vaginal tract.[55] Without the animals voicing their experiences, it is not clear what signs the researchers read besides visible rashes to indicate irritation.

Ley explained, "The only appropriate and final test for this type of product, once the animal studies have been completed, is studying use in humans under an experimental or investigative protocol as Procter & Gamble did."[56] In its initial testing, 1,332 women completed the study, in which he described "there were 9,500 cycles, menstrual cycles of use of Rely tampons, which if you divided by thirteen cycles per year, you arrive at a figure of approximately 730 woman years of experience with

Rely tampons." This math created the impression of long-term studies as well as representing a broad swath of the population. He also added that "this amount of clinical experience, 730 woman years of experience with Rely tampons, is very comparable to the amount of clinical experience with a new drug substance that FDA would require for approval of such a substance in the form of a medicine on the market." The lawyers used his voice to express that P&G had done everything right.

Furthermore, Martin Cannon, a manager in research and development at P&G, confirmed the nature of this testing. Reinforcing Ley's testimony to further explain the company's scientific rigor, Cannon noted that a physician supervised the clinical tests of women wearing tampons, thus indicating that if something were awry, the doctor would surely have caught it. For the Rely prototypes, he recalled that researchers tested polyurethane foam by implanting it "underneath the tissue inside the body" in "certain types of animals," which remained unnamed. Though Cannon personally believed polyurethane to be safe, the product received bad publicity in its rollout in Rochester, New York, where women there challenged its appropriateness in a tampon when it was a cancer-causing agent. He testified that it was easier to replace the ingredient to spare the reputation of the product than to fight what he believed was a misinformed consumer. As he explained: "In products that you're selling to the consumer, you can know scientifically that things are quite appropriate and satisfactory, but if you're—if you're not able to explain that, to describe that in a way that people can understand, then you can't maintain the confidence on the part of the consumer to continue to use the product in that circumstance."[57] With this statement, he sidestepped the cancer concerns, yet moved ahead with the replacement material of polyester, considered to be "a very pure material" and "used extensively in a lot of medical applications internally." With this change, researchers fed polyester to laboratory animals to test for its safety. Cannon added, "We've even made up small little pledgets and used them vaginally in mice through an entire life cycle to insure that even in that usage, in attempting to have a vaginal model for it, we can assure that these—this unique component introduces no risk to the user of the product."[58]

For these particular tests, researchers chose not to use women at all but substituted mice instead. By the 1970s P&G included the commonly held practice of testing chemicals and components on mice to determine whether they promoted birth defects. From any ethical or epistemological standpoint regarding science, questions must be posed about usefulness of the data gleaned from the mouse tampons, especially since mice are rodents without monthly menstrual periods. Mice really then cannot act as a suitable understudy to a human woman in replicating the dynamics of a vagina with its requisite ecosystem and fluctuating microbiome. To enact such a substitution is to deny a vast array of physical factors and tolerate a tremendous amount of extrapolation between test conditions and consumer use. Yet animal testing is a common practice to prevent some of the very abuses exercised by research physicians and scientists at the turn of the twentieth century and later, thus sparing humans from pain and suffering.

Mouse testing, however, provided a comforting reproduction of the scientific method and its ability to produce data, but the data points revealed little about conditions or even safety for women. Both artifacts and bodies—of animals and women—were tested in different ways to gauge product efficacy during a menstrual period. Neither may have provided much sound evidence to make safety claims because of gendered assumptions that the tampon remained inert in the vagina, and that (for a moment in suspended imagination) mouse and woman body parts were interchangeable.

Beyond testing on mice, scientists' attempts to assay changes in vaginal microflora proved more difficult. As Martin Cannon described it, "What we find is that the microflora of the vagina . . . it just changes, changes for an individual woman and it changes in spite of what product habits that, you know, we were able to observe."[59] His is not an unusual reaction to the vagina as a vexing site for scientific analysis and control. The history of medicine and gynecology is rife with examples to subdue women's reproductive health, including pregnancy, fertility, and menstruation.[60] In this case, women's bodies were unable to conform to the dictates of the lab to remain fixed; for the scientists, there were just too many variables related to the fluctuating, permanent, and transient microorganisms to isolate. Thus, lab conditions were different than environmental conditions, and the scientists were not required by any regulating body, whether internal or external, to rectify these differences. The complexity of the vaginal ecosystem loomed, and was summarily dismissed, as just too unwieldy for study.

By July of 1980, another member of the P&G science team, only mentioned by his last name, Dzialo, expressed concern about this very problem of isolating more elements to test. In a memo to a supervisor, R. L. Stone at Procter & Gamble, Dzialo lamented "an inadequate understanding of menstrual fluid characteristics and of the functional anatomy of the vagina has complicated an already difficult task. An improved understanding of both areas would significantly reduce the need for a trial by error mode of operation."[61] Dzialo seemed to be the lone voice at P&G who recognized shortcomings, many of which he could not even name because he lacked a more robust understanding of menstruation and women's bodies in order to articulate them. What he confronted was the tyranny of the androcentric male as a proxy for all matters of health, leaving the researchers in a knowledge vacuum and without the aid of women researchers to point out fundamental understandings about menstruation (though this knowledge was not unique to them). He also disparaged the inefficient process he called "trial by error." Though there are plenty of examples of errors leading to scientific discovery, in this case the errors seemed to be stemming from active ignorance.

Others within the company remarked about this difficulty of testing. James Stone Widder, the director of the human safety division of the Miami Valley Laboratories, a research arm of P&G, was appointed in October 1980 as associate director of the special programs division once TSS became an issue for the company. He remarked, "We don't have a vagina in the laboratory that we can study, in this case, menstrually associated toxic shock." Here, he was careful to call it "menstrually associated toxic shock" and not tampon-associated TSS, which deflected culpability away from the company. It was almost as if because they could not just go out and get a vagina, this inability rationalized why they could not be held accountable for proper testing. Widder asserted, "It has to be done really in an animal, ideally in a human, to study it."[62] The ethics protecting human (women) test subjects rationalized another reason for the company's inability to fully understand TSS.

In essence, the scientists could not identify the known unknowns, or fix the variables when so many existed. The challenges of a multivariant environment overwhelmed the methods at hand that required a quarantine on a specific set of conditions and reagents. This constructed, artificial condition—exactly because it was limiting—became the case on which conclusions were drawn about larger systems and environments. Except it was the exact artificiality, the simulacrum of a laboratory or rodent vagina, that betrayed the scientists because it was not a sufficient stand-in for "field" conditions. Women possessed variable bodies, immune systems, and different flora, fauna, and bacterial constituents, including the *Staphylococcus aureus* bacterium responsible for TSS. Individual vagaries of women's bodies remained unaccounted for in lab conditions. Without accounting for difference, it created an illusion that Rely was safe. The company reported that no women fell ill during the in vivo phase of testing, but this should not have been interpreted as exoneration from fault. Rather, it indicated that women prone to TSS (those carrying *S. aureus* and without the immunity to the TSST-1 toxin) were not part of the testing pool. Omitted from the set, the women could not possibly manifest symptoms and report problems. The research was not comprehensive enough to account for microbial variables, though they knew they existed, but scientists chose to dismiss them as both too wild to control and too insignificant to raise concerns.

Experts on Trial

The Kehm trial exemplified a modern trend in many court cases of using scientific experts to testify on behalf of the plaintiff or defendant in order to bolster the arguments of the lawyers and also to provide evidence. There are multiple levels of validation at work: (1) claims of truth within the court case itself; (2) scientific claims (which may or may not be "truth"); (3) claims of expertise, reified by that very same work as a paid witness; and (4) claims of "justice" and the court's ability to deliver it, thus engendering trust in the system of law.

Simon Cole and Rachel Dioso-Villa analyze the relationship of science to the court of law in the United States with the "CSI effect," the name inspired by the CBS forensic television drama that aired from 2000 to 2015. Their work points to the somewhat uneasy relationship between science and the courts, which is exacerbated by the lay public's perception that both are truth-producing institutions. Science, they note, is "popularly associated with such positive values as truth, certainty, goodness, enlightenment, progress, and so on." In addition, "While law has often held high hopes that science would prove effective at resolving disputes without ambiguity, this very potential to be truth-producer is a cause for understandable anxiety on the part of the law," in part because jurors have been taught to expect that science can deliver unequivocal certainty. The concerns about this "truth-producing institute called 'science'" indicate that lawyers perceive that other kinds of evidence, besides those produced by science, are losing favor.[63] Yet it does point to the power that scientific evidence, as well as testimony of scientists, can have on a court of law.

Sheila Jasanoff offers a critique about the ways in which the growing incorporation of scientific evidence into courtroom proceedings has raised issues about expertise, valid data sets and results, and "certifiable knowledge." This highlights the difficult issue about what science is "good" science, and how judges or juries should discern credible yet opposing data from expert witnesses. As she puts it, "The legal system has as great a stake in distinguishing admissible from inadmissible claims of expertise as science itself."[64] The law needs experts to reify its credibility, but as scholars of science and technology studies make so amply clear, science is not necessarily neutral. In addition, the way that scientists might frame a problem to generate data may not generate "facts" appropriate for a trial. The absence of an occurrence, for example, may have meaning in some scientific experiments, but it does not translate into direct evidence, proof, or causality, which are hallmark components of a court case.

Jasanoff's model of the "game board of expertise" demonstrates the intersections of expertise, objectivity, and experience, and how plaintiffs and defendants alike succumb to the bolstering and stripping of witnesses' credibility and integrity to raise doubt about knowledge they may produce for the court. This game's model is a useful tool in gauging the tactics used by lawyers in the Kehm trial, as well as how science was presented, manipulated, undermined, contested, confirmed, and by whom. Important to keep in mind are the kinds of witnesses called on to testify, which of those had been paid as consultants and by whom (used to show that evidence was tainted by association, regardless of how sound the findings might be), and then how their credibility was undermined or bolstered. As Jasanoff points out in the silicone breast implant cases of the 1990s, defense claims and arguments reflected the position that there was no good science linking the implants to connective tissue disease, and "the plaintiffs, by contrast, claimed that epidemiology was too blunt an instrument to establish a definite relationship between silicone and [atypical connective tissue disorders]."[65] In this version for the sufferers, the epidemiological studies had not been careful and precise enough, but that did not negate the link between implants and illness. In regard to the plaintiffs in *Kehm v. Procter & Gamble*, epidemiology was not dismissed but embraced. Here, both the defense and the plaintiffs used science and scientific methods for their own argumentative ends to frame injury suffered by women. Jasanoff does not label damage wrought by silicone breast implants as a gendered technological injury, but doing so provides a useful case for sake of comparison with tampon-related TSS. Understanding them both as unique health hazards to women, the injuries did not follow typical forms of bodily damage measured against a "universal male." They each required different arguments and different kinds of scientific evidence to produce claims of damage and injury.

* * *

As a result of the trial, the jury found P&G partially guilty, not in terms of negligence, but in having prior knowledge about TSS the summer preceding Patricia Kehm's death. The jury awarded Michael Kehm $300,000 in compensatory damages in the liability case, but it chose not to award punitive damages for reckless disregard of rights. It was "the highest verdict in Iowa's history for the death of a housewife," though it should have been more.[66] According to Riley, the jury felt that P&G was negligent but did not want to financially harm the company with a large payout to the Kehm family. They worried that workers in Cincinnati might lose their jobs because of the payout and instead opted for the lesser award.[67] The sense of protection granted to perceived male wage earners outweighed the compensation to remedy Kehm's death.

The jury failed to punish the company financially, though the case made clear that current testing methods did not prevent the manufacture of risky tampons. It also highlighted the fact that P&G had not provided sufficient warning of danger, and that more needed to be accomplished. Through a federal trial, the Kehm case unearthed and made public corporate memos and documents that would have otherwise remained inaccessible. These documents detail numerous unknowns related to TSS and tampons, and how corporate public relations worked to protect profit. These same issues would emerge in attempts to establish uniform labeling, balancing corporate rights and their "trade secrets" with women's health and their right to know. Accurate labeling proved to be the necessary missing element to protect both corporations and women if tampons were to remain on the market.

5

Health Activism and the Limits of Labeling

Even after litigation, the resulting settlements to women and their families, and the withdrawal of Rely from market shelves, more was still needed to protect women from the danger associated with superabsorbent tampons. That toxic shock syndrome (TSS) could be identified by its symptoms, and that tampon-related TSS was stabilized as a legitimate illness, aided in diagnoses of patients. Women, however, wanted to be assured that they would not unintentionally die from a tampon. To reduce the problem to a "choice" between brands, as marketing so often did by equating it with freedom and equality, was misleading and unfair. Who would willingly choose to use a tampon knowing they might be dead three days later when they could have simply selected brand X, Y, or Z instead and remained alive?

Corporations could no longer act is if tampons were inert, especially because epidemiology provided clear data that TSS rates were linked to superabsorbent tampons. Short of banning tampons altogether, an immediate necessity was to warn women and tell them to use the least absorbent one possible. The Centers for Disease Control (CDC) and the Food and Drug Administration (FDA) provided this initial message, but companies would need to shoulder that responsibility if they wanted to keep selling tampons and not be held liable. The most conscientious woman following the CDC's advice to use the least absorbent tampon in order to reduce the risk of TSS had to base her decision on marketing propaganda, the language for which was inconsistent between brands. Even the text on the sample box of Rely depended on imprecise definitions of absorbency when it boasted "if you now use the Super size of another tampon, you may find that you can completely depend on Rely Regular—it works that well!" Though this promotional material crafted these differences as beneficial, the slippery terminology was a problem. While companies made it their business to determine the absorbency rates of each and every tampon including their competitors, they withheld this information from consumers, instead offering terms such as "super" or "regular" to indicate absorbency, which were not meaningful. There was no systematic rating, ranking, or basic gram weight indicated on tampon boxes.

The politics of nondisclosure and the withholding of information are not unusual in the history of women's health. The women's health movement of the late 1960s and early 1970s played a large role in exposing the costs of silence, the hubris of some physicians in controlling medical treatment, and the lack of basic knowledge and information about women's reproductive life course. In addition, feminist health advocacy organizations, such as the Boston Women's Health Book Collective (BWHBC), worked to fill the void by reclaiming information and distributing it, most notably in the form of the book *Our Bodies, Ourselves* (*OBOS*). The collective was interested in menarche, pregnancy, menopause, birth control, abortion, and sexuality, while discussing these topics openly and promoting practices that favored women's health. As such, it included tampon safety in its mission. Thus, absorbency labeling carried political stakes, and women's health advocates sought a role in shaping federal policy about risk and tampon-related TSS.

The politics of tampon labeling were surprisingly contentious. A triad of competing interests sought very different outcomes. The FDA, under new direction by the Reagan administration to reduce regulations, sought a simple warning with the least resistance all around. The corporations fought to maintain the status quo, which meant they could determine the language and terms as they wished. The consumer groups and women's health advocates saw an opening to engage the federal labeling process and provide legible and meaningful warnings, while also pressing for broader regulation of tampon safety. The Tampon Task Force first convened in 1982 to promote formal dialogue between these groups and negotiate labeling, but owing to irreconcilable differences it disbanded in 1985. This chapter demonstrates the deep political stakes involved in labeling by tracing the debates within the task force, charged to establish the standardization of a test to measure absorbency, and the standardization of language to categorize and label tampons.[1] The results of these decisions would lead to routine practices and, once formalized and entrenched, they would be difficult to amend for any stakeholder. Thus, the negotiations and outcomes of the

Tampon Task Force held significant consequences for tampon manufacturers, federal regulators, and women tampon users alike.

A New Tool: The Syngyna

Though there was no official rating system for tampon absorbency that
women were aware of, companies had been doing their own in-house
testing since the 1950s. One particular method of measurement circulated among industrial labs by the 1960s and 1970s: the syngyna test.
The syngyna, known as a synthetic vagina, was lab apparatus devised
to simulate menstrual flow in a controlled lab environment to determine tampon absorbency. It originated in 1958, when Campana, the
maker of Pursettes tampons, commissioned G. W. Rapp, a professor of
biochemistry and physiology at Loyola University Chicago, to conduct
comparative tests on tampons in order to create scientifically verifiable
evidence supporting the claim that its tampons were superior to others.[2]
In part, the Pursettes tampon was twisted closed, and, as advertisements
described it, when exposed to moisture "Pursettes blossom out to absorb
more fully, more effectively."[3] This reference to flower blooms was a
signifier of both femininity and (the problematic) cultural notion that
women are closer to nature; thus by association this product was good
for women. Pursettes were different from the lengthwise-expanding
Tampax because it tended to cup fluid at its base. For these reasons, a
methodical comparison between tampons based on the design differences made sense, and after the tests, a 1963 advertisement in *Ebony*
magazine said that "Pursettes actually proved more absorbent than
super sizes of other leading tampons in an independent laboratory
test."[4] These results were derived from the syngyna test, and they also
reveal the lack of meaning concerning the term "super" as an indicator
of absorbency, because Pursettes not labeled with that moniker actually
absorbed more.

The unpublished 1958 lab report submitted to Campana, and later
shared among manufacturers, is instructive in understanding how tampon absorbency, and later standards, came to be established. As such,
the report shows how Rapp conceptualized menstruation as a type of
fluid, considered women's bodies as mechanical, and then erased the
myriad differences and real-life variables of the vaginal ecosystem with

the syngyna lab-based apparatus. The creation of lab equipment to help answer questions about problems is deeply rooted in scientific practice, so the syngyna was not unusual in this regard. Adele Clarke and Joan Fujimura, sociologists of health and science, describe how tools are co-constructed alongside scientific practice, with the need to produce the "right" tool to do the job at hand. They take note of the ways tools are disciplined to "produce rightness" and, furthermore, the stabilizing and disciplining of tools to create continuity.[5] This perspective is useful in understanding how the syngyna test first appeared, and then became the standard equipment by which tampon absorbency would be measured.

In his report "A Comparison of the Absorptive Efficiency of Commercial Catamenial Tampons," Rapp first noted that there were both "subjective and objective" factors in assessing tampon absorbency, but his study made no consideration of "the psychologic aspects since these would presumably not be relevant." With this broad stroke, he eliminated even the most rudimentary understanding that women might have a preference for one style of tampon over another, based on their bodily experiences with them. With feelings and opinions about tampons summarily dismissed, Rapp attended to the work at hand as a scientist in building an instrumentalized synthetic vaginal canal as a laboratory tool for the purpose of scientific experimentation.[6]

He did, however, discern between subjective and objective variables and how these related to menstrual fluid absorption in relation to tampons. Subjective factors equated to variables that the company could not control, such as the insertion of the tampon, and how far into the vaginal canal a woman lodged the tampon. Affecting this also was the "adaptation pressure" and how well the vaginal tissue and muscles held the tampon in place. Rapp referred to this as the "tonus of the vaginal walls" and "the tonus or adaptational pressure" exerted on a tampon. Likening it to the stomach, whose walls expand to the content and volume of food, the vagina was "a collapsed container" and when "a tampon is introduced into the vagina, the walls adapt themselves about it." This pressure was also something that could be determined by "introducing collapsed balloons and measuring the hydrostatic pressure needed to force the walls apart," ascertained by measurements garnered from "25 normal women aged 23 to 30" and how they "yielded a pressure of 135 to 180 mm of water." Here, the vaginal canals of twentysomething women presumably with elastic tissue, pried open with water balloons, established a "norm" for tone and strength. This ignored other age groups and women who had multiple vaginal deliveries, thus the set of women was quite circumscribed in establishing a "norm."

So-called objective factors focused on the physical properties of the tampon itself. The report noted that "nearly all of the commercial tampons available are made from pure cotton," though absorbency rates varied as a result of heat and pressure applied to the tampon during the manufacturing process, the length of the fibers, and the "direction in which the fibers run." Physical dimensions included size, but also "the relationship between long and short axis," which Rapp hypothesized "may affect the degree of permeability of the Tampon." Additionally, how the tampon acted as it began to take on fluid, including its "saturated shape," also influenced its overall performance.

Rapp referred to four different methods to measure the absorptive capacity of tampons. The first was the "in situ method" in which women were the test subjects. The tampon was weighed before and after during a specific time interval to determine the absorptive capacity rate. Rapp commented, "It seems clear that this method while giving 'proof of the pudding' kind of evidence is not suitable for precise comparative purposes. It is not possible to control any of the subjective factors outlined above." This, arguably, was the most important test, but it did not produce the valued "scientific" evidence for which he sought. Women were not the right tool, and they could not be modified to eliminate variables. The second method was the "total immersion method," which "gives unrealistic values." Just like it sounds, the tampon was immersed in fluid and then weighed to see what it had absorbed. The third technique, the "vertical drop method," entailed "dropping fluid drop by drop" onto the tampon in a predetermined position and at a predetermined rate. For Rapp, these methods did not yield useful data, because many factors could not be controlled.

The fourth method, and one that Rapp designed, was the "syngyna" (or sometimes spelled with an "i" as "syngina") method. This synthetic vagina simulated a woman's vaginal canal, re-created the internal pressure exerted by the vaginal walls on a tampon, reproduced body temperature, and mimicked the rate and flow of menstrual fluid. As he put it, "It consists of applying to a properly positioned Tampon an adaptation pressure of physiologic magnitude and then allowing a fluid of proper consistency to flow at its tip at a controlled rate." The apparatus consisted of "a thin rubber membrane," that is, a condom, "which holds the Tampon. A glass device around the membrane serves to introduce water about the membrane," the overflow managed by a "hydrostatic head." Lastly, "[a] reservoir of 'Syngyna' fluid with a flow regulator leads to an 'eyedropper' tip inside the membrane, which introduces the fluid at a predetermined rate of 2 drops per second." This rate seems a bit rapid for menstrual flow, nonetheless, it was the rate he determined to be correct for the test. The end point of the experiment was marked when "the *first drop* of fluid begins to fall from the open end," whether or not the tampon was fully saturated. Rapp noted a high degree of fluid channeling by some of the tampons, so that none came close to reaching their full absorptive capacity. The tampon was removed and then weighed, subtracting the dry tampon weight from the saturated tampon weight, to generate its absorption capability.

Rapp justified the relative accuracy of the syngyna test by comparing the results from the real-life female subjects. He reported that the values were "realistic" because from the study of thirty-five women, "the average fluid absorption was 11.3 grams, with a range of 6.6–12.3. The values obtained with the 'Syngyna' on the same brand of Tampons were an average of 12.6 with a range of 7.8–13.4." He concluded, "In the face of these findings, and because of the evident superiority of the 'Syngyna' method over the others, this device was used throughout these tests for obtaining the values reported herein." At one level, the test relieved women from being test subjects. At another, the syngyna proved to be a stand-in for the real, a simulation that ultimately eliminated all bodily differences and vagaries into glass and tubing.

Besides the laboratory equipment assembled to run the tests, it also required a menstrual-like fluid for the tampons to absorb. Referred to as "syngyna fluid," it included the following:

Cellulose Gum (Hercules CMC 70 Medium) 10 grams
Glycerol 100 grams
Sodium Chloride 10 grams
Sodium Bicarbonate 4 grams
Water, to make 1000ml

It contained many common ingredients: table salt, baking soda, water. In addition, glycerol is often referred to as glycerine and serves as a thickening agent. It is found in lotions, soap, and as a thickener in food. The cellulose gum, or carboxymethylcellulose, is another hydrophilic ingredient and is one and the same as what is found in Rely tampons.

Management at Campana was very proud of the findings produced by the scientized vagina, and its company president, I. Willard Crull, was known to highlight the syngyna during VIP tours of the headquarters located west of Chicago. Jerry Della Femina, an advertising executive and chairman of Della Femina Travisano & Partners (and whose memoir was purportedly the inspiration for the television show *Mad Men*), recalled a story about accountants from New York arriving at the Campana headquarters and taking the tour:

> With the president leading the way, they drift through the factory and suddenly the group comes across a very strange, *very strange*-looking thing. The president proudly explains that this *thing* is an artificial vagina, in fact its name is the syngina, and naturally it tests how good Pursettes are. The guys from New York are looking at these synginas and they're biting through their lips to keep from laughing. The president keeps carrying on about how good these synginas are and finally one New Yorker says, "And if you're real nice, they let you take the syngina to dinner." Here are guys collapsing on the floor of a factory in Batavia, Illinois, the president turning white with rage, the advertising manager petrified with fear, the agency guys still too stoned to worry.[7]

The syngyna had multiple interpretations, from absurd and strange to sexualized, so that its intended creation as a lab instrument was not self-evident. The president's anger juxtaposed with the ad guys' laughter shows a range of emotions about the tampon business, and also the stark omission of women in any role except that of consumer.

Procter & Gamble Modifies the Syngyna

During the post-Rely fallout, the FDA began exploring issues of tampon safety, including absorbency. In 1981, Gordon Hassing, an associate director at Procter & Gamble (P&G) responsible for product safety, provided a copy of Rapp's 1958 lab report to Don Marlowe in the Bureau of Medical Devices at the FDA when it pursued a means to evaluate the absorptive capacity of tampons.[8] What was unusual were the modifications that P&G scientists made to the syngyna test and apparatus, for which Hassing provided the protocol that they used. The procedures were problematic at best, reflecting the company's need to inflate the attributes of the tampon rather than assess its compatibility with actual use.[9] Hassing explained, "We have found Dr. Rapp's 'syngyna' method, with minor modification noted, to be an accurate means of predicting the maximum in vivo fluid uptake of tampons." However, researchers implemented three other modifications. In Rapp's test, the syngyna chamber tilted downward, correlating with the angle of the vagina in a woman sitting or standing. In the P&G test, researchers tilted the chamber upward at a forty-five-degree angle. This would resemble a woman lying down on her back, and tilting her pelvis upward. This meant that with the P&G test, drops of fluid worked against gravity and wicked upward toward the opening in the chamber. This may have created more time for the tampon to absorb fluid. P&G also slowed down the flow rate, and increased the hydrostatic pressure at the valve. Hassing noted, "P&G's modifications reduce the probability of premature failure due to channeling of the fluid around the tampon. Data obtained by the P&G syngyna method are more precise but yield similar overall results." With the contraption in essence opening upward, in the exact opposite direction of a woman's vagina while standing, it made sense that there were fewer incidents of "premature failure," because it collected pooling fluids rather than catching flowing liquids. The angle of the chamber to face upward is simply counterintuitive. The practice indicated the importance of serving the needs of the lab and favorable test results, rather than the commonsense notion that women spend most of their days upright, and would need a tampon to work in these kinds of normal circumstances.

P&G also had detailed instructions for producing syngyna fluid, which they referred to as "blue goo."[10] The blue shade provided by vegetable coloring provided a stark contrast to the white tampons in the syngyna test chamber, offering a visual cue concerning fluid channeling as well as the saturation point with the first drip from the chamber. Many who have watched television commercials and seen print advertisements in magazines recall the blue liquid dripped onto sanitary pads, tampons, and baby diapers to demonstrate the product's ability to absorb massive amounts of fluid without leaking. While providing a strong visual image and a sanitized representation of menstrual fluid, the ads referenced historical lab practices and did not solely emanate from the imagination of creative marketing executives.

The syngyna fluid also differed from Rapp's in composition. Rapp mixed sodium bicarbonate with the other ingredients, while P&G used sodium carbonate, more commonly seen in water softener pellets. It can be used as a descaler in heating elements or boilers, an acidity regulator in pools, or an anticaking component in food. There was no rationale provided for this change in components by P&G. However, there was a warning attached to the making of this fluid: "This solution is caustic and could cause eye injury or skin irritation. Safety goggles, rubber apron, and gloves must be worn during preparation."[11] Though menstrual fluid has been vilified, identified as a biohazard, and circumscribed through cultural practices, it neither is caustic nor requires protective equipment for a woman to handle on her own. It is ironic, then, that the menstrual simulacra would be dangerous to touch, but "better" as a lab tool.

Testing the Test

In the wake of tampon-related TSS, a glaring issue acknowledged by the FDA and the Bureau of Medical Devices was the lack of standardization among tampon absorbencies. This was very important, because the FDA recommended that women use the least absorbent tampon possible, and, according to the CDC, superabsorbent tampons were a contributing factor in TSS. The superabsorbent materials of polyester foam and carboxymethylcellulose in Rely were eliminated, polyacrylate was discontinued in 1985, and rayon is still used, but only the absorbency capacities and not the composition of the tampons were questioned.[12] The message conveyed was that superabsorbent tampons should be limited during a woman's menstrual cycle. At issue were a variety of absorbencies across different manufacturers, within a brand, and even sometimes between different lots of tampons produced for the same product line. Companies took liberties embellishing the absorptive capacity of tampons in their advertising claims, but there was no way for consumers to gauge the assertions. There simply were no standards.

In light of TSS developments, and the lack of accessible data about tampon absorbency rates, in 1981 scientists at the Bureau of Medical Devices reconstructed the syngyna test and the P&G modified test.[13] The rationale for the bureau getting involved was to "test the test" as it were, because epidemiologic studies indicated a relationship between absorbency of tampons correlating with an increased risk of TSS, yet there were no clear markers of what constituted "high" absorbency. The bureau noted "absorbency characteristic of tampons is a performance parameter which is little understood outside the group of tampon manufacturers."[14] Specifically, "the Center for Medical Device Analysis (CMDA), under the direction of the Toxic Shock Working Group, Bureau of Medical Devices, has conducted an evaluation of the 'Syngyna Test' along with two other methods based upon it."[15] In its report, researchers questioned the P&G practices, specifically the angle of the chamber, and also the temperature of the water bath in the chamber, and that of the syngyna fluid itself. In the P&G protocol, the water was kept at a steady state of 27° Celsius or 80.6° Fahrenheit, making it thicker. This is far below the average human body temperature of 98.6° Fahrenheit. The researchers commented, "We did not understand the rationale for the 27°C test temperature as called out in the Procter & Gamble protocol. We were not able to clarify this point even with a conversation with the technical staff at Procter & Gamble." In addition, the fluid of Dr. Rapp's test "contained more than twice the amount of cellulose gum as that which P&G specifies and we subsequently used."[16] They surmised that Rapp ran the tests at 37°C, roughly that of body temperature, and that this required adjusting viscosity of the fluid with thickening agent at the warmer temperature.

In addition, the researchers at the Bureau of Medical Devices conducted a third test, using the downward-facing apparatus and a greatly reduced flow rate, going from 120 ml/hour to only 12 ml/hour. This still seemed like a relatively fast rate compared to actual menstrual flow, but it was more realistic than the former. What they found, not surprisingly, was that all the tampons tested absorbed less fluid at the slower rate. The tampon would "backfill" from the downstream end and would be only 25–30 percent saturated before the first droplet appeared, thus ending

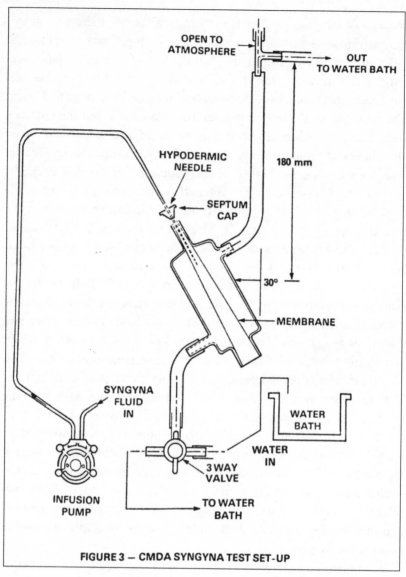

OPEN TO ATMOSPHERE

OUT TO WATER BATH

HYPODERMIC NEEDLE

180 mm

SEPTUM CAP

30°

MEMBRANE

SYNGYNA FLUID IN

WATER BATH

WATER IN

3 WAY VALVE

INFUSION PUMP

TO WATER BATH

FIGURE 3 — CMDA SYNGYNA TEST SET-UP

Figure 5.1. Syngyna test setup. This diagram details the syngyna lab apparatus and setup to test tampon absorbency, as described by the Center for Medical Device Analysis, Bureau of Medical Devices, Food and Drug Administration. A condom pulled taut serves as the faux vagina, referred to in the diagram as the "membrane." Source: D. E. Marlowe, R. M. Weigle, and R. S. Stauffenberg, "Measurement of Tampon Absorbency: Test Method Evaluation," FDA, Bureau of Medical Devices, CMDA Report 81-013, May 1981. Arthur and Elizabeth Schlesinger Library, Boston Women's Health Book Collective, Box 29, Folder 2.

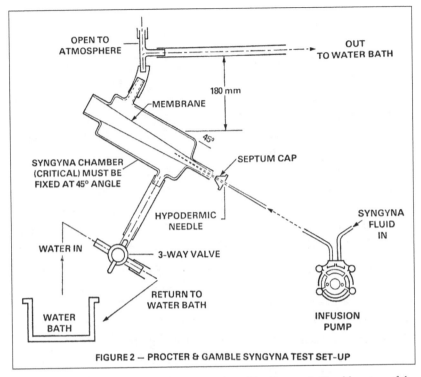

OPEN TO ATMOSPHERE

OUT TO WATER BATH

180 mm

MEMBRANE

45°

SYNGYNA CHAMBER (CRITICAL) MUST BE FIXED AT 45° ANGLE

SEPTUM CAP

HYPODERMIC NEEDLE

SYNGYNA FLUID IN

WATER IN

3-WAY VALVE

RETURN TO WATER BATH

WATER BATH

INFUSION PUMP

FIGURE 2 — PROCTER & GAMBLE SYNGYNA TEST SET-UP

Figure 5.2. Procter & Gamble syngyna test setup. The Procter & Gamble setup of the syngyna apparatus, as replicated by the Bureau of Medical Devices, has been articulated upward to promote tampon absorbency. Source: D. E. Marlowe, R. M. Weigle, and R. S. Stauffenberg, "Measurement of Tampon Absorbency: Test Method Evaluation," FDA, Bureau of Medical Devices, CMDA Report 81-013, May 1981. Arthur and Elizabeth Schlesinger Library, Boston Women's Health Book Collective, Box 29, Folder 2.

the test. This indicated that the tampons were failing prematurely or the syngyna may have not been an ideal tool for the job after all. In addition, the P&G method of the inversed chamber created a pool of fluid, "a deep pocket at the upstream end," that produced a "flowering" in the shape of the tampon. What the researchers concluded was that the downward-facing chamber did a better job of measuring absorption in relation to the infusion rate, and that the syngyna fluid should be modified to an appropriate viscosity in relation to the average human body temperature. This set of tests was not to provide a rank order of tampons and their absorbencies, but rather to "test the test" and see how the methodology yielded results, as well as determine the pros and cons of each test method.

The Tampon Task Force

With this information in hand, the FDA requested that a special committee known as the Tampon Task Force—composed of corporate representatives, consumer groups, and women's health advocates—convene to offer recommendations about tampon absorbency for future regulation and policy making.[17] The FDA worked with an organization called ASTM (American Society for Testing and Materials) that specifically engaged various stakeholders in setting terms and processes of standardization. Founded in 1898 to address railroad deficiencies in materials and inconsistencies in specifications that hampered the efficiency of travel and movement of cargo, it was concerned with shoddy materials and poor construction that caused downright dangerous conditions that could be easily rectified with agreed-on gauge widths or steel quality. The ASTM continues to be an international body that helps to establish voluntary consensus around standardization and specifications within industry, but it has no authority to carry out implementation. That is left to corporate, federal, and governing bodies.

In 1981, Alan Anderson, the acting associate director for standards at the Bureau of Medical Devices, sent a formal request to ASTM and its medical and surgical materials devices division. The letter did not dictate terms but used the less heavy-handed language of "urge" to make the entreaty. "The Bureau of Medical Devices urges the ASTM to form . . . a subcommittee to develop a standard which would include performance requirements, disclosure requirements, and appropriate labeling to control, to the extent possible, the mechanical and material properties of tampons."[18] Anderson also cautioned that "until a specific cause and effect relationship between TSS and tampons is established, we believe a specific requirement cannot be developed in a standard." Part of the impetus for standards came from the increased attention that tampons received due to media coverage of TSS, leading to increased reports of problems and concerns with tampons across the board. Anderson continued:

> The unexpected outbreak of TSS and the national attention that has been focused on this device has stimulated considerable public awareness about tampons. This has resulted in an increased number of complaints which have been filed with our Agency. These complaints are not only

associated with TSS but include other problems associated with tampons. The Device Experience Network has accumulated over 745 reports associated with tampons. Of that number, 701 were not related to TSS.[19]

Complaints included "broken strings, particulates, cleanliness, shredding sharp edges, allergies, absorption and mispackaging." Anderson concluded that "all of these items, we believe can be addressed in a performance standard." In early 1982, the ASTM coordinated its first meeting in St. Louis, followed by Philadelphia, with "at least seven task force meetings" for the year.[20] The group continued meeting regularly until 1985, when irreconcilable differences caused its dissolution.

At the beginning, there was great optimism because nonproducers were included in the standard-setting discussions for the first time. The ASTM partnered in a new cooperative program with the National Consumers League (NCL) to include layperson consumer input into the standard-setting process. Becky LeBuhn (at the time Cohen) was the consumer representative from the NCL on the medical devices committee. She encouraged the committee, also referred to as F-4, to agree to the FDA's request to develop a tampon standard, but she pointed out that she was the only qualified user with no other women on the committee besides herself. A group purporting to represent consumers needed actual tampon users in the standards development effort; an all-male chorus was inadequate. Through the NCL, LeBuhn volunteered to "assemble a group of women, including representatives of women's health and advocacy organizations," to participate on the task force and make sure women's health and safety concerns were on the table.[21] In this case it was not just competing industries potentially vying to maintain the upper hand of a design or process, but consumers and feminist activists who had a stake in their personal health and safety.

LeBuhn reached out to Esther Rome, a founder of BWHBC and a cowriter of *OBOS,* to serve on the Tampon Task Force. Rome was a well-informed feminist activist, and an important voice to include. Her colleague and co-author of the 1984 edition of *OBOS,* Jill Wolhandler, participated intermittently as well. The BWHBC was a significant feminist activist group; with its heft representing women, calling on them for letter-writing campaigns, and publishing *OBOS,* the FDA and manufacturers could not easily dismiss their concerns.

From the start, the stakeholders held very different goals. The manufacturers, including Johnson & Johnson, Kimberly-Clark, Tampax, and Playtex, sought the least intrusive labeling and the fewest modifications to their own products. The consumer representatives including BWHBC, Coalition for the Medical Rights for Women, Empire State Consumer Association, NCL, National Women's Health Network, and Woman Health International saw their inclusion on the committee as an opportunity not only to set standards for absorbency, but also to address safety and follow-through on the FDA's grand charge.[22]

In addition to the consumer representatives, lawyers for the different parties attended meetings as well. David Swankin was general counsel for the NCL, and Becky LeBuhn recruited him to the task force. Swankin was the first executive director of the White House Office of Consumer Affairs under Lyndon Johnson, and he later worked at the U.S. Department of Labor. He attended all the meetings, corresponded with the FDA and manufacturers, and represented their interests. In my interview with him, Swankin emphasized the dramatic divide between the consumers and manufacturers: "I cannot overstate the cultural gap that governed this entire thing. So, there were legal considerations because of what was going on with Toxic Shock, [and] the cultural thing that just was overwhelming, *overwhelming* [emphasis in original]."[23] It became evident that the promise for far-reaching standards and regulations would not be easily agreed on, in large part due to the cultural differences between the manufacturers who wanted the least change possible and the consumer advocates who had their sights on substantive policy.

Rome and Wolhandler from the BWHBC pushed to require biocompatibility tests "to assess the effects of tampons and tampon ingredients on living tissue." Importantly for Rome and Wolhandler, these tests would "measure such factors as irritation, drying, tissue injury, effects of chemicals, which might leach out of tampons during use, effects of repeated long-term use, toxicity, and carcinogenicity."[24] The FDA urged cooperation among the participants, stressing the importance of developing "voluntary standards."[25] This is why the umbrella of the ASTM was crucial as neutral ground with its long history in negotiating standards. However, the activists found neutrality to be a false claim, and they ran in to irreconcilable differences favoring corporate needs rather than women's health.[26]

The tension was apparent from the very beginning, despite the FDA's clear goals. Handouts, detailed outlines, and "working documents," as they referred to them in the Tampon Task Force meetings, at first encompassed most of the issues mentioned in the FDA dispatch. The working document entitled "Standard for Performance Characteristics of Menstrual Tampons" contained a statement of scope in terms of requirements for "the mechanical, chemical, biocompatibility, and material characteristics of these devices" and their need to be tested with appropriate methods. Key issues included withdrawal string length, tensile strength, and failure when the string pulled away from the absorbent section, wicking, leaching, inserter strength and rigidity, particulates, and outer box labeling. The document also proposed absorbability categories, from 1 to 3, from low, medium, to high, with the exact fluid capabilities yet to be determined.[27] Manufacturers were keen on neither the extra tests nor the labeling in general, which had the potential to name it a dangerous product, or perhaps worse, suggest its reclassification as a medical device.

This concern about reclassification was not a moot point. Elayne Clift from the National Women's Health Network urged Lillian Yin, the director of the division of OBGYN and radiology devices at the FDA, to "label tampon and sanitary napkin boxes for content" as well as include a warning about TSS. Furthermore, Clift stated that she and the network's 10,000 members "wish to see tampons classified as Class III" because "they represent a significant risk to users, as evidenced by the CDC and other research findings."[28] The difference between Class II and Class III was significant: Class II acknowledged that a device could cause harm, but that careful use and controlled application managed it; Class III required special handling, understanding the benefit outweighed the risk, but also that limited data about safety provided no assurances. A shift to Class III would have challenged the tampon industry, and it is interesting to imagine whether or not the companies would have been more creative in predicting risk and engineering safety after such a shift.

By 1983, clear divisions had formed, evident by these kinds of tensions. John Villforth of the National Center for Devices and Radiological Health (NCDRH) from the FDA opened the March 28, 1983, meeting by beseeching the groups to come to a compromise, because they needed an absorbency test method to move forward with absorbency labeling.

If necessary, he urged the committee to consider "a separate effort from the rest of the tampon standard, e.g., standards on string parameters, biocompatibility, etc." in order to advance. For advocates, expedience sacrificed safety and a whole set of issues related to the uncertainty of tampons. Manufacturers were equally unhappy about the extent to which they would have to redesign not only graphics on boxes, but also the actual tampon itself to conform to standards of absorbency. It meant a possible overhaul on the manufacturing line. The memo that recounted the meeting stated that "it was clear that at the current time, manufacturers are not in agreement on how tampons should be labeled to inform women of tampon absorbency and that it will take some negotiations and compromise to reach a consensus. It is likely that a uniform labeling standard will require that some manufacturers either change their product's absorbency or change their product's labeling."[29] For the manufacturers, the science did not suggest that redesigning the tampon and overhauling the production line would be a fruitful use of capital, if the labeling only served to deter consumers from purchasing a product deemed dangerous by federal standards. In addition, each had begun to label boxes in their own way with information about TSS.

Consumer groups realized they needed to coordinate efforts after observing the way that meetings proceeded. In a letter to Commissioner Arthur Hayes of the FDA, the women's health activists and consumer groups lamented that "the tampon manufacturers have chosen to work out a unified position in private as the basis for discussion in the task force, rather than each company speaking individually." Furthermore, they "then 'block vote' this position. The effect of this strategy is to freeze industry positions before task force discussion, cause delays and impede progress."[30] The consumer groups copied the tactic and began communicating with each other before the ASTM meetings and working on a platform piece. In a memo to "Consumer Members of Tampon Task Force," dated October 1, 1983, LeBuhn and Swankin cast broad strokes characterizing accomplishments, difficulties, and expectations. Handwritten comments by Esther Rome filled the margins.[31] Her penciled notations highlighted concerns: "Industry unified most positions outside of ASTM before TTF [Tampon Task Force] discussion," indicating that negotiation and bargaining were off the table before they even started. There was a lack of information, "no data presented by industry," and "we expected to evaluate their data, not have to generate our own." As worrisome as the lack of a standard was to the activists, they were equally concerned about becoming complicit with manufacturers' desires for the status quo, their presence thus endorsing ineffective regulations. Point V of the outline, "Levels below which we cannot go and still in good conscience support a standard," foreshadowed an exit strategy, in essence drawing their own terms of withdrawal rather than capitulating. Their list included record keeping, biocompatibility tests, ingredients disclosure, bacteriology, mechanical operation and integrity, labeling, and absorbency. They also sought "acknowledgments that our concerns are legitimate"; however, that desire would remain unmet.[32]

Fighting Science with Science

As talks progressed, it became clear to the activists that the science of the syngyna test was problematic in its poor simulation of the vaginal canal and that of menstrual fluid; if it were to become the test by which all ratings would be established, it needed some changes in both method and materials. Manufacturers countered, complaining that "some consumer representatives lacked scientific knowledge" and that this deficit caused delays with the ASTM standard. This, however, was far from the truth. The manufacturers tried to dismiss consumer advocates due to their lack of perceived expertise, but Rome and Wolhandler amassed impressive expertise about women's bodies through the writing of *OBOS*. A memo outlining the progress of the committee reported that "some consumers have requested the ASTM committee to develop standards that the manufacturers said are not feasible at this time, e.g., a tampon package wrap that does not break in purses, a syngyna test that uses menses blood, etc."[33] Characterized as "not feasible," testing the standard with menses blood and even heparinized blood challenged assumed lab practices.

For many scientists, standardized saline seemed intuitive as a fluid to use in the syngyna. With so many variables, and different tampons being the significant unknown to measure, a standardized fluid eliminated error. Menstrual blood from different bodies and different points during the menstrual cycle was inconsistent. The troubling part was that health advocates and consumer groups were not expected to question this rationale. They had to take any given manufacturer's word that the corporate science was correct because they did not have a lab back at their offices to run any kind of tests. In many ways, this was an example of what David Hess, a sociologist of science, refers to as "undone science." This term "refers to an unequal power that involves a conflict between reformers, such as social movement leaders, and industrial and political elites, and that is associated with absent knowledge." The reformers look to science for answers, but "their better funded adversaries often have much more research available to support their claims."[34] Yet in this case the reformers challenged the undone science by conducting their own.

Without human menstrual fluid in the protocol, the advocates argued, the standardized method did not actually provide context-specific data relevant to women's bodies. The women's health advocates and the consumer groups realized that they needed their own scientists to conduct experiments, but "funding that the manufacturers promised to give to ASTM to pay for technical consultants was canceled."[35] They therefore needed a volunteer researcher sympathetic to the cause to carry out feminist-based science. Rome remembered Nancy Reame, whom she met at an annual conference of the Society for Menstrual Cycle Research. Reame, a professor of nursing at the University of Michigan, studied reproductive physiology and the endocrinology of menstruation. Reame recalled her conversation with Rome, in which Rome pitched her the job, stating, "'You are the only person in the country that's ever worked with menstrual blood! We don't want an epidemiologist, we don't want someone who can crunch the numbers, we want someone who's actually done some clinical research.' I said of course! I love it! This sounds like such an adventure!"[36] Reame began her work for the task force, and one of the corporate labs sent her the syngyna lab equipment, including instructions to use a "Sheik" unlubricated #9 condom as the faux vagina, a point she found particularly galling.[37] She set about to incorporate heparinized blood (blood treated with heparin so it does not coagulate quickly) as the test fluid to compare it to the saline as the "standard." Based on her data collection, she reported findings to the task force in the report "Comparison of Syngyna Fluid and Venous Blood Using the Syngyna Absorbancy [sic] Test."[38] The differences were significant.

Reame found that "the degree of greater absorbancy [sic] of blood when compared to syngyna fluid varies from 2–25%" and the higher absorbencies had the greatest difference of all. For her, the findings were similar on a relative basis, but she warned that her report "in no way implies these findings are directly applicable to absorbancy [sic] characteristics on menstrual fluid which may be quite different due to differences in viscosity, pH, specific gravity, etc.," or rather the in-field variables.[39] Reame stated that she "approved of this protocol as an acceptable absorbancy [sic] measurement standard," but—there was a qualifier—there were "significant differences between blood and saline absorbancies [sic]."[40] This raised questions about the efficacy of the syngyna test to accurately measure tampon absorbency.

Rome and Reame also presented these findings to a broader audience in an editorial to the *Journal of the American Medical Association*, in which they described a "discrepancy between the actual differences in absorbency comparing saline use and the one trial using heparinized blood." The issue at stake was not so much the relative rankings of the tampons, which remained the same, but rather that "the differences in absolute absorbency seem significantly different at the higher absorbencies, with much more blood absorbed than saline."[41] If the tampons tested actually absorbed more blood than saline at the higher absorbencies, there was an intrinsic error in the standard. There was a distinct possibility that some tampons would be miscategorized and mislabeled as less absorbent despite their higher absorptive capacity, thus defeating the purpose to help women choose the least absorbent tampon for their needs.

Shifting Tactics

By the spring of 1984, it was clear the women's health activists and consumer groups had reached their limit. The coalition of consumer groups and women's health organizations wrote a joint letter to Mark Novitch, the acting commissioner of the FDA, outlining their grievances and requesting a different form of action. They described how the task force could agree only on "the most insignificant portions of an overall product standard" and, worse, "we are at an impasse when it comes to developing tests and performance requirements for the important health and safety aspects of the device." The coalition blamed manufacturers who were withholding data and were "unwilling to disclose the results of in-house research," notably on TSS.[42] They also saw no way to find consensus with manufacturers, especially when they summarily dismissed an offer from Anderson to "convene a balanced and independent panel of experts to assess the status of tampon research and propose research to generate the data needed to answer the many questions about possible adverse health effects from tampon use."[43] Without that kind of agreement, they saw no way that the task force could find any common ground about absorbency standards, especially without data to make informed recommendations.

They settled on a new tactic. Due to the delays and because of the continued risk to women who still had no way of assessing tampon absorbency, the coalition made a formal request to the commissioner to "initiate immediately a Section 514 proceeding to develop an absorbency labeling standard," which would draw the FDA into taking regulatory action without the input of ASTM.[44] Later, and on reflection, Esther Rome commented that "this is the only area in which the FDA has taken any action," in large part she felt because of the activists.[45]

It still did not come easily. By the fall of 1984, the FDA did hold a hearing on a petition proposed by Women's Health International seeking a safety standard, but this was unsuccessful. The consumer groups began corresponding with government officials through their lawyers to pressure the FDA to generate data and information. Specifically, the lawyers informed Frank Young, the commissioner of food and drugs at the FDA, about this problem concerning skewed data: "We have reason to believe that the tampon manufacturers are now conducting user surveys to support their company's preferred labeling method. Unfortunately, none of our consumer or women's health organizations has the resources to conduct a statistically valid, nation-wide survey. Otherwise, the agency's hearing record is unlikely to contain any data except what is generated by industry-sponsored surveys which, however useful, cannot be considered unbiased."[46] The women's health activists and consumer groups were getting squeezed out. They later learned that Alan Anderson from the FDA met the manufacturers without the consumer groups, and moreover, withheld data from them. The advocates' lawyer David Swankin wrote to him saying, "I understand that you and Mr. Phil White met with the tampon manufacturers earlier this week (at their request), and that certain information was shared with them," including proposed tampon labeling, the current timetable for labeling regulations as well as public hearings, and data from the "Winchester Study."[47] Conducted at the Medical Device Laboratory at the Winchester Engineering and Analytical Center, the purpose was "to confirm the tampon absorbency measurements made in 1981 at the Center for Medical Device Analysis" so that "a realistic absorbency index may be formulated for tampon packaging." This study, more accurately named "Determination of the Fluid Capacity of some Commercial Catamenial Tampons" by M. Louis Arin, was likely conducted in the spring of 1984. The difference this time was that the experiment used the syngyna method to compare tampons, such as Playtex Regular, Playtex Deodorant, and Kotex Super Stick Tampons, rather than to "test the test" of the syngyna method.[48] This was exactly the type of information that women's health advocates and consumer groups needed to know.

The data from this test were not immediately forthcoming, and it is unclear when the BWHBC members received it. For Nancy Reame, who had conducted tests on behalf of the consumer groups, the lack of data sharing was quite troublesome. She wrote to Villforth in regard to unfair practices on the Tampon Task Force. As she described it, "I have found it difficult at times to participate in the work of a committee where data is available to group members on a selective basis; because of propriety constraints, the consumers and other non-producer members of the Task Force have clearly been informationally-disabled in terms of their ability to make appropriate recommendations for standard development." Furthermore, she stated, "as an active Task Force member, I was therefore surprised and somewhat embarrassed to learn by happenstance of an FDA-conducted 'syngyna study' recently completed and presented at a scientific meeting." The FDA carried out the study, comparing 1,000 tampons, which had direct relevance and bearing on the task force. "I am most interested," she continued, "in the rationale for the FDA's failure to disclose this information to the Task Force." Finally, she requested that the FDA's representative to the task force, Mr. Kobrin, present the findings at the upcoming meeting on April 18 in Philadelphia.[49]

Villforth replied, but with a chastising tone. He agreed with Reame in the most perfunctory way that they both sought labeling rulings about tampon absorbency. The FDA proposed a numerical index, but he conveyed in an accusatory manner that "this action was taken only after a failure on the part of the ASTM tampon task force to successfully address absorbency labeling," pushing the blame on the Tampon Task Force and the consumer groups. The testing to which Reame referred, he added, was only conducted to confirm that "data could be used to generate a numerical index," and he indicated that data would be available in the proposal. Furthermore, "Any release of information prior to that time will be governed by the obligations under the Freedom of Information Act," which would, of course, mean further delays for the advocates. Villforth hid behind protocol, and with one last jab he concluded, "I hope this clarifies the matter."[50] Indeed, it clarified that the FDA favored corporate interests, and the consumer advocates would remain in the dark about comparative tampon absorbency studies and data.

These actions demonstrated that FDA officials were not neutral and would not hear appeals from the consumers. It probably should not have been a surprise. The Reagan administration ushered out many officials sympathetic to women's health, and more specifically, it discouraged any more business regulations. Mandatory standards were considered part of government overreach. As early as 1981, a top FDA official was quoted in the *Chicago Tribune* saying that "there will be very little emphasis on regulatory standards" for medical devices, so in essence "voluntary" standards would be the only option.[51] With such institutional momentum, it was no wonder that the Tampon Task Force disbanded like a hung jury, or that the women's health groups were left to their own political devices to influence change.

Advocacy beyond the Tampon Task Force

Even though the task force "met for over three years, it became inactive in April 1985 without producing any kind of standard."[52] The nonmanufacturing members decided to employ a different set of tactics to persuade the FDA to take a stand. Esther Rome corresponded with her senator, Ted Kennedy, and regaled him with evidence concerning the importance of labeling and how the lack of information continued to be an ongoing threat to women's health.[53] She cited the report authored by Al Gore, titled "Medical Device Regulation: The FDA's Neglected Child," which examined "tampons as one of four case studies of how FDA inaction has harmed the public health." Though manufacturers had agreed to a numerical scale correlated to absorbency (based on the syngyna test),

Figure 5.3. A Public Health Service poster, "Toxic Shock Syndrome." Despite the Tampon Task Force disbanding in 1985, the FDA distributed posters reminding women not to forget about TSS, since it was no longer circulating as a national current event in the news. The poster omits the recommendation to use the least absorbent tampon possible, however. Source: Health and Human Services Publication No. (FDA) 85-4192, 1985. Courtesy of the Food and Drug Administration.

the terms used to describe absorptive capacity were still off the table. According to Rome and Wolhandler, "This system would have allowed a 'Regular-13' that is more absorbent than a 'Super-9,' a situation the consumers strongly opposed."[54] Kennedy responded by letter to Rome, noting, "My staff has spoken with the FDA officials responsible for developing the new labeling, and shared with them your concern that the number system (similar to sunscreen rating) would be potentially confusing to consumers if tampons also maintained the non-uniform labels of 'Super' or 'Regular' absorbency." With the comment period still to come, he felt she could "respond to the proposed regulations before they become final."[55] But by this point, the consumer groups had had enough.

On June 1, 1988, the Public Citizen Health Research Group, an arm of Public Citizen originally founded by Ralph Nader, filed a lawsuit against the FDA for illegal delays of more than seven years concerning required tampon labeling.[56] The lawsuit sought a judicial order to force the governmental agencies to act and to "require tampon manufacturers to display standardized absorbency information on tampon boxes along with an accompanying warning about the association between tampon absorbency and toxic shock syndrome."[57] The same problem of sloppy terminology among descriptors such as Regular, Super, and Super Plus remained, and the lawsuit asserted that "women cannot intelligently choose among tampons to select the ones that would minimize their risk of contracting toxic shock syndrome."[58] The outcome of the lawsuit the following year favored the plaintiffs, with the judge ruling that "the FDA had to publish a final regulation by October 31, 1989."[59]

Concurrent with this lawsuit was yet another proposal by the FDA during the fall of 1988 for a dual-labeling system, one that still retained the vagaries of inconsistent nomenclature. Some manufacturers supported it because it allowed them to retain their own product labeling while incorporating a numerical scale, with the benefits of only changing packaging without altering the product. During this comment period, Playtex Family Products, which made Playtex tampons, laid out its concerns, arguing for test methods that allowed for averaging. This method required that the average grams absorbed per sixteen tampons serve as the "number." The FDA proposed labeling a specified range, since any given tampon did not always meet the criteria, but it called for 95 percent of all the tampons within a particular product line to fall within it.

Playtex argued for the single number, within the A, B, C category system, rather than the numerical system correlating with standardized terminology such as Regular, Super, and Super Plus. Otherwise, the company believed that new rules would "arbitrarily force Playtex to increase the absorbency of its Super Plus product, which is used by about 1.5 million consumers, by more than 1 full gram."[60] In the new categorization, the product would be a "Super," requiring only modification of the box graphics; this was not the path the company wanted to take. Yet if the company insisted on the current tampon remaining "Super Plus," the tampon needed to be materially redesigned and bulked up to fall within that category. While Playtex advocated for its own product, hundreds of handwritten notes from women arrived at the FDA during the comment period, prompted by a grass-roots effort from the BWHBC, demanding standardized terminology for tampon labeling. The dual systems of numbers and letters provided no clarity and increased confusion.

The Paperwork Reduction Act, managed through the Office of Management and Budget (OMB), also slowed down meaningful labeling. In general, this sounded like a sensible idea to decrease extraneous paperwork and its initial intent was to apply to regulations with significant economic impact, but its neoliberal intent grew to review all regulations before they went to print. Many viewed this as a political means to slow down the approval of policies that were not supported by the broader Reagan administration. Thus, tampon labeling would have to have approval from not only the FDA, but the OMB as well, because the OMB oversaw official publications. During congressional meetings and hearings on the OMB, the BWHBC testified that the OMB "not only delayed regulation of tampons but had insisted on a labeling system that was confusing and contradictory" by not allowing the FDA to move forward on labeling in a substantive manner.[61] Thus, 1988 proved yet one more year in which tampons would still not be labeled in a consistent fashion.

As the October 1989 deadline from the Public Citizen lawsuit against the FDA approached, the consumer groups still worked behind the scenes, but this time they allied with some of the manufacturers, particularly Tambrands (formerly Tampax, Inc.). Throughout the summer of 1989, Rome lobbied FDA Commissioner Frank Young, corresponded with the NCL's lawyer, David Swankin, and also sent letters to Steven

Fellman, who represented Tambrands with his firm Loomis, Owen, Fellman & Howe, and whom she knew from their introduction on the Tampon Task Force. The greater threat was now the intransigence of the FDA, and even some companies recognized basic labeling was good for business. Among all the corporate lawyers on the Tampon Task Force, Fellman was more sympathetic to the consumer advocates, and as a result of meeting Rome, he even gave a copy of *OBOS* to his wife.[62] Arguably Tambrands, who still held a majority share of the market and picked up former Rely users, may have had more to gain in the end by making its products legible to consumers.

Fellman used his leverage, and the influence of Tambrands, to urge the other manufacturers to agree to primary absorbency ranges, thus offering the FDA language and recommendations for labeling. In correspondence to Rome, Fellman offered a glimpse into the difficulty in reaching consensus by referencing the "junior" category of tampons. He stated: "With regard to 'junior,' the manufacturers couldn't reach a consensus on what to call 'junior' and so we intentionally left this up in the air. Junior accounts for less than 1% of the market and has such a low absorbency that it is really only effective for first time users. I hope you find this is agreeable as I am having a difficult time holding my crew in line."[63] Fellman sought a concession. He would hold the "crew in line," that is, the other manufacturers concerning all the other categories, if the consumer groups would let go of a new name for "junior." Indeed, the name "junior" remained, and it signaled the least absorbent range. Sacrificing a better term for the benefit of agreement about the category in general proved to be efficacious. With all the other concerns dropped (biocompatibility, tensile strength, particulate residue, etc.) the ranges and nomenclature were the final two points.

Johnson & Johnson, the holdout, refused to sign the joint letter, but the other companies now encouraged the FDA to standardize terminology. In a draft letter to Commissioner Young summarizing the consensus that they had reached, Rome stated:

> Hundreds of consumers, medical professionals, and the manufacturers of the majority of the tampons of the market have supported this position in letters to the FDA over a period of several years. In response to the September 22, 1988 Federal Register proposal alone, over 250

consumers and Kimberly-Clark and Tambrands wrote the FDA favoring standardization of the terms "regular," "super," and "super plus."[64]

Based on the number of women represented by all the consumer groups, and the agreement finally hammered out with most of the manufacturers, she reiterated the "common position among such a widely representative group mandates that FDA incorporate this position as its final rule."

The OMB dropped its indefinite hold on the passage of tampon regulations, and the FDA approved a final ruling on October 26, 1989, just days before the judge's deadline ordered the previous year.[65] Federal ruling 801.430 outlined labeling for tampons as well as absorbency ranges as the following:

6 grams and under—junior absorbency
6–9 grams—regular absorbency
9–12 grams—super absorbency
12–15 grams—super plus absorbency
15–18—none
above 18—none[66]

The Federal Register summarized comments from consumer groups, medical practitioners, and industry representatives, documenting their arguments for and against regulations. It provided guidelines for labeling, which still offered the manufacturers a great deal of leeway except for the terms "junior absorbency," "regular absorbency," "super absorbency," and "super plus absorbency." Now, required components on packaging included a description of TSS, its risks, how to avoid TSS by "not using tampons," and its legibility and positioning on the box. More specifically in a small victory for the consumer groups, the Federal Register detailed the absorbency ranges in grams and defined the associated terms, those very elements that were so contested among members of the Tampon Task Force from the beginning. It also indicated that the syngyna test and a saline syngyna fluid would be used to determine tampon absorbencies. Finally, failing to include such labeling, the tampon would be considered "misbranded." Thus, standardized labeling for tampons became effective in March of 1990.[67]

Limits of Labeling

Among spurious revisions and without pressure from litigants and judges, it is doubtful the FDA would have moved forward on these specific regulations. After their experience with the Tampon Task Force, Rome and Wolhandler surmised that

> because women's health issues are not a research priority and because the FDA is limited in its effectiveness, product liability lawsuits will continue to be the single most effective way to make public results of manufacturers' proprietary research and to get questionable products off the market. This is why legislation to limit product liability awards is not in the public interest.[68]

Kehm v. Procter & Gamble in 1982 exemplified the importance of product liability lawsuits because the trial proved that Patricia Kehm was not warned of any danger, and the company had information prior to her death that tampons were associated with TSS and continued to sell the product anyway. With the new FDA regulations publicized and made into law in the Federal Register, the corporations were somewhat protected from litigation, even though the conditions suitable for TSS had not substantially changed. Labels on every box now informed women about TSS, and the burden fell on women consumers to prove that the product harmed them, even when in essence they were told not to use it.

S. Lochlann Jain argues, in *Injury*, that this is part of the very foundation of capitalism: "Injury laws determine when an individual's right not to be injured has been infracted by incidents caused by poor design, lack of warning, or corporate malevolence."[69] Furthermore, damage to bodies is part and parcel of capitalist structures, the "cost" shouldered by individuals with injury or disability, or pushed back to the manufacturer in the form of compensation payments. What is significant about the 1980s was the ways in which tactics shifted when the FDA requirements for labeling were not well defined. No longer was causal damage an argument available to plaintiffs because women now had been duly warned; however, the ways in which they were warned raised some important questions.

The 1988 case *Krystal H. Rinehart v. International Playtex*, U.S. District Court, Southern District of Indiana, Indianapolis, Indiana, foreshadowed the constraints of product liability. Ruled even before the 1989 regulations about absorbency were finalized, the case nonetheless hinged on whether or not women had been sufficiently warned. The defendants sought a summary judgment—a judgment by the court without a jury—because Playtex could argue that Rinehart had assumed the risk of the product and tampons were not defective. Conversely, the plaintiffs sought to invoke "Rule 11 Sanctions" against the defendant's lawyers for improper action by failing to "advise the Court of a recent, relevant Ohio decision." Basically, they argued on a technicality, which did not hold much weight in terms of the safety or quality of tampons. More substantively, Playtex lawyers argued that "because of the warning statement on the package insert, and danger of toxic shock syndrome due to tampon use was patent, and that when the risk of harm is thus open and obvious, the product is not defective as a matter of law." The plaintiffs disagreed, stating the "alleged risk of toxic shock syndrome from tampon use is not open and obvious, but latent." Furthermore, the "defendants had a duty to warn and, indeed, this is why the FDA has imposed a duty to warn." The judge denied both motions and sided with Playtex, likely due to its compliance in labeling.[70]

While this was not a good outcome for those who suffered from TSS, the plaintiff's lawyers deployed a novel tactic: demonstrate that the labeling was not a warning but merely "important information," which was inadequate because it did not convey urgency or danger about tampons and TSS. The lawyers secured Roger Shuy on their behalf, a linguist and expert in reading, discourse, and language. He wrote about his experience as a witness for this case, and he argued that the warning was not really a warning and therefore women were not informed by the labeling. An important element to the FDA guidelines was the difference between a warning and an alert. Significantly, Shuy noted that "the FDA does not specify the exact wording to be used on most of this warning label" but that it must be prominent and legible. Furthermore, the two sentences required "are referred to as an 'alert' statement that is to use the word 'attention' rather than 'warning.'" Manufacturers did not need to warn about the product, but they had to "warn about the signs and danger of toxic shock syndrome."[71] Shuy argued that "alert" and "attention" pointed to different levels of concern in which outcomes could be good, while a warning nearly always connoted that something bad could happen. At question was whether or not the alert accomplished its goal.

In order to demonstrate the indirect nature of tampon warnings and the relative lack of urgency and directness, Shuy created a comparison to a very familiar situation: what to do at a railroad crossing. With this example, he demonstrated "how a railroad crossing sign might have been written" if it had followed the same formula that manufacturers used for toxic shock syndrome. The alert would read like this:

1. Important information about accidents.
2. Read this sign.
3. People can get hit by trains. If you are on the tracks and see a train coming, drive faster to get away.
4. Or avoid the train by stopping first.
5. Danger!
6. Avoid danger by stopping, looking, and listening.
7. If you have been hit by a train, call for medical assistance.
8. Trains are not the only causes of accidents.
9. If you have questions, call Amtrak.[72]

Shuy conceded that, yes, pedestrians are warned and advised in this scenario, but "the problem here is not whether they were warned, but where and how this warning was given." He felt that since his vignette actually used the word "danger" it was clearer than what Playtex used; the manufacturer's label stated "there is a risk to all women using tampons during the menstrual period. TSS is a rare but serious disease that *may* cause death [emphasis added]." Here he explained that "the text does not make explicit" the relational danger; it must be inferred, in part with the subjunctive "may." His analysis is quite insightful concerning the language of an alert versus a warning, and how women have been left to their own devices to interpret exactly what it means for themselves. And, as Jain reminds us, the language shifts the burden of risk to the consumer, in this case menstruators who use tampons.

* * *

The intent to alert women about tampon-related TSS demonstrates a nexus of conflicting interests, with women ultimately bearing the brunt of the consequences. During the 1980s, there was closure around two significant points: the standardization of a testing method that sets standards, and the standardization of nomenclature concerning absorbency. Standardizing standards is a contested practice and is recursive work; how these questions are answered makes a big difference in how standards are agreed on and created, and what facts are stabilized.[73] Those groups and individuals that have a place at the negotiating table hold important reins of power in affecting how processes, systems, and transactions take shape and are routinized, and how tools of measurement are stabilized to create meaning.[74] Thus, the inclusion of consumer groups and women's health advocates was absolutely crucial in challenging a corporate-centric interpretation of tampon technologies.

Tampon labeling for absorbency and the naming of ranges carried political stakes, both in terms of financial output for companies, but more importantly for health outcomes for women. Women's health advocates well understood the consequences for safety, testing, and consistent labels in reducing injury and decreasing TSS. The neoliberal tone of the Reagan administration thwarted commonsense labeling, and corporations' interests were favored. Only after constant grassroots activism, letter writing, and lawsuits did basic labeling appear on tampon boxes. Despite their optimistic list of issues, which were not addressed, the women's health advocates' efforts were not in vain. They challenged the standardization of the syngyna lab test before it became stabilized and entrenched, and they argued against the omission of menstrual fluid or blood as key factors in the protocol. Unfortunately, the manufacturers and the FDA renounced Reame's data and the incorporation of feminist science approaches into the methodology. They ignored the inherent error discovered by Reame, that superabsorbents absorbed more blood than saline. This omission remains, yet the contemporary absorbency scale was absolutely strong-armed into existence by the women's health advocates. Choosing the least absorbent tampon for menstrual flow remains a cornerstone of reducing incidents of TSS, but more work to personalize understandings of risk needs to be undertaken.

Conclusion

Managing Menstruation and Beyond

Tampon-related toxic shock syndrome (TSS) is important to understand in its own right, because millions of women use tampons and it is a possible outcome of their use. Though the illness is linked to both menstruation and tampon technologies, burdened with historical associations of shame and impropriety, it has not garnered widespread compassion or a pink ribbon campaign like breast cancer. It is misguided to brush aside the illness as insignificant because it is related to women's health and menstrual hygiene management, especially since it provides an important lesson about the relationship of technology and health to us all. TSS is a harbinger of other biocatalytic injuries to come. Though the poor outcome seemed unanticipated, it should not have been a surprise. There are ways to imagine biocatalytic consequences, but our system of corporate manufacturing and scientific knowledge production will need to change to accommodate them, as well as include input from women users toward the common good. The moral of the story is not to forbid tampons, but to be far more thoughtful. For the case of tampon-related TSS, there are three main changes that would prevent illness. The first is to better disclose risk about materials and chemicals used in tampons, and the effects they have on humans; the second is to have a better understanding of our own bodies in terms of our individual immune system and its antibodies; the third is a broader knowledge of microbial inhabitants as technological users, and how we might work together with them more productively.

Managing Menstruation

The technological fix of tampons is very powerful in modern American society. Tampon technology fixes the problem of an unacceptable menstruating body. My book *Under Wraps* argued that these technologies help women pass as nonmenstruants, when there are no unearned privileges but mostly slights to be gained from a menstruous body. Modern technologies have been quite successful managing menstruation, to the extent that "accidents" are not the technology's but the woman's fault. Menstrual management technologies are so normalized that it is hard to imagine a woman not using them. A woman's purposeful exposure of menstrual fluid is so far outside the expected norm that she has to deliberately announce she is challenging menstrual anathema, the cover of the pass so well assumed. Online images of menstrual fluid, and reactions to them, trended in 2015; they seemed innocuous enough to some, simply revealing a woman having a period, and absolutely inappropriate to others, so much so that Instagram twice pulled down the photo of Rupi Kaur sleeping, which depicted her menstrual blood seeping through her leggings.[1] During the Boston Marathon, Kiran Gandhi ran during her period, free bleeding to the finish line.[2] The Chinese swimmer Fu Yuanhui, who won the bronze medal for the one-hundred-meter backstroke during the 2016 Olympics, openly discussed competing with menstrual pain during her period in an interview after another race.[3] All purposely outed themselves and challenged norms of concealment. That menstrual etiquette kicks in to both actively censor menstruation as well as manage it speaks to the ubiquity of its construction as a social, rather than technological, problem.

Underpinning this notion that menstruation is a social phenomenon is the sheer number of menstruators actively concealing their periods each and every day. A discussion thread on the Society for Menstrual Cycle Research email list began when one person asked, what percentage of women in the United States, between the ages of eighteen and forty, are menstruating at any given time? This question, so simple, made me realize that it is a huge number of women! Sure, there are women using menstrual suppressing hormones, others in early menopause, those with hysterectomies, others pregnant and lactating, and the age range does not even cover teenagers or women past forty and into their fifties who still menstruate. There are other qualifiers, too, such as who "counts" as a woman since most transgender women do not menstruate but transgender men might. And corporations that sell menstrual management technologies likely have a precise sense of this number as well. The conversation in the thread settled on about 1 in 9, or perhaps 13 percent (a twenty-eight-day cycle of roughly four weeks, divided by four weeks in a month for 25 percent, divided in half again to account for pharmaceutical regulation and other reasons for not menstruating). With this logic, it is pretty amazing to think that more than 10 percent of women are menstruating at any given time in the contemporary United States, with figures higher in many countries abroad.[4]

Thus, the technological fix is a powerful paradigm to manage the recurrent absorption of menstrual fluid and the social problem of its concealment.[5] Therefore, new technologies inevitably emerge to "fix" this problem. One such emergent technology, announced in 2017, is an app and Bluetooth belt-clip menstrual monitor called My Flow. Aimed to eliminate "menstrual mortification," the app tracks tampon saturation, so that the wearer will know when to change it. The menstruator must wear a tampon with a very long, strong string encased in medical-grade steel, attached to the "wearable device," to be clipped to a waistband or underwear. By creating menstrual bio data, the company claims that users will better know when to change tampons and, furthermore, prevent infection. Amanda Brief, the creator, says My Flow eliminates the problem of forgetting to change a tampon and will therefore help prevent TSS (because the manufacturers' recommendation is to change tampons frequently).[6] This claim is dubious, and unfortunately it exemplifies a lack of clear information available about TSS. This also seems to be a technological fix for something that is really not a problem for most women. A new tampon connected to lights and data is not the solution for TSS or menstrual mortification.

The technological fix for better tampons does not solve the social problem of unacceptable, out-of-control menstrual bleeding. At every turn containment of menstrual fluid is reinforced, and it is no wonder that corporate scientists have been charged to create better tampons. The problem is that this fix does not address the deeply held and charged issue of menstrual blood being out of place and uncontained. It is clear from the policy makers within government agencies, as well as feminist advocates, that tampons were and continue to be important to the feminist toolbox of physical mobility. The real-world pragmatism of tampons is well grounded, but so is the risk to some women. We are asked to heed the warnings and participate in the scare tactics about TSS, and for many of us this is unnecessary. Thus, we must think about them more carefully and differently.

Material Safety and Risk

Even though tampons do not directly cause TSS, that does not mean that manufacturers are off the hook. The responsibility has been offloaded onto women, and they simply do not have enough information to determine their own risk. Esther Rome and the Boston Women's Health Book Collective (BWHBC) knew this, and they worked very hard to get boxes labeled concerning absorbency to at least regularize tampons across brands so that women could compare them and follow Food and Drug Administration (FDA) guidelines to use the lowest absorbency for their menstrual flow. Yet this is such a gross guideline and does not acknowledge the biocatalytic impacts of tampons. There is simply not enough accessible and meaningful information for menstruators to make informed decisions, and the fix is both political and scientific.

There is a significant need for accurate labeling concerning the composition of tampons specifically, and medical devices more broadly speaking. As consumers and users we are disadvantaged by the lack of a mere list of ingredients. The consequences of this can be quite significant. For instance, it was not until my friend and colleague Siobhan Somerville sent me the obituary of Bruce Dan, who had worked at the Centers for Disease Control (CDC) on the TSS Task Force and who also testified as an expert witness in *Kehm v. Procter & Gamble* for the plaintiffs, that I came to recognize a small detail. The obituary stated that "one study, in which Dr. Dan played a central role, showed that one brand of tampon, Rely, made by Procter & Gamble, carried an elevated risk because its lubricant, Pluronic L92, greatly increased the level of toxins in the bacterium."[7] This Pluronic L-92 substance was not part of the early epidemiologic studies pursued by the CDC. I began searching and found patent 4,239,043 issued to P&G in 1980, describing how Pluronic L-92 (from BASF Wynandotte Corp., Industrial Chemical Group, Wyandotte, Michigan) would be used in making the polyester foam for the tampons, along with the copolymers polypropylene glycol and polyethylene glycol.

In order to better understand the significance of Pluronic L-92, I reached out to Sam H. Au, a research fellow at Harvard Medical School's BioMEMS Resource Center, focusing on BioMicroElectroMechanical Systems. More specifically he wrote an article about Pluronic L-92 and cell damage.[8] He explained to me that the name L-92 indicates its hydrophilic and hydrophobic components. As he put it in an email, "The first digit, '9' in L-92 designates a total length of the copolymer. The second digit, '2' in L-92 designates the percent of the copolymer that is the hydrophilic PEO [polyethylene oxide or polyethylene glycol] in this case 20%, the remaining 80% is comprised of hydrophobic PPO [Polyphenylene Oxide]." He went on to note, "This second digit is what we found to be important for damage to cells. A hydrophobic dominant copolymer such as L-92, causes a lot of damage to cells, while hydrophilic dominant copolymers such as F-68 or F-88 do not."[9]

The thing I found interesting was not only did L-92 lead to cell death, but Au mentioned that "pluronics and other surfactants may also aid in bringing other components into cells," since they permeate into cell membranes. What this means for TSS is that L-92 may have contributed to cell death, as well as accelerated the spread of the TSST-1 toxin (toxic shock syndrome toxin-1) through mucus membranes to enter damaged cells, thus accelerating the effects leading to multisystem shock. Thus, L-92 was a poor choice to use within biosystems, and particularly for those women harboring the S. aureus strain capable of producing TSS.

In correspondence with Pat Schlievert, a microbiologist and expert on TSS, he confirmed that Pluronic L-92 in tampons increased toxin production, and that has been written about in numerous journals.[10] A team of researchers led by Marian Melish, who specializes in infectious diseases, also found that "PL-92 is a potent stimulator of TSST-1 production and increases mortality in in vivo rabbit vaginal and SC (subcutaneous) models. PL-92 may have been responsible for the epidemic of TSS which occurred in 1980."[11] Schlievert felt that many scientists discovered the link to Pluronic L-92 at the same time; it was not an exclusive find by Bruce Dan or any of the other teams. He noted that after his publications, "The FDA has asked me to test products that are used vaginally for effect on TSST-1. I have done this for companies up to and including the present time."[12] This is assuring to a degree, as long as he is kept on board to do this work. But we are still left in the dark about the material components of tampons and, for that matter, other chemicals that may be part of tampon production or processing and their biocatalytic effects.

The significance of this points to the urgent need for better policy and truth in labeling. No one person should go to the lengths that I have in order to learn about tampon ingredients and potential harm due to the chemicals involved in their manufacture and processing. Pluronic L-92 is a fabulous engineering solution to make fibers more absorbent, but no woman would willingly choose more absorption over death. Pluronic L-92 is not likely used anymore because most tampons are not made of polyester with surfactants, but without any formal components label on the box, one cannot know. Requirements for labeling with the Robin Danielson Act, proposed by Carolyn Maloney, a U.S. House Representative for New York, would offer a step forward in moving from "proprietary" knowledge to truth in labeling. But, categorized as a medical device, tampons are not like food or cosmetics that require disclosure of ingredients. Many argue that it is difficult for consumers to adjudicate health risks even with labeling since they do not understand chemistry. Yet, without labeling, it is impossible.

The desire for more specific labeling stems from the rather vague language currently approved to be printed on boxes and available as product inserts. In general, most women know not to "leave in a tampon too long" and manufacturers generally recommend wearing a tampon for no longer than eight hours. This, however, is spurious. I have found no recommendations from the CDC or FDA that suggest a length of time. I inquired about this omission at the CDC-sponsored "We Were There" lecture series, where both Kathryn Shands and Arthur Reingold, epidemiologists at the CDC during the height of the TSS health crisis, offered their perspectives on this time period. I specifically asked them about the basis for the length of wear, and both concurred that this was not included in their studies.[13] I then sent an email to Nancy Buc, the legal counsel to the FDA who brokered the terms of withdrawal for removing Rely from the market. She also indicated this was not part of the language crafted to warn about risk.[14] I then reached out to Harry Finley, curator of the Museum of Menstruation, to determine when time limits were first suggested. He directed me to some of the earliest examples of tampons. Language on packaging of Fax, Nunap, and Moderne Woman tampons from the 1930s instructed women to wear a tampon from six to twenty-four hours, with one woman tester for Fax wearing hers for forty-eight hours.[15] It is unclear how these times were determined, but manufacturers' instructions about duration of wear have been included in the tampon narrative from the beginning.

Probably more surprising was locating the federal labeling requirements from the Code of Federal Regulations, updated in April 2017. Surely, I thought, I could find the recommended length of wear in this document. To my surprise, there is nothing. According to code 801.430, "User Labeling for Menstrual Tampons," the following statement "shall appear prominently and legibly on the package label": "Attention: Tampons are associated with Toxic Shock Syndrome (TSS). TSS is a rare but serious disease that may cause death. Read and save the enclosed information."[16] The code requires that there must be a package insert that describes symptoms of TSS, provides estimates of its incidence, and advises women to use minimum absorbencies. The insert must include a statement that risk can be avoided altogether by "not using tampons" (which is unusual for a product to recommend against its own use) and "alternating tampon use with sanitary napkin use during menstrual periods." The absorbency ranges and terms, thanks to the women's health advocates, must be represented as well. But there is no time limit. A generous reading of this omission is that industry scientists have conducted correlation studies between the amount of time a tampon is worn to TSS, allergic reactions, or product integrity, and that these studies are proprietary and not for public dissemination. A more cynical reading is that the time limit is a legal protection for the companies to avert product liability lawsuits. A time recommendation also ensures that women change their tampons often, thus increasing sales. Mike Osterholm, an epidemiologist working for the state of Minnesota in 1980 and who directed the state's TSS studies, explained that the frequent changing of Rely only exacerbated TSS; pulling out a used tampon squeezed out some of the menstrual fluid, including the S. aureus, thus priming the next tampon, and offering an even better set of environmental circumstances suitable for the bacterium to grow. In this case, changing tampons actually made things worse. Thus, the time limit is not a protection against TSS.

What Can We Do? (and Why We Do Not)

What if you could learn whether or not you have the antibody for the TSS toxin? With the antibody, a person can neutralize the toxin and eliminate it from the body. Obtaining this knowledge is already possible through a blood test and could be part of preventative care, but it is not. It should be part of a "well-child" visit to the pediatrician for girls, as a way to gauge their immunity to the TSST-1 toxin. As early as 1986, Richard Novick, the director of the nonprofit Public Health Research Institute, developed a blood test to screen for the antibody. Leo Harrison from the CDC commented on its efficacy but also its impracticality to the *Journal of Commerce*, saying, "You're talking about doing millions of lab tests, which would cost quite of bit of money," with the implication being that the benefits would not outweigh the costs, except, of course, for the person who does not have the antibody.[17] At a certain level, this makes sense because TSS is such a rare disease, occurring in about 1 in 100,000 women or 1 to 17 per 100,000 menstruating women, depending on the source.[18] In 1986, this may have seemed like overkill. But, during the first decades of the twenty-first century, we have moved well into the realm of individualized medicine, with genetic tests for breast cancer, and prenatal tests for cystic fibrosis, to name just two. Children undergo a battery of recommended vaccines and various eye and hearing tests in order to be fit for admission to elementary school. Adding an antibody test to a well-child visit by age ten would be a simple way to see if a young person has the ability to ward off the toxin production of *S. aureus*. If not, the person could be easily counseled to avoid wearing tampons. Schlievert explained that "80% of humans have antibodies to TSST-1 and are thus protected from TSS. However, 20% of young adults (>12 years old) do not, and never will, develop protective antibodies to TSST-1. The reason is their immune systems become too dysfunctional in the presence of the toxin, suppressing the ability of their B cells to make protective antibodies."[19] Testing for an antibody is not foolproof, but it is more tangible than vague alerts, which we mostly ignore because they have little meaning.

Jeffrey Parsonnet, an infectious disease specialist who has studied TSS, reiterated the importance of the antibody. If a person has the protective antibody, he or she will not contract TSS. Even if the person supports *S. aureus* as a permanent constituent of the body, such as in the nasal cavity, the neutralizing antibody is protective.[20] Thus, recommendations about length of wear, frequent changes, and even absorbency do not exactly get at the real issue. Most people are absolutely fine and will not contract TSS because of their immune systems or the absence of the particular bacterial strain producing TSST-1. Yet for those few who lack the antibody and have the TSST-1-producing strain of bacterium in their bodies, and who also use a tampon or nasal pack that introduces oxygen, the consequences can be dire. The ability for TSS to express the toxin under these conditions points back to the need for the antibody test, one that Parsonnet developed and uses in his lab.

Parsonnet tried to get corporations on board for a self-administered test, which he proposed could be available for purchase at a pharmacy, requiring a finger prick of blood. This would be similar to an over-the-counter HIV test. As he sought support, there were more concerns than interest, mostly in terms of liability, administering it properly, and interpreting results. Another concern was the false sense of security provided by the test in the off chance that a person might contract strep-based TSS rather than staph-based TSS, or that TSS might develop at a different site on the body rather than through tampon use.[21] These liability concerns are unfortunate because I think many would gladly get a test to see if they fall within the 80 percent, and then they could let go of the fear of "dying from a tampon."

In addition, there is news of a vaccine to prevent TSS, announced in *Lancet Infectious Disease* on June 10, 2016.[22] In general, this would seem to be a good idea, and vaccines have prevented many horrible illnesses and deaths. The problem is that for 80 percent of the population, this vaccine is redundant. If a person has developed the antibodies, they do not need the vaccine. The body has already successfully accomplished its protective work. When I asked Parsonnet about this, he commented that even if the vaccine were administered, there are those healthy people where the vaccine simply does not "take," whether given once or multiple times. For them, it will not work either. For this last 20 percent, the strain of *S. aureus* responsible for TSS may not even be present, again posing no threat. Thus, a recommendation for a blanket vaccine is questionable.

If a TSS vaccine were to become recommended, it is not in the best interest for the majority. A better approach from the patient's perspective would be to pair both: administer a blood test first and if it returns negative, health providers could move forward with a vaccine and counseling. This question of "who benefits?" is crucial here. The individual, and not the hospital, insurer, or pharmaceutical company, should be the focus. The patient should be the one to benefit through new knowledge about the workings of his or her individual body, and then be able to make real choices because of it.

Embracing Our Bacterial Selves

For the most part, we have constructed an antagonistic relationship with bacteria, and this has proved to be shortsighted. This is not to dismiss their danger, but to acknowledge we need some fresh thinking in the face of the declining efficacy of antibiotics, the difficulty of keeping hospitals free of MRSA (methicillin-resistant *Staphylococcus aureus*), and the futility of disinfecting our homes. We continue to lose this battle, every time. There are, however, some approaches that challenge this antagonism, reshaping ideas about hygiene, cleanliness, and sterile environments. There is discussion about the health effects of absent bacteria on newborns delivered via C-section, who do not pass through the vaginal canal and pick up the four microbes Lachnospira, Veillonella, Faecalibacterium, and Rothiaare; diabetes may be linked to chronic overexposure to *S. aureus* on the skin; allergies related to super-cleanliness and the body's lack of exposure to a variety of bacteria may be an overreactive immune response.[23] Ravi Mantha, in his TEDx talk "All about Bacteria," argues for human health by promoting bacterial health; imbalance within the microbiome leads to poor health outcomes, not necessarily recognized by western medicine or attributed to bacteria per se.[24] He argues that antibiotics have wiped out numerous bacterial colonies within the body, leaving certain bacteria to run amok. In addition, because bacteria have "quorum sensing" and the ability to detect other counterparts, they regulate their reproductive rates. With this in mind, it is easy to see how antibiotics or other elements have the ability to skew the balance of bacterial entities, allowing bacteria such as *Clostridium difficile* (*C. Diff*) to take over in the gut, or MRSA to overcome hospitals.

Manthra suggests something different than more rigorous sterilization. He asks, what if we populated operating rooms with friendly bacteria, to crowd out the more troublesome pathogens? As counterintuitive as it sounds, his idea is to add a friendly form of cow manure to hospital surgical rooms to swamp the area with harmless bacteria and challenge the unfettered growth of MRSA, for example. For years people in India have plastered their homes with cow dung, and some have theorized that this has protected them from outbreaks of *E. coli.* There are lots of questions for sure, and it flies in the face of revolutionary sterilization practices that are the foundation of modern medicine, but the idea is provocative to help us think differently. For instance, there is a company called Mother Dirt that produces a no-soap shampoo stocked full of bacteria. By repopulating skin with benign bacteria that have been formerly killed with traditional soap and shampoo, the stink-producing ones have less influence. The reintroduction of bacteria eliminates a number of body products all together.[25] This same concept of the microbial effect on TSS was studied by a team of researchers led by Roderick MacPhee, who suggests that the presence of vaginal lactobacilli reduces the virulence of *S. aureus.*[26]

For this very reason the context of the vaginal microbiome matters, especially for the sheer number of women menstruating every single day in our collective biorhythm. That biorhythm has in general been underappreciated, at times vilified, and either given too much credit in dictating women's essentialized bodies, or too little respect as a consideration for overall health. Furthermore, the intricate relationship of bacterial organisms to this cyclical menstrual cycle has not been well understood either, leaving many unanswered questions in regard to menstrual health and its relationship to menstrual management. It is a whole realm in which we must learn more, and understand better, before we run roughshod over delicate ecosystems, synergies, and chemistries of which we have no prior knowledge.

Uncharted Biocatalytic Technology

The niggling feeling remains that there is still something wrong with this whole thing. Tampons have been part of the liberation toolbox, and instead of securing bodily freedom with benefits of full public engagement they now seem to offer a technological roulette of death without our consent. Because women expect the right to a safe, healthy, and technologically mediated period, what to do about tampons presents a difficult policy question, both immediately after the first TSS cases were reported and identified, and still today as health advocates protest for disclosure about tampon materials. What specifically to tell women, and how this message is conveyed, is contested and orchestrated and remains a troubling casualty of the lack of attention to the effects from biocatalytic technologies.

These technologies are already here. A headline in an article from the *New York Times* reads "A Shocking Diagnosis: Breast Implants 'Gave Me Cancer.'"[27] The specific name for this cancer is "breast-implant associated anaplastic large-cell lymphoma." This implant, a technology and a particularly gendered one, has a roughened texture rather than a smooth one. The texturing was incorporated to promote tissue growth around it and to "help anchor the implant." Physicians suspect either that the immune system responds to the surface texture or that a possible reaction to bacteria remaining on the silicone surface triggers the lymphoma. Regardless, the implants are catalyzing cancer, an ironic and cruel development since many of the women used the implants in their reconstructive surgery following mastectomies to halt breast cancer. Here again, an "unexpected" outcome with the supposedly inert technology precipitated a horrible illness. But we do know better, and must create a system that traces, measures, and accounts for biocatalytic harm, for it will certainly strike again.

Understanding bacterial interactions with implanted technologies of the body is necessary to our health and welfare. Bacteria are incredibly robust and skilled at becoming users of the technological interfaces presented to them. Life is impossible without bacteria and is highly influenced by their presence or lack thereof. Because of this interrelationship, we must be thoughtful and conscientious about interactions of bacteria with internal technologies and their biocatalytic potential. Tampon-related TSS is a forewarning of other relational illnesses between medical devices and our microbiome.

ACKNOWLEDGMENTS

This book has benefited from so many people and influences. My husband, Ray Fouché, has had a large imprint on this book, from reading the manuscript more than once to making sure that I took breaks from it as well. He is the first person I thanked in *Under Wraps*, and he is the first person I must thank here. I am delighted when he dishes out bits about menstrual hygiene at the apropos moment, just like I find great pleasure interjecting about scratching and turntables at the right occasion. I treasure and value our partnership in so many ways.

I have been employed at various universities and departments, and at each I have expanded my knowledge base and learned from tremendous scholars and individuals. I earned my science and technology studies (STS) chops at Rensselaer Polytechnic Institute, where Nancy Campbell, Linda Layne, and Langdon Winner were my colleagues. Nancy and Linda have been great supporters of my work and thoughtful with their comments to me. Langdon was not thinking about tampons when he wrote "Do Artifacts Have Politics?" but the power of his question undergirds this book. The Rensselaer connection is a welcome network at conferences, and those years in the STS department deeply shaped my research agenda. I also met Katherine Isbister while there, and we have remained in contact and friends ever since. She has helped me set writing goals, and she asks about my progress in a way that imparts care.

At the University of Illinois, I kept my attention on STS and matched it with gender studies. The Department of Gender and Women's Studies embraced the idea that the history of menstrual hygiene technologies mattered. Siobhan Somerville, Teri Barnes, Chantal Nadeau, Sam Frost, Karen Flynn, Cris Mayo, Stephanie Foote, Mimi Nguyen, Fiona Ngo, Vicki Mahaffey, Pat Gill, and Antoinette Burton all imparted insight and support. C. L. Cole encouraged me to reach out to New York University Press (as did Rebecca Herzig who had nothing but compliments for the editors and their work). Lisa Nakamura, Christian Sandvig, Melissa

Littlefield, Spencer Schaffner, Jodi Byrd, Cynthia Oliver, and Jason Fin-
kelman were also good-spirited audiences when I regaled them with
tampon patents and the like. Esther Some was my research assistant for
one semester, and she left me with a dropbox full of documents and
the framework for my Survey Monkey questionnaire (which the social
network of Chris Bobel and the Society for Menstrual Cycle Research
helped to distribute). While at Illinois, I earned an Illinois Program
for Research in the Humanities Fellowship, and a Center for Advanced
Studies Fellowship, both of which offered me time off from teaching to
think through ideas and conduct research on the first book, which had
ramifications for this one as well.

The move to Purdue University brought me back to history, but also
allowed me to branch out with affiliations in the programs of Women's,
Gender and Sexuality Studies, American Studies, and also the College
of Engineering Education. Wendy Kline accepted a position at Purdue
University about a year after I arrived, and she suggested that I take a
look at the finding aid for the Boston Women's Health Book Collective
papers. Her hunch delivered the last chapter into my hands. She introduced me to Judy Norsigian, one of the collective's co-founders and a
co-author of *Our Bodies, Ourselves*. It was so lovely to be trusted to tell
one small part of their tremendous history. Yvonne Pitts kept my spirits
up in the arduous days of revisions, and I have appreciated her friend-
ship. I have benefited from Nancy Gabin's wise counsel, with advice a
few shorts steps away in her office directly across the hallway from mine.
Lauren Haslem was a research assistant for me, contributing another
dropbox full of annotated files. I also won a National Science Foundation STS Scholars Award, which helped me to take a leave from teaching
for one semester and focus solely on writing. The current dean of the
College of Liberal Arts, David Reingold, connected me to his brother
Arthur Reingold, who happened to be a TSS expert at the Centers for
Disease Control. This introduction was a fortuitous consequence of his
arrival at Purdue.

I received input from many anonymous reviewers, not only for this
book, but also for journal articles and grants. I am awed by their collective insight and generosity, and the work it takes to cross disciplines
despite the risks for misunderstandings. The breadth of knowledge they
possess inspires me to keep pushing and keep making connections. I

have also been graciously received as a guest speaker at the University of California at Los Angeles, the University of California at Santa Barbara, and Indiana University–Purdue University Indianapolis, and as a keynote speaker at the Society for Menstrual Cycle Research and the Indiana Historical Bureau, where I spoke about various themes from this book. I have delivered research papers at numerous conferences as well. All of the venues have offered thoughtful audiences full of questions that have helped me hone the contours of this book. As menstrual matters have more recently risen in social media and the news, journalists have reached out to me for input. Their questions have helped me think about my own research and how to frame it for a broader audience beyond the academy.

I also am grateful for people who helped me to not think about this book all the time. The women soccer players of my scrimmage league, whose ages range from fortyish to sixtyish, inspire me every week. Some benefited from Title IX and played soccer in college, and others like me did not even have a rec league experience to draw on. They give me a space to be present and in the moment, and to keep learning and moving. It is no place for work creep, but a welcome respite from all the responsibilities and trials of the day.

My son, Eads, is no longer a little boy, as he was when I finished my first book, but now a fully fledged teenager. He has heard my ramblings about this topic long enough to joke "call the CDC!" if he gets a scrape or hangnail. He, too, has kept me grounded and honest about my work and my time. Both Ray and Eads are my greatest supporters, and it means the world to me. Thank you.

* * *

Sections from the following articles I have authored contributed to the content of this book:

"Rely and Toxic Shock Syndrome: A Technological Health Crisis," *Yale Journal of Biology and Medicine* 84.4 (December 2011): 447–459.

"Toxic Shock Syndrome, Tampons and Laboratory Standard-Setting," *Canadian Medical Association Journal* 189.20 (May 23, 2017): E726–E728.

"Toxic Shock Syndrome, Tampon Absorbency, and Feminist Science," *Catalyst: Feminism, Theory, Technoscience* 3.1 (2017), doi: http://dx.doi.org/10.28968/cftt.v3i1.127.

APPENDIX

SOURCES AND EVIDENCE
Sources for this research are varied and disparate. There is no one library that houses all these documents, and I have had to create my own personal archive about toxic shock syndrome (TSS) and tampons. Primary sources, including scientific journal articles, reports, and memos from the Centers for Disease Control (CDC), and biographies of scientists have provided insight toward the discovery of TSS and the identification of reagents in tampon-related TSS. Oral histories with employees at the CDC and the Food and Drug Administration (FDA), and FDA documents in the public domain have shed light on decision making and guidelines about policy. Newspapers, magazines, and periodicals address the events as they unfolded in the 1980s and capture the healthscape of TSS, while the archives for the Boston Women's Health Book Collective, located at the Arthur and Elizabeth Schlesinger Library at Harvard University, provide ample documentation of efforts to regulate tampon absorbency in the name of safety for women.

A rich yet unintended archive is found in the trial documents generated by lawsuits against tampon-producing manufacturers, holding them to blame for deaths and injuries resulting from TSS. I do not use these cases to establish legal precedent concerning product liability, but to read TSS historically and culturally. In particular, the three-thousand-page transcript, court proceedings, exhibits, and trial records of the 1982 federal product liability suit, *Kehm v. Procter & Gamble*, has been quite informative. In order to preserve these documents for future researchers, I convinced Tom Riley, who tried the case (and passed away in 2011), to donate his papers to the University of Illinois archives, where they now reside in its permanent collection (Kehm vs. Procter and Gamble Case File, 1976–1996). I cite the trial and exhibits to my own personal collection, however, since the accession at Illinois occurred after Riley allowed me the privilege of photocopying his papers at his law office in Cedar Rapids, Iowa. I also purchased from Stephen Kaufman—the attorney who pursued the first lawsuit against P&G that was subsequently settled out of court—the five-volume binder set he collated, copied, and sold during the height of TSS litigation: "A Lawyer's Handbook on Toxic Shock Syndrome, 1981" and "A Lawyer's Supplemental Handbook on Toxic Shock Syndrome, 1982."

In addition, I created a Survey Monkey questionnaire with open-ended questions called "Toxic Shock Syndrome Survey," in which I collected anonymous online responses from February 21, 2012, to February 21, 2013. The call for the survey was shared with online list-servs and were intended for qualitative use. I also conducted a limited set of semi-structured oral histories with women who wanted to share their stories of Rely tampons. I have chosen to maintain their anonymity by using first names only, and in some cases first-name pseudonyms. These histories are by no means comprehensive or indicative of larger trends; they are specific to certain individuals at certain times. I also conducted oral histories with physicians, scientists, epidemiologists, and FDA representatives, and their names are listed in full throughout the book because they are known public figures of record. It is from this disparate set of interviews, documents, and court cases, as well as numerous other sources, that I have drawn this book together. I made every effort to represent the scientists' ideas as accurately as possible, but as with much of scientific writing, ideas may have been "lost in translation" and mistakes are my own.

ORAL HISTORY INTERVIEWS AND EMAIL CORRESPONDENCE
Sam Au, research fellow, Harvard Medical School's BioMEMS Resource Center
Joan Z. (Jodie) Bernstein, general counsel, Food and Drug Division of Health and Human Services
Nancy Buc, chief counsel, Food and Drug Administration
Steve Fellman, counsel to Tambrands, with his firm Loomis, Owen, Fellman & Howe
Harry Finley, director and curator, the Museum of Menstruation
Becky LeBuhn, consumer representative from the National Consumers League on the medical devices committee and participant on the Tampon Task Force
Judy Norsigian, co-founder of the Boston Women's Health Book Collective and contributor to Our Bodies, Ourselves
Mike Osterholm, epidemiologist, Minnesota Department of Health
Jeffrey Parsonnet, M.D., infectious disease specialist, with a research focus on TSS
Arthur Reingold, M.D., Centers for Disease Control, Epidemiology Intelligence Service

Nancy Reame, nursing professor and research scientist for the Tampon Task Force

Sara Riley, daughter of Tom Riley, law student and research assistant for *Kehm v. Procter & Gamble*

Tom Riley, Cedar Rapids lawyer for plaintiffs in *Kehm v. Procter & Gamble*

Pat Schlievert, professor of microbiology and immunology, with a research focus on TSS

Kathryn Shands, M.D., Centers for Disease Control, Epidemiology Intelligence Service, 1979–1981, TSS Task Force

David Swankin, general counsel, National Consumers League, Swankin & Turner Law Firm

NOTES

INTRODUCTION

1 Susan Okie, "Toxic-Shock Syndrome Cases Show Decline," *Washington Post* (May 26, 1981).

2 Gloria Steinem, "If Men Could Menstruate," *Ms. Magazine* (October 1978).

3 Code of Federal Regulations, Title 21, Volume 8, Sec. 801.430, "User Labeling for Menstrual Tampons" (April 1, 2017); Jeffrey Parsonnet, "To Build a Better Mousetrap: Pitfalls on the Path to Improving Tampon Safety," *Clinical Infectious Disease* 49 (December 1, 2009): 1718–1720.

4 Jeffrey Davis, "The Investigation of TSS in Wisconsin and Beyond, 1979–1980," in Mark Dworkin, ed., *Outbreak Investigations around the World: Case Studies in Infectious Disease Field Epidemiology* (Boston: Jones and Bartlett, 2009), 79–102.

5 Molly Katchpole, "It Happened to Me: I Got Toxic Shock Syndrome," *XOJane*, September 16, 2011, http://www.xojane.com.

6 "Michelle's Toxic Shock Syndrome Story," *My Thoughts, Ideas, and Ramblings*, January 6, 2013, https://mythoughtsideasandramblings.com.

7 Kenneth Todar, "*Staphylococcus aureus* and Staphylococcal Disease," *Todar's Online Textbook of Bacteriology*, accessed November 13, 2009, http://www.textbookof bacteriology.net.

8 Merlin Bergdoll and P. Joan Chesney, eds., *Toxic Shock Syndrome* (Boca Raton, FL: CRC Press, 1991).

9 Joan Rothchild, *Design and Feminism: Re-Visioning Spaces, Places, and Everyday Things* (New Brunswick, NJ: Rutgers University Press, 1999); Judy Wajcman, *Feminism Confronts Technology* (University Park: University of Pennsylvania Press, 1991); Anne Balsamo, *Technologies of the Gendered Body: Reading Cyborg Women* (Durham, NC: Duke University Press, 1996); Nina Lerman, Ruth Oldenziel, and Arwen Mohun, eds., *Gender and Technology: A Reader* (Baltimore, MD: Johns Hopkins University Press, 2003); Jennifer Terry and Melodie Calvert, eds., *Processed Lives: Gender and Technology in Everyday Life* (New York: Routledge, 1997); Linda Layne, Sharra Vostral, and Kate Boyer, eds., *Feminist Technology* (Urbana: University of Illinois Press, 2010); Andrea Tone, *Devices and Desires: The History of Contraceptives in America* (New York: Hill and Wang, 2001); Leslie Reagan, *When Abortion Was a Crime: Women, Medicine, and Law in the United States, 1867–1973* (Berkeley: University of California Press, 1998); Judith Walzer Leavitt, ed., *Women and Health in America: Historical Readings*, 2nd revised ed. (Madison: University of Wisconsin Press, 1999); Anne Fausto-Sterling, *Sexing the*

Body: Gender Politics and the Construction of Sexuality (New York: Basic Books, 2000); Wendy Kline, *Bodies of Knowledge: Sexuality, Reproduction, and Women's Health in the Second Wave* (Chicago: University of Chicago Press, 2010); Sandra Morgen, *Into Our Own Hands: The Women's Health Movement in the United States, 1969–1990* (Piscataway, NJ: Rutgers University Press, 2002); Charles Rosenberg, "Framing Disease: Illness, Society, and History," in Charles Rosenberg and Janet Golden, eds., *Framing Disease: Studies in Cultural History* (New Brunswick, NJ: Rutgers University Press, 1992): xiii–xxvi; Joan Jacobs Brumberg, *The Body Project: An Intimate History of American Girls* (New York: Vintage, 1998); Sharra L. Vostral, *Under Wraps: A History of Menstrual Hygiene Technology* (Lanham, MD: Lexington Books, 2008); Lara Friedenfelds, *The Modern Period: Menstruation in Twentieth-Century America* (Baltimore, MD: Johns Hopkins University Press, 2009).

10 Carsten Timmermann and Julie Anderson, eds., *Devices and Designs: Medical Technologies in Historical Perspective* (New York: Palgrave Macmillan, 2007); S. Lochlann Jain, *Injury: The Politics of Product Design and Safety Law in the United States* (Princeton, NJ: Princeton University Press, 2006); Londa Schiebinger, ed., *Gendered Innovations in Science and Engineering* (Stanford, CA: Stanford University Press, 2008); Nelly Oudshoorn and Trevor Pinch, eds., *How Users Matter: The Co-Construction of Users and Technology* (Cambridge, MA: MIT Press, 2003); Fausto-Sterling, *Sexing the Body*.

11 Robert Bud, "Biotechnology in the Twentieth Century," *Social Studies of Science* 21.3 (August 1991): 415–457.

12 Sheila Jasanoff, "The Idiom of Co-Production," and "Ordering Knowledge, Ordering Society," in Sheila Jasanoff, ed., *States of Knowledge: The Co-Production of Science and Social Order* (London: Routledge, 2004): 1–12, 13–45; Oudshoorn and Pinch, *How Users Matter*.

13 Nancy Friedman, *Everything You Must Know about Tampons* (New York: Berkley Books, 1981); Brian Schmaefsky, *Deadly Diseases and Epidemics: Toxic Shock Syndrome* (New York: Chelsea House, 2004).

14 Christopher H. Foreman Jr., *Plagues, Products, and Politics: Emergent Public Health Hazards and National Policymaking* (Washington, DC: Brookings Institution, 1994), vii, 7–8.

15 Doug Levy, "When Fear Becomes an Unintended Public Health Problem," NPR Shots, February 23, 2016, http://www.npr.org.

16 M. T. Osterholm, J. P. Davis, R. W. Gibson, J. S. Mandel, L. A. Wintermeyer, C. M. Helms, J. C. Forfang, J. Rondeau, J. M. Vergeront, and the Investigative Team, "Tri-State Toxic-Shock Syndrome Study. I. Epidemiologist Findings," *Journal of Infectious Diseases* 145.4 (April 1982): 431–440; Michael T. Osterholm and Jan C. Forfang, "Toxic-Shock Syndrome in Minnesota: Results of an Active-Passive Surveillance System," *Journal of Infectious Diseases* 145.4 (April 1982): 458–464; Mike Osterholm, interview with author, April 29, 2016.

17 Osterholm et al., "Tri-State Toxic-Shock Syndrome Study," 435.

18 Philip Tierno, *The Secret Life of Germs: Observations and Lessons from a Microbe Hunter* (New York: Pocket Books, 2004), 79–80.

19 Gabrielle Olya, "Are Super-Absorbent Tampons to Blame for Toxic Shock Syndrome? Experts Weigh In," *People*, February 8, 2016, http://www.people.com.

20 Laurie Garrett, *The Coming Plague: Newly Emerging Diseases in a World Out of Balance* (New York: Penguin, 1994), 404.

21 Patrick M. Schlievert, "Comparison of Cotton and Cotton/Rayon Tampons for Effect on Production of Toxic Shock Syndrome Toxin," *Journal of Infectious Diseases* 172.4 (October 1995): 1112–1114.

22 "Bacterial Toxins Cause Deadly Heart Disease," *Medical Xpress*, August 20, 2013, https://medicalxpress.com.

23 Parsonnet, "To Build a Better Mousetrap," 1719.

24 Sophie Jamart, Oliver Denis, Ariane Deplano, Georgios Tragas, Alexandra Vandergheynst, David De Bels, and Jacques Devriendt, "Methicillin-Resistant *Staphylococcus aureus* Toxic Shock Syndrome," *Emerging Infectious Diseases* 11.4 (April 2005): 636–637.

25 Elizabeth Wilson, *Gut Feminism* (Durham, NC: Duke University Press, 2015). Excerpt from the introduction found at *Catalyst: Feminism, Theory, Technoscience* 1.1 (2015), http://catalystjournal.org.

26 Denise Riley, *Am I That Name? Feminism and the Category of Women in History* (Minneapolis: University of Minnesota Press, 1988).

27 Chris Bobel, *New Blood: Third-Wave Feminism and the Politics of Menstruation* (New Brunswick, NJ: Rutgers University Press, 2010).

28 SugaDaddyStyles, Twitter, accessed July 31, 2012, http://inagist.com/all /230176621003431936/.

CHAPTER 1. UNEXPECTED CONSEQUENCES

1 I use "technobiological" to focus on the artifactual component and avoid confusion with "biotechnology." Robert Bud discusses the etymology of the term and how it means something different to various communities, among them engineers, molecular biologists, and even venture capitalists. While he confirms that there is no one universal meaning, "in practice the word often refers vaguely to technologies associated with genetic engineering," though we often think of processes ranging from "biochemical engineering" to "recombinant DNA." See Robert Bud, "Biotechnology in the Twentieth Century," *Social Studies of Science* 21.3 (August 1991): 415–457.

2 Roger Silverstone, *Consuming Technologies: Media and Information in Domestic Spaces* (London: Routledge, 1992); Maren Hartmann, Thomas Berker, Yves Punie, and Katie Ward, eds., *Domestication of Media and Technology* (Berkshire, UK: Open University Press, 2005).

3 Sharra L. Vostral, "Advice to Adolescents: Menstrual Health and Menstrual Education Films, 1946–1982," in Cheryl Warsh, ed., *Gender Health and Popular Culture: Historical Perspectives* (Waterloo, ON: Wilfrid Laurier Press, 2011), 47–64.

4 Vostral, *Under Wraps*.

5 Sharra L. Vostral, "Tampons: Re-scripting Tampons as Feminist," in Layne, Vostral, and Boyer, *Feminist Technology*.

6 Vostral, *Under Wraps*.

7 F. S. Richardson, inventor, Catamenial Plug, U.S. Patent 1,932,383, filed January 28, 1931, and issued October 24, 1933; Vostral, *Under Wraps*, 96.

8 George C. Graham, inventor, Personal Products Co. assignee, Flexible Product, U.S. Patent 2,815,756, filed October 12, 1955, and issued December 10, 1957.

9 George C. Graham, inventor, Personal Products Co. assignee, Catamenial Device, U.S. Patent 3,005,456, filed July 3, 1956, and issued October 24, 1961.

10 George C. Graham and Vincent H. Barlow, inventors, Personal Products Co. assignee, Tow Tampon, U.S. Patent 2,934,068, filed June 21, 1956, and issued April 4, 1960.

11 William H. Burger, Howard N. Nelson, Carl H. Rowe, inventors, Kimberly-Clark Corporation assignee, Cellulosic Product, U.S. Patent 2,926,667, filed April 9, 1956, and issued March 1, 1960.

12 Karen Houppert, "Pulling the Plug on the Sanitary Protection Industry," *Village Voice* (February 7, 1995): 31.

13 Jeffrey Parsonnet, Paul A. Modern, and Kristine D. Giacobbe, "Reply," *Journal of Infectious Disease* 177 (April 1998): 825–826.

14 Barbara Lauze, "Getting to Know Our Neighbors—A Tour of Tambrands in Auburn," Good Shepherd Food-Bank, April 5, 2012, http://gsfb.org.

15 Billy Gene Harper, Robert Niles Bashaw, Bobby Leroy Atkins, inventors, Dow Chemical Co. assignee, Absorbent Product Containing a Hydrocelloidal Composition, U.S. Patent 3,669,103, filed May 31, 1966, and assigned June 13, 1972.

16 Russell L. Johnson, inventor, Kimberly-Clark Corporation assignee, Digital Tampon, U.S. Patent 4,212,301, filed August 14, 1978, and assigned July 15, 1980.

17 Anne Marie Helmenstine, "How Do Disposable Diapers Work? Why Do They Leak?" March 16, 2017, https://www.thoughtco.com.

18 Makoto Shinohara and Nathan D. Field, inventors, International Playtex, Inc. assignee, Preparation of Water-insoluble Carboxymethyl Cellulose Absorbents, U.S. Patent 4,200,736, filed May 5, 1978, and assigned April 4, 1980.

19 Leonard M. Kaczmarzyk, James J. Hlaban, Leo J. Bernardin, inventors, Kimberly-Clark Corporation assignee, Compressed Catamenial Tampons with Improved Capabilities for Absorbing Menstrual Fluids, U.S. Patent 4,044,766, filed February 27, 1976, and assigned August 30, 1977.

20 Dale A. Gellert, inventor, Procter & Gamble Company assignee, Absorbent Devices, U.S. Patent, 4,475,911, filed April 13, 1981, and assigned October 10, 1984.

21 Dale A. Gellert, inventor, Procter & Gamble Company assignee, Absorbent Means for Catamenial Devices, U.S. Patent, 4,239,043, filed November 29, 1978, and assigned December 16, 1980. This patent includes Pluronic L-92. According to Pat Schlievert and others, high concentrations of Pluronic L-92 stimulate the production of exotoxins in *S. aureus*. Pat Schlievert, "Effect of Merocel

Vaginal Sponge on Growth of Staphylococcus aureus and Production of Toxic Shock Syndrome–Associated Toxins," *Journal of the American College of Surgery* 183 (1996): 19–24. Bruce Dan's obituary in the *New York Times* notes that he demonstrated that Pluronic L-92 increased the level of toxins that the bacteria produced.

22 Patrick M. Schlievert, James R. Deringer, Michael H. Kim, Steven J. Projan, and Richard P. Novick, "Effect of Glycerol Monolaurate on Bacterial Growth and Toxin Production," *Antimicrobial Agents and Chemotherapy* 36.3 (March 1992): 626–631; Schlievert, "Comparison of Cotton and Cotton/Rayon Tampons."

23 "Superabsorbents Seek Markets That Are Super," *Chemical Week* 125.3 (July 18, 1979): 40.

24 Juliana DeCarvalho Anderson, "Thalidomide," *Toxipedia*, May 20, 2013, http://toxipedia.org; Linda Bren, "Frances Oldham Kelsey: FDA Medical Reviewer Leaves Her Mark on History," *FDA Consumer Magazine* 35.2 (March–April 2001): 24–29.

25 Gina Kolata, "The Sad Legacy of the Dalkon Shield," *New York Times* (December 6, 1987); Jim Szaller, "One Lawyer's 25 Year Journey: The Dalkon Shield Saga," *Ohio Trial* 9.4 (Winter 1999): 7–20.

26 Jennifer Couzin-Frankel, "Contraceptive Comeback: The Maligned IUD Gets a Second Chance," *Wired Magazine* (July 15, 2011).

27 Morton Mintz, "A Crime against Women: A. H. Robins and the Dalkon Shield," *Multinational Monitor* 7.1 (January 15, 1986); Morton Mintz, *At Any Cost: Corporate Greed, Women, and the Dalkon Shield* (New York: Pantheon, 1985).

28 Szaller, "One Lawyer's 25 Year Journey."

29 Langdon Winner, "Do Artifacts Have Politics?" *Daedalus* 109.1 (Winter 1980): 121–136.

30 Morgen, *Into Our Own Hands*; Elaine Tyler May, *America and the Pill: A History of Promise, Peril, and Liberation* (New York: Basic Books, 2011).

31 Kline, *Bodies of Knowledge*.

32 "The American Experience: The Pill," DVD, PBS (2003); Elizabeth Siegel Watkins, *On the Pill: A Social History of Oral Contraceptives, 1950–1970* (Baltimore, MD: Johns Hopkins University Press, 2001).

33 Susan Reverby, "Feminism & Health," *Health and History* 4.1 (2002): 5–19. Reverby characterizes this tension of women's bodies to health policy during this time in the stages of victimization, resistance, attacks against institutions, and finally the histories and lessons of political forces and political actions.

34 David M. Worthen, "Reflections on the FDA's Intraocular Lens Regulations," *IRB: Ethics and Human Research* 2.4 (April 1980): 1; Jamie Kohen, "The History of the Regulation of Menstrual Tampons," accessed July 31, 2012, http://leda.law.harvard.edu.

35 David A. Kessler, Stuart M. Pape, and David N. Sundwall, "The Federal Regulation of Medical Devices," *NEJM* 317.6 (August 6, 1987): 357–366.

36 Ibid., 358.

37 Jeffrey Shapiro, "The Medical Device Amendments of 1976: The Statute That Went Awry," July 3, 2013, http://www.fdalawblog.net.

38 *Michael L. Kehm v. Procter & Gamble*, United States Courthouse, Cedar Rapids, Iowa (April 5, 1982), 1143.

39 Nelly Oudshoorn, "The Vulnerability of Cyborgs: Sensing and Taming the Unwanted Agency of ICDs," paper delivered at the Society for the Social Studies of Science annual meeting, Denver, CO (November 12, 2015).

40 J. Johnson (Bruno Latour), "Mixing Humans and Nonhumans Together: The Sociology of a Door-Closer," *Social Problems* 35.3 (1998): 298–310.

41 Stephen J. Collier and Aihwa Ong, "Global Assemblages, Anthropological Problems," in Aihwa Ong and Stephen Collier, eds., *Global Assemblages: Technology, Politics, and Ethics as Anthropological Problems* (Malden, MA: Blackwell Publishing, 2005), 3–21 (quoted on p. 4). See also Bruno Latour, *We Have Never Been Modern* (Cambridge, MA: Harvard University Press, 1993). Latour is well known for theorizing Actor Network Theory (ANT), which could be used to explain tampons and bacteria and their processes of interaction. ANT is a useful framework, but where it fails is in acknowledging systems of power at play, such as race and gender, and how networks privilege and dismiss certain ways of knowing.

42 Jane Bennett, *Vibrant Matter: A Political Ecology of Things* (Durham, NC: Duke University Press, 2010), viii.

43 National Institutes of Health Human Microbiome Project, accessed July 12, 2012, http://www.hmpdacc.org.

44 Rob Stein, "Finally, a Map of All the Microbes on Your Body," NPR Shots, June 13, 2012, accessed July 12, 2012, http://www.npr.org; Michael Pollan, "Some of My Best Friends Are Germs," *New York Times Magazine* (May 14, 2013); David Salisbury, "The Pronoun 'I' is Becoming Obsolete," Research News @ Vanderbilt, August 19, 2015, http://news.vanderbilt.edu.

45 Bret Stetka, "The Human Body's Complicated Relationship with Fungi," NPR Shots, April 16, 2016, http://www.npr.org.

46 Interview with Karen Barad, "Matter Feels, Converses, Suffers, Desires, Yearns, and Remembers," in Rick Dolphijn and Iris van der Tuin, eds., *New Materialism: Interviews and Cartographies*, doi: http://dx.doi.org/10.3998/ohp .11515701.0001.001.

47 Michael Wilson, *Microbial Inhabitants of Humans: Their Ecology and Role in Health and Disease* (New York: Cambridge University Press, 2005), 2–3.

48 Ibid., frontispiece.

49 Ibid., xviii.

50 Linda Nash, *Inescapable Ecologies: A History of Environment, Disease, and Knowledge* (Berkeley: University of California Press, 2006), 6–8.

51 Heather Paxson, "Post Pasteurian Cultures: The Microbiopolitics of Raw-Milk Cheese in the United States," *Cultural Anthropology* 23.1 (2008): 15–47.

52 Stefan Helmreich, "*Homo Microbis*: The Human Microbiome, Figural, Literal, Political," *Thresholds* 42 (2014): 52–59 (quote from p. 56); Heather Paxson and Stefan

Helmreich, "The Perils and Promises of Microbial Abundance: Novel Natures and Model Ecosystems, from Artisanal Cheese to Alien Seas," *Social Studies of Science* 44.2 (2014): 165–193. There is still controversy about the ratio of other cells to human cells. See Ed Yong, "You're Probably Not Mostly Microbes," *The Atlantic*, January 8, 2016, http://www.theatlantic.com.

53 Banu Subramanium, "The Aliens Have Landed! Reflections on the Rhetoric of Biological Invasions," *Meridians: Feminism, Race, Transnationalism* 2.1 (2001): 26–40.

54 Informal conversations with Jodi Byrd, a scholar of American Indian studies, helped me to think about this relationship. See also Philip J. Deloria, *Indians in Unexpected Places* (Lawrence: University of Kansas Press, 2004).

55 Rob Stein, "Disinfect All ICU Patients to Reduce 'Superbug' Infections," NPR Shots, May 29, 2013, http://www.npr.org.

56 D. Boone, comment section, "Finally, a Map of All the Microbes on Your Body," NPR Shots, accessed June 14, 2012, http://www.npr.org.

57 Sally Wyatt, "Non-Users Also Matter: The Construction of Users and Non-Users of the Internet," in Oudshoorn and Pinch, *How Users Matter*, 67–79.

58 Nathanael Bassett, "'A Sound of Thunder': Technology, Silence, and Non-Humans in the Anthropocene," talk given at the 42nd Annual American Studies symposium, Purdue University, West Lafayette (April 29, 2017). Bassett discussed the concept of a "technological bystander," which prompted me to develop the category of unintended users.

59 Marissa Wenzke, "Menstrual Pads Could Be Getting a Long Overdue Make-over," Mashable, October 8, 2016, http://mashable.com.

60 On these cofactors and relationships, see Brian Pfaffenberger, "Technological Dramas," *Science, Technology & Human Values* 17.3 (1992): 282–312; Jasanoff, "Idiom of Co-Production," 1–12; Jasanoff, "Ordering Knowledge, Ordering Society," 13–45.

61 James K. Todd, "Toxic Shock Syndrome—Scientific Uncertainty and the Public Media," *Pediatrics* 67.6 (June 1981): 921–923 (quoted on p. 922).

62 John C. Burnham, *Accident Prone: A History of Technology, Psychology, and Misfits of the Machine Age* (Chicago: University of Chicago Press, 2009), 193.

63 Henry Petroski, *To Forgive Design: Understanding Failure* (Cambridge, MA: Harvard University Press, 2012).

64 Arwen Mohen, "Designed for Thrills and Safety: Gender, Technology, and the Commodification of Risk in the Amusement Park Industry," *Journal of Design History* 14.4 (Fall 2001): 291–306; Ulrich Beck, *Risk Society: Towards a New Modernity* (New Delhi: Sage, 1992); Anthony Giddens, "Risk and Responsibility," *Modern Law Review* 62.1 (January 1999): 1–10; Deborah Lupton, *Risk*, 2nd ed. (New York: Routledge, 2013).

65 Paul Slovic, *The Perception of Risk* (New York: Routledge, 2000); Sheila Jasanoff, *Risk Management and Political Culture: A Comparative Analysis of Science* (New York: Russell Sage Foundation, 1986).

66 Alvin M. Weinberg, "Science and Trans-science," *Minerva* 10.2 (1972): 209–222.

67 Ibid., 210.

68 Karen L. Henwood, Karen Anne Parkhill, and Nick F. Pidgeon, "Science, Technology and Rick Perception: From Gender Differences to the Effects Made by Gender," *Equal Opportunities International* 27.8 (2008): 662–676.

69 Jain, *Injury*, 52.

70 Gerald Markowitz and David Rosner, *Deceit and Denial: The Deadly Politics of Industrial Pollution* (Berkeley: University of California Press, 2002); Rachel Maines, *Asbestos and Fire: Technological Tradeoffs and the Body at Risk* (Piscataway, NJ: Rutgers University Press, 2005); Phil Brown, *Toxic Exposures: Contested Illness and the Environmental Health Movement* (New York: Columbia University Press, 2007).

71 Gregg Mitman, "Introduction: A Cloud over History," in Gregg Mitman, Michelle Murphy, and Christopher Sellers, eds., Osiris, 2nd Series, Vol. 19, *Landscapes of Exposure: Knowledge and Illness in Modern Environments* (Chicago: University of Chicago Press, 2004), 2.

72 Paul Israel, comments, Life of New Materials conference, cosponsored by the Chemical Heritage Foundation and the Hagley Museum and Library, October 2011; David B. Morris, *Illness and Culture in the Postmodern Age* (Berkeley: University of California Press, 1998).

73 "EPA to Set Limit on Chemicals in Drinking Water," CNN Health, February 2, 2011, http://www.cnn.com.

74 Alix Spiegel, "Why Radiologists Can Miss a Gorilla Hiding in Plain Sight," NPR Shots, February 11, 2013, http://www.npr.org.

75 Jennifer L. Croissant, "Agnotology: Ignorance and Absence or Towards a Sociology of Things That Aren't There," *Social Epistemology* 28.1 (2014): 4–25 (quoted on p. 5). See also Robert N. Proctor and Londa Schiebinger, eds., *Agnotology: The Making and Unmaking of Ignorance* (Stanford, CA: Stanford University Press, 2008).

76 Kathy Ferguson, *The Man Question: Visions of Subjectivity in Feminist Theory* (Berkeley: University of California Press, 1993), 7.

77 "China Bad Milk Recalls Now Global," CBS News, September 24, 2008, http://www.cbsnews.com.

78 David Ehrenfeld, "The Cow Tipping Point," *Harper's Magazine* 305.1829 (October 2002): 13–20.

79 Ibid., 18.

80 David Harvey, *A Brief History of Neoliberalism* (Oxford: Oxford University Press, 2005).

81 Philip Doughety, "Advertising: A look at the Rely Campaign," *New York Times*, September 24, 1980.

82 Shreya Dixit, Gayle Fischer, and Corola Wittekind, "Recurrent Menstrual Toxic Shock Syndrome Despite Discontinuation of Tampon Use: Is Menstrual Toxic Shock Syndrome Really Caused by Tampons?" *Australasian Journal of Dermatology* (August 17, 2012), doi:10.1111/j.1440-0960.2012.00938.x.

CHAPTER 2. MYSTERY

1 Christian Schrock, "Disease Alert," *JAMA* 243.12 (March 3, 1980): 1231. In the Kehm trial, Woodside, the lead counsel for Procter & Gamble, said that Schrock dubbed it "sad madam" syndrome.

2 Lawrence K. Altman, *Who Goes First? The Story of Self-Experimentation in Medicine* (Berkeley: University of California Press, 1987), 195–197.

3 "Toxic Shock Syndrome—United States, 1970–1980," *MMWR* 30.3 (January 30, 1981): 25–36.

4 "Update: Toxic Shock Syndrome—United States," *MMWR* 32.30 (August 5, 1983): 398–400.

5 "Estimates of Deaths Associated with Seasonal Influenza," *MMWR* 59.33 (August 27, 2010): 1057–1062; "Toxic Shock Syndrome—United States, 1970–1980," 28.

6 "Study Links Toxic Shock Illness to Middle-Class White Families," *New York Times* (March 7, 1981).

7 Rosenberg, "Framing Disease," xiii. Annemarie Goldstein Jutel provides a good sociological interpretation of diagnosis in *Putting a Name to It: Diagnosis in Contemporary Society* (Baltimore, MD: Johns Hopkins University Press, 2011).

8 *Kehm v. Procter & Gamble*, 1800.

9 Mark Pendergrast, *Inside the Outbreaks: The Elite Medical Detectives of the Epidemic Intelligence Service* (New York: Houghton Mifflin Harcourt, 2010), xii.

10 Mark Dworkin, *Outbreak Investigations around the World: Case Studies in Infectious Disease Field Epidemiology* (Sudbury, MA: Jones and Bartlett, 2010), 2.

11 Ibid., 17.

12 Steven Epstein, *Impure Science: AIDS, Activism, and the Politics of Knowledge* (Berkeley: University of California Press, 1996), 3, 256–258.

13 Ibid., 255.

14 Garrett, *Coming Plague*, 183.

15 Patrick Di Justo, "The Last Great Swine Flu Epidemic," *Salon*, April 28, 2009, http://www.salon.com.

16 Garrett, *Coming Plague*, 189. See also Pendergrast, *Inside the Outbreaks*; Elizabeth Etheridge, *Sentinel of Health: A History of the Centers for Disease Control* (Berkeley: University of California Press, 1992).

17 "Current Trends Update on Acquired Immune Deficiency Syndrome—United States," *MMWR* 31.37 (September 24, 1982): 507–508, 513–514.

18 Garrett, *Coming Plague*, 293; Alan Whiteside, *HIV/AIDS: A Very Short Introduction* (Oxford: Oxford University Press, 2008), 1–2.

19 Priscilla Wald, *Contagious: Cultures, Carriers, and the Outbreak Narrative* (Durham, NC: Duke University Press, 2008), 218–219.

20 Institute of Medicine, American College of Physicians, Institute of Medicine Committee on Toxic Shock Syndrome, "The Toxic Shock Syndrome: A Conference Held 20–22 November 1981," *Annals of Internal Medicine* 96.6, pt. 2 (June 1982): 831–996.

21 James Todd, Mark Fishaut, Frank Kapral, and Thomas Welch, "Toxic-Shock Syndrome Associated with Phage-Group-I Staphylococci," *The Lancet* 312.8100 (November 25, 1978): 1116–1118.

22 Ibid., 1116.

23 *Kehm v. Procter & Gamble*, 111.

24 Philip Tierno, *The Secret Life of Germs: Observations and Lessons from a Microbe Hunter* (New York: Pocket, 2004), 74.

25 Garrett, *Coming Plague*, 408. Schlievert has studied *S. aureus* for his whole career, and he currently proposes that it is responsible for the autoimmune response of Type II diabetes. See "Common Bacteria May Be One Cause of Type II Diabetes," MedicalResearch.com interview with Patrick Schlievert, June 4, 2015, http://medicalresearch.com.

26 Jeffrey Davis, "The Investigation of TSS in Wisconsin and Beyond, 1979–1980," in Dworkin, *Outbreak Investigations*, 79–102 (quoted on 80–81).

27 Nancy Friedman, *Everything You Must Know about Tampons* (New York: Berkley, 1981), 61–62.

28 Susan Okie, "'Toxic-Shock Syndrome' Disease Is Striking Young Women," *Washington Post*, May 30, 1980.

29 Davis, "Investigation of TSS," 82.

30 Ibid.

31 Friedman, *Everything You Must Know*, 63–64.

32 Davis, "Investigation of TSS," 83.

33 Neil Rosenberg, "Fever, Signs of Shock, Puzzle Girl's Doctors," *Milwaukee Journal* (February 14, 1980): 1, 3; Davis, "Investigation of TSS," 83.

34 Kathryn Shands, interview with author, November 9, 2016, Atlanta, GA.

35 Davis, "Investigation of TSS," 87.

36 Tierno, *Secret Life of Germs*, 83.

37 Richard V. McCloskey, "Scarlet Fever and Necrotizing Fasciitis Caused by Coagulase-Positive Hemolytic *Staphylococcus aureus*, Phage Type 85," *Annals of Internal Medicine* 78.1 (1973): 85–87; Altman, *Who Goes First?*, 196.

38 Kathryn Shands, email correspondence with author, July 24, 2017.

39 Altman, *Who Goes First?*, 198.

40 "Toxic-Shock Syndrome—United States," *MMWR* 29.20 (May 23, 1980): 229–230.

41 Jeffrey P. Davis, P. Joan Chesney, Philip J. Wand, and Martin LaVenture, "Toxic-Shock Syndrome: Epidemiologic Features, Recurrence, Risk Factors, and Prevention," *NEJM* 303.25 (December 18, 1980): 1429–1435.

42 *Kehm v. Procter & Gamble*, 113–116.

43 Ibid., 116.

44 Shands, interview with author.

45 "Follow-up on Toxic-Shock Syndrome—United States," *MMWR* 29.25 (June 27, 1980): 297–299.

46 The June 27 *MMWR* report stated that there were no significant differences in terms of "marital status, parity, contraceptive methods used, frequency of

sexual intercourse, frequency of sexual intercourse during menstruation, brand of tampon or sanitary napkin used, absorbency or use of deodorized tampons." What was statistically significant was tampon use. "However, 50 of 50 cases with onset [of TSS] during menstruation (100%) used tampons as compared to 43 of 50 controls (85%) (p = .02 by McNemar test with continuity correction)." This meant that if forty-four of fifty had used tampons, there could be no conclusion drawn. But this slight difference was enough to link tampon use to TSS.

47 Kathryn Shands, "Toxic Shock Syndrome: A Lasting Legacy," *We Were There* lecture series, October, 19, 2017, Centers for Disease Control, Atlanta, GA.

48 "Follow-up on Toxic-Shock Syndrome," *MMWR* 29.37 (September 19, 1980): 441.

49 Ibid., 442.

50 Davis, "Investigation of TSS," 96.

51 Garrett, *Coming Plague*, 393–394; Tom Riley, *Price of a Life: One Woman's Life from Toxic Shock* (Bethesda, MD: Adler & Adler, 1986), 108–109. Riley counts ten to fifteen complaints per month in his assessment of the call log to P&G.

52 *Kehm v. Procter & Gamble*, 2196.

53 Ibid., 2196–2197.

54 "History of Vaccines," College of Physicians of Philadelphia, accessed October 22, 2014, http://www.historyofvaccines.org.

55 "Koch's Postulates," Wikipedia, accessed October 22, 2014, http://en.wikipedia.org.

56 *Kehm v. Procter & Gamble*, 2200.

57 Garrett, *Coming Plague*, 403–404.

58 *Kehm v. Procter & Gamble*, 1453–1456.

59 "Follow-up on Toxic-Shock Syndrome—United States" (June 27, 1980).

60 *Kehm v. Procter & Gamble*, 1454.

61 Riley, *Price of a Life*, 161.

62 "Toxic Shock Case Weighed by Court," *New York Times* (November 4, 1982).

63 *Kehm v. Procter & Gamble*, 2560.

64 Ibid., 2568.

65 Ibid., 2650–2652.

66 Thomas Laco to Edward Harness, September 11, 1980, Tom Riley Papers, personal possession (hereafter referred to as Tom Riley Papers).

67 TSS Microbiology memorandum, September 22, 1980, Tom Riley Papers.

68 Report prepared by Gordon Hassing, "Toxic Shock Syndrome and Tampon Usage," September 5, 1980, Tom Riley Papers. The contacts included two meetings at the CDC (on August 21 and August 27), and with numerous scientists including James Todd (pediatrician), Paul Iannini (Infectious Diseases, Danbury Community Hospital), Jim Davis (Wisconsin Department of Health and Social Services), Mike Osterholm (Minnesota Department of Health), Shirley Fannin (Los Angeles County Public Health Office), Frank Kapral (Ohio State University), and Patrick Schlievert (UCLA).

69 Marjorie Sun, "Lawyers Flush Out Toxic Shock Data," *Science* 224 (April 13, 1984): 132–134; Riley, *Price of a Life*, 106, 264.

70 Patrick Schlievert, Kathryn Shands, Bruce Dan, George Schmid, and Russell Nishimura, "Identification and Characterization of an Exotoxin from *Staphylococcus aureus* Associated with Toxic-Shock Syndrome," *Journal of Infectious Diseases* 143.4 (April 1981): 509–516.

71 *Kehm v. Procter & Gamble*, 1806; Sun, "Lawyers Flush Out Toxic Shock Data," 132.

72 Sun, "Lawyers Flush Out Toxic Shock Data," 132–134.

73 Merlin Bergdoll and P. Joan Chesney, eds. *Toxic Shock Syndrome* (Boca Raton, FL: CRC Press, 1991), 6.

74 Ibid., 1.

75 Susan Okie, "Tampons Only One Clue in Toxic-Shock Mystery," *Washington Post* (October 6, 1980).

CHAPTER 3. THE MEDIA SOUNDS THE ALARM

1 Sandy Rovner, "Toxic Shock: Fighting over Tampon Labels," *Washington Post* (August 1, 1989), Health, p. Z7.

2 Armand Lione and Jon Kapecki, "Testing Tampons in Rochester: Just What Can You Rely On?" *Rochester Patriot* (July 23–August 5, 1975).

3 "P&G to Remove Plastic in Controversial Tampon," *Rochester Patriot* (December 11, 1975–January 13, 1976).

4 M. C. to Procter & Gamble Consumer Services and Lillian Yin, August 26, 1979, Tom Riley Papers.

5 Rosenberg, "Fever, Signs of Shock, Puzzle Girl's Doctors."

6 *Kehm v. Procter & Gamble*, 483–484.

7 "Toxic-Shock Syndrome—United States," 229–230.

8 Okie, "'Toxic-Shock Syndrome' Disease Is Striking Young Women."

9 Shands, interview with author.

10 Etheridge, *Sentinel of Health*. Though Etheridge traces the story, her dates are incorrect. She linked the June 27 *MMWR* report to Kennedy's hearing, but it was the May 23 report instead. The congressional hearing occurred on June 6, 1980. "Toxic Shock Syndrome, 1980," Hearing before the Subcommittee on Health and Scientific Research of the Committee on Labor and Human Resources, U.S. Senate, 96th Congress, June 6, 1980.

11 "Toxic Shock Syndrome, 1980," Hearing, June 6, 1980, 1.

12 Ibid., 11.

13 Ibid., 7.

14 "Hazardous Waste," *CBS Evening News* (June 6, 1980), Vanderbilt Television News Archive, http://tvnews.vanderbilt.edu.

15 UPI, "Toxic-Shock Disease Probed," *Bangor Daily News* (June 7–8, 1980), 4; "New Disease Strikes Women, Report Claims," *Tuscaloosa News* (June 7–8, 1980); "New Mystery Disease Striking Women of Childbearing Age," *Indianapolis Star* (June 7, 1980); 7; Bayard Webster, "7 Are Dead of a Baffling, Newly Discovered Disease," *New York Times* (June 7, 1980), 6.

16 Julianne Cheek identifies ten categories to code newspaper headlines concerning TSS. These include shock (grab attention), discreditory (cast doubt), neutral (remain impartial), reassuring (restore confidence), bizarre (sensationalize), poignant (evoke emotion), informative (convey facts), warning (give notice of danger), speculative (raise questions), and legal (convey content about litigation related to TSS). See "(Con)textualizing Toxic Shock Syndrome: Selected Media Representations of the Emergence of a Health Phenomenon 1979–1995," *Health: An Interdisciplinary Journal for the Social Study of Health, Illness and Medicine* 1.2 (1997): 183–203; and *Postmodern and Poststructural Approaches to Nursing Research* (Thousand Oaks, CA: Sage Publications, 1999), 97–98.

17 "Follow-up on Toxic-Shock Syndrome—United States" (June 27, 1980), 297.

18 Susan Okie, "Mystery Disease in Women Tied to Tampon Use," *Washington Post* (June 28, 1980); "Tampons Are Linked to a Rare Disease," *New York Times* (June 28, 1980), 17.

19 *CBS Evening News*, interview with Kathryn Shands (June 27, 1980), Vanderbilt Television News Archive, http://tvnews.vanderbilt.edu.

20 "Tampon Firms Fear Publicity, Say Study on Toxic-Shock Doesn't Show Causal Link," *Wall Street Journal* (June 30, 1980).

21 Riley, *Price of a Life*, 53.

22 Wayne L. Pines, "Rely Tampons: Universal Media Coverage," in *Communicating in a Healthcare Crisis* (Falls Church, VA: FDA News, 2007), 156.

23 Nancy Buc, interview with author, April 10, 2011, Arlington, VA.

24 Pines, "Rely Tampons: Universal Media Coverage," 156.

25 Ibid.

26 Riley, *Price of a Life*, 54.

27 Buc, interview with author.

28 Jere Goyan, "The Rely Case," address delivered to the Health Industry Manufacturers Association, Washington, DC, October 2, 1980, Food and Drug Administration.

29 Buc, interview with author.

30 Ibid.

31 Patricia Roberts Harris, "The New Women at H.H.S.," letter to the editor, *New York Times* (November 25, 1980), p. A18.

32 Pines, "Rely Tampons: Universal Media Coverage," 158.

33 "Tampons," *ABC Evening News* (September 17, 1980), Vanderbilt Television News Archive, http://tvnews.vanderbilt.edu.

34 "Production of Tampons Halted Pending Review," *New York Times* (September 19, 1980), p. A17.

35 *Kehm v. Procter & Gamble*, 1604.

36 Ibid.

37 Riley, *Price of a Life*, 56–57.

38 Ibid., 57.

39 Michael T. Osterholm, *Deadliest Enemy: Our War against Killer Germs, the Fight We Cannot Afford to Lose* (New York: Little, Brown, 2017), chapter 3.

40 *Kehm v. Procter & Gamble*, 1605.

41 Pines, "Rely Tampons: Universal Media Coverage," 159; Steven Fink, *Crisis Management: Planning for the Inevitable* (New York: Amacom, 1986); Matt Haig, *Brand Failures: The Truth about the 100 Biggest Branding Mistakes of All Time* (London: Kogan Page, 2003).

42 Goyan, address, p. 4.

43 Buc, interview with author.

44 Ibid.

45 Ibid.

46 Ibid.

47 Jasanoff, *Risk Management*, 2.

48 Ibid., 5.

49 "Follow-up on Toxic-Shock Syndrome" (September 19, 1980).

50 Memo, Jere Goyan to the Secretary, "FDA-Procter & Gamble Consent Agreement on Rely—Information," October 1, 1980, Department of Health, Education and Welfare.

51 BLS Reports, "Women in the Labor Force: Databook" (December 2015), 13, https://www.bls.gov. The 1980s witnessed an expansion of demographics with both teenagers and men watching soap operas. There was also a slight decline in real-time viewership due to the growing popularity of VCRs, which allowed for shows to be recorded and watched at a later time, while skipping through commercials.

52 Goyan, "FDA-Procter & Gamble Consent Agreement," 4.

53 Ibid., 5–6.

54 Rely commercial, https://youtu.be/IpSUJUZpLAs, accessed April 16, 2016.

55 Pines, "Rely Tampons: Universal Media Coverage," 161.

56 Ibid., 162.

57 "Tampon Brand Tied to Shock Syndrome," *New York Times* (September 18, 1980).

58 Nadine Brozan, "Toxic Shock: New Theories Arise and Scientists Differ," *New York Times* (October 10, 1980).

59 "Rely Tampons Taken off Market," *Boston Globe* (September 9, 1980).

60 Rosalie Rayburn, "Peaceful Warrior: Retired PR Pro, '60s Protester Now Champions Veterans' Causes," *Albuquerque Journal* (October 2, 2016).

61 James Todd, "Toxic Shock Syndrome, Scientific Uncertainty and the Public Media," *Pediatrics* 67.6 (June 1981): 921–923.

62 Tom Brokaw, *Boom! Voices of the Sixties* (New York: Random House, 2007), 248; *Larry King Live*, interview with Tom Brokaw (November 8, 2002), http://transcripts.cnn.com.

63 Art Athens, *Check It Out! Great Reporters on What It Takes to Tell the Story* (New York: Fordam University Press, 2004), 38.

64 "Tampons," *NBC Evening News* (September 27, 1980), Vanderbilt Television News Archive.

65 Rebecca Ginsburg, "'Don't Tell, Dear': The Material Culture of Tampons and Napkins," *Journal of Material Culture* 1.3 (1996): 366–375. Ginsberg explains the contours of "menstrual etiquette."

66 Joyce Leviton, "Federal Disease Detectives Close in on the Killer Known as Toxic Shock Syndrome," *People Weekly* 14.17 (October 27, 1980): 39.

67 Shands, interview with author.

68 Leviton, "Federal Disease Detectives," 39. On television appearances, see "Toxic Shock Syndrome," *CBS Evening News* (October 6, 1980); "Toxic Shock Syndrome," *ABC Evening News* (October 10, 1980); "Toxic Shock Syndrome," *CBS Evening News* (October 11, 1980), all at the Vanderbilt Television News Archive.

69 Okie, "Toxic-Shock Syndrome Cases Show Decline."

70 "Complaints Fuel Debate over Research into Tampons," *Chicago Tribune* (May 4, 1981).

71 Ibid.

72 Ibid.

73 "Disease Linked to Tampons Is Still Elusive," *New York Times* (August 30, 1980), 14.

74 "Toxic Shock Syndrome Survey," online responses collected via Survey Monkey from February 21, 2012, to February 21, 2013.

75 Chris, interview with author, December 1, 2009, Urbana, IL.

76 Sean McCormally, "Government Moves to Put Warning Labels on All Tampons," UPI (September 26, 1980), http://www.upi.com.

77 Nan Robertson, "Toxic Shock," *New York Times Magazine* (September 19, 1982). She also reflects on this in a C-SPAN interview, Nan Robertson, 0:24:35, http://www.c-span.org.

78 Roger Wolmuth, "After Surviving Toxic Shock, Journalist Nan Robertson Takes a Firm Grip on Life," *People* 18.24 (December 13, 1982).

79 Walter Annenberg to Howard Rusk, September 24, 1982, Nan Robertson Papers at the Arthur and Elizabeth Schlesinger Library (hereafter referred to as Robertson Papers), Box 7, Folder 2.

80 "Betty" to Nan Robertson, October 15, Robertson Papers, Box 7, Folder 2.

81 Nan Robertson to "Betty," October 20, 1982, Robertson Papers, Box 7, Folder 2.

82 Esther Rome to Nan Robertson, Robertson Papers, Box 7, Folder 6.

83 Rovner, "Toxic Shock: Fighting over Tampon Labels."

84 Okie, "Toxic-Shock Syndrome Cases Show Decline."

85 Eleanor Johnson Tracy et al., "Back to the Old; Tampax after Toxic Shock," *Fortune* (March 23, 1981): 21.

86 Cynthia Bendoraitis, "Tampon Regulation Remains Lax Despite Rely Controversy," *Chicago Tribune* (May 5, 1981).

87 Michael T. Osterholm and Jan C. Forfang, "Toxic-Shock Syndrome in Minnesota: Results of an Active-Passive Surveillance System," *Journal of Infectious Diseases* 145.4 (April 1982): 458–464.

88 Mike Osterholm, interview with author, April 28, 2016, Minneapolis, MN.

89 Osterholm et al., "Tri-State Toxic-Shock Syndrome Study"; Osterholm and Forfang, "Toxic-Shock Syndrome in Minnesota."

90 Press release, HHS News, October 20, 1980, Health and Human Services. For a discussion of the technical and legal elements of the emerging policy, see Jamie Kohen, "The History of the Regulation of Menstrual Tampons," LEDA at Harvard Law School (April 6, 2001), https://dash.harvard.edu.

91 Okie, "Toxic-Shock Syndrome Cases Show Decline."

92 UPI, "U.S. Sets New Rules for Warning Labels on Tampon Boxes," *New York Times* (June 22, 1982).

93 U.S. Congress, House Committee on Energy and Commerce, FDA Oversight: Medical Devices, Hearings before the Subcommittee on Oversight and Investigations, July 16, 1982, serial no. 97-144 (Washington, DC: U.S. G.P.O., 1982), 11–13.

94 Ibid., 141.

95 Michael deCourcy Hinds, "Panel Debates Tampon Labels," *New York Times* (July 24, 1982); Medical Devices Hearings.

96 Medical Devices Hearings, 124.

97 Wayne Pines, *Communicating in a Healthcare Crisis* (Falls Church, VA: FDA News, 2007), vii.

98 Goyan, "FDA-Procter & Gamble Consent Agreement."

99 Pines, "Rely Tampons: Universal Media Coverage," 161.

100 Rob Daumeyer, "P&G's Bob McDonald Tells a Story about Integrity and Trust," *Cincinnati Business Courier* (February 8, 2013).

101 Hinds, "Panel Debates Tampon Labels."

102 Dean Rotbart, "State of Alarm: Tampon Industry Is in Throes of Change after Toxic Shock," *Wall Street Journal* (February 26, 1981).

103 Okie, "Toxic-Shock Syndrome Cases Show Decline."

104 Adele Clarke, "From the Rise of Medicine to Biomedicalization: U.S. Healthscapes and Iconography, Circa 1890–Present," in Adele E. Clarke, Janet K. Shim, Laura Mamo, Jennifer Ruth Fosket, and Jennifer R. Fishman, eds., *Biomedicalization: Technoscience, Health, and Illness in the U.S.* (Durham, NC: Duke University Press, 2009), 104–146 (quoted on p. 105).

105 Ibid., 131.

106 "Disease Calls an Industry into Question," *New York Times* (November 16, 1980).

107 Gary L. Kreps, Ellen W. Bonaguro, and Jim L. Query Jr., "The History and Development of the Field of Health Communication," in L. D. Jackson and B. K. Duffy, eds., *Health Communication Research: Guide to Developments and Directions* (Westport, CT: Greenwood Press, 1998), 1–15.

108 Marcia Angell, *Science on Trial: The Clash of Medical Evidence and the Law in the Breast Implant Case* (New York: W. W. Norton 1997), 170.

109 Denise Grady, "A Shocking Diagnosis: Breast Implants 'Gave Me Cancer,'" *New York Times* (May 14, 2017).

CHAPTER 4. GROUNDS FOR LIABILITY

1 "A Verdict on Tampons," *Time* 119.13 (March 29, 1982): 75; Okie, "Toxic-Shock Syndrome Cases Show Decline."

2 William Gruber, "After 8 Years, Procter Still Not Free of the Rely Controversy," *Chicago Tribune* (March 27, 1989); "Procter & Gamble Settles a Toxic Shock Suit," *New York Times* (August 25, 1982).

3 Paul Hutchinson, "Jurors Deliberated 1 Hours [*sic*] Tuesday and Retired without a Verdict," UPI (March 16, 1982), http://www.upi.com.

4 "Procter & Gamble Settles a Toxic Shock Suit"; "Verdict on Tampons," 75.

5 Hutchinson, "Jurors Deliberated."

6 "Firm Negligent in Toxic Shock Syndrome Case," *Chicago Tribune* (March 20, 1982).

7 I, too, purchased a package from their law firm called "A Lawyer's Handbook on Toxic Shock Syndrome, 1981," and "A Lawyer's Supplemental Handbook on Toxic Shock Syndrome, 1982."

8 Riley, *Price of a Life*.

9 Ibid., 18–19.

10 Gordon Hassing to Lillian Yin, August 1, 1980, Tom Riley Papers; Owen Carter, File Memorandum, "Telephone Call Report, Dr. Lillian Yin—FDA," August 1, 1980, Tom Riley Papers.

11 *Kehm v. Procter & Gamble*, 38.

12 Ibid., 38–39.

13 Ibid., 50.

14 Ibid., 2027. The ensuing discussion is a great example of a technology in flux. The Court: "Will it play on Betamax?" Mr. Calder: "I don't know. I'll have to ask my expert."

15 Ibid., 120.

16 Ibid., 43.

17 Walter Schlech, Kathryn Shands, Arthur Reingold, Bruce Dan, George Schmid, Nancy Hargrett, Allen Hightower, Loreen Herwaldt, Marguerite Neill, Jeffrey Band, and John Bennett, "Risk Factors for Development of Toxic Shock Syndrome Association with a Tampon Brand," *JAMA* 248.7 (1982): 835–839; Kathryn N. Shands, George P. Schmid, Bruce B. Dan, Deborah Blum, Richard J. Guidotti, Nancy T. Hargrett, Roger L. Anderson, Dianne L. Hill, Claire V. Broome, Jeffrey D. Band, and David W. Fraser, "Toxic-Shock Syndrome in Menstruating Women—Association with Tampon Use and *Staphylococcus aureus* and Clinical Features in 52 Cases," *NEJM* 303 (December 18, 1980): 1436–1442.

18 *Kehm v. Procter & Gamble*, 125.

19 Ibid., 127.

20 Sheila Jasanoff, "Expert Games in Silicone Gel Breast Implant Litigation," in Michael Freeman and Helen Reece, eds., *Science in Court* (Dartmouth: Ashgate, 1998), 85.

21 *Kehm v. Procter & Gamble*, 117–118.

22 Alvan Feinstein, Wikipedia, accessed July 15, 2017, https://en.wikipedia.org/wiki/Alvan_Feinstein.

23 Mary Harvey, Ralph Horwitz, and Alvan Feinstein, "Toxic Shock and Tampons: Evaluations of the Epidemiologic Evidence," *JAMA* 248.7 (August 20, 1982): 840–846. See also Alvan Feinstein, "Scientific Standards in Epidemiologic Studies of the Menace of Daily Life," *Science* 242.4883 (December 2, 1988): 1257–1263.

24 Harvey et al., "Toxic Shock and Tampons," 846.

25 Riley, *Price of a Life*, 75–76.

26 *Kehm v. Procter & Gamble*, 2077.

27 Shands, interview with author.

28 CDC Study #2, September 16, 1980, Tom Riley Papers.

29 Riley, *Price of a Life*, 76.

30 *Kehm v. Procter & Gamble*, 862–866.

31 Riley, *Price of a Life*, 85.

32 Ibid., 86.

33 *Kehm v. Procter & Gamble*, 873.

34 Ibid., 879.

35 Ibid., 905.

36 Ibid., 883–884.

37 Ibid., 848.

38 Philip Tierno, "Cellulase Activity of Microorganism on Carboxymethylcellulose from Tampons," *The Lancet* 2.8249 (October 3, 1981): 746–747; Philip Tierno, Bruce Hanna, and Megan Davies, "Growth of Toxic-Shock-Syndrome Strain of Staphylococcus Aureus after Enzymic Degradation of 'Rely' Tampon Component," *The Lancet* 321.8325 (March 19, 1983): 615–618.

39 *Kehm v. Procter & Gamble*, 949.

40 Ibid., 940–941.

41 Ibid., 950–951.

42 Ibid., 923.

43 Michael Sierks and Peter Reilly, "Application of Cross-Linked Carboxymethyl Cellulose Degradation by Beta-glucosidase and Vaginal Microbes to Toxic Shock Syndrome," *Applied Environmental Microbiology* 50.3 (September 1985): 634–637.

44 Riley, *Price of a Life*, 220; *Kehm v. Procter & Gamble*, 2495, 2500.

45 *Kehm v. Procter & Gamble*, 2397–2399.

46 Ibid., 1077–1078. This instance of "not feeling too good" may have been a milder form of TSS. By the time it recurred again in September, it was far more virulent and deadly.

47 *Kehm v. Procter & Gamble*, 1120.

48 Ibid., 1441.

49 Ibid., 784.

50 Ibid., 786.

51 Ibid., 816.

52 Ibid., 642.

53 Harry Collins and Trevor Pinch, *The Golem at Large: What You Should Know about Technology* (Cambridge: Cambridge University Press, 2002), 2.

54 *Kehm v. Procter & Gamble*, 2457–2458.

55 Ibid., 2457.

56 Ibid., 2455–2456.

57 Ibid., 2259.

58 Ibid., 2261–2262.

59 Ibid., 1348–1350.

60 There are numerous examples of attempts to control women's bodies and their health, from delimiting knowledge of midwives and controlling gynecology; to restricting access to healthcare, birth control and abortion; to dismissing illnesses and minimizing side effects of pharmaceuticals.

61 *Kehm v. Procter & Gamble*, 2390–2391.

62 Ibid., 2193, 2215.

63 Simon A. Cole and Rachel Dioso-Villa, "Investigating the 'CSI Effect': Media and Litigation Crisis in Criminal Law," *Stanford Law Review* 61.6 (April 2009): 1335–1373 (quoted on p. 1373).

64 Jasanoff, "Expert Games," 85; Simon Cole, *Suspect Identities: A History of Fingerprinting and Criminal Identification* (Cambridge, MA: Harvard University Press, 2002).

65 Jasanoff, "Expert Games," 99.

66 Riley, *Price of a Life*, 248, 250–252.

67 Tom Riley, interview with author, January 10, 2007, Cedar Rapids, IA.

CHAPTER 5. HEALTH ACTIVISM AND THE LIMITS OF LABELING

1 There is a growing body of literature concerning standards and the role of science in their legitimization. Xaq Frohlich outlines the functions of standard setting as measurement, interoperability, performance, product safety, coordination of the marketplace, and gatekeeping. See Xaq Frohlich, "An Age of Standards: The Rise of the FDA's Food 'Standards of Identity' System, 1930s–50s," paper delivered at the Society for the History of Technology annual meeting, Philadelphia, PA (October 26–29, 2017); Sarah Vogel, *Is It Safe? BPA and the Struggle to Define the Safety of Chemicals* (Berkeley: University of California Press, 2012); JoAnne Yates and Craig Murphy, "The Role of Firms in Industrial Standards Setting: Participation, Process, and Balance," accessed October 29, 2017, http://mitsloan.mit.edu.

2 G. W. Rapp, Professor of Biochemistry and Physiology, Loyola "A Comparison of the Absorptive Efficiency of Commercial Catamenial Tampons" (n.d.), Boston Women's Health Book Collective Collection at the Arthur and Elizabeth Schlesinger Library (hereafter referred to as BWHBC), Box 29, Folder 2.

3 Pursettes advertisement, "No Bulky Applicator—Prelubricated Tip," *Ebony* 13.9 (July 1963): 44.

4 Ibid.

5 Adele E. Clarke and Joan H. Fujimura, "What Tools? Which Jobs? Why Right?," in Adele E. Clarke and Joan H. Fujimura, eds., *The Right Tools for the Job: At Work in Twentieth-Century Life Sciences* (Princeton, NJ: Princeton University Press, 1992), 3–44.

6 Sharra Vostral, "Toxic Shock Syndrome, Tampon Absorbency, and Feminist Science," *Catalyst: Feminism, Theory, Technoscience* 3.1 (2017): 1–30, doi:http://dx.doi.org/10.28968/cftt.v3i1.127.

7 Jerry Della Femina, *From Those Wonderful Folks Who Gave You Pearl Harbor: Front-Line Dispatches from the Advertising War* (New York: Simon and Schuster, 2010), 84.

8 Gordon Hassing to Don Marlowe, Bureau of Medical Devices, February 9, 1981, BWHBC, Box 29, Folder 2.

9 Ibid.

10 "Finished Product—Physical," Procter & Gamble (n.d.), BWHBC, Box 29, Folder 2.

11 Ibid.

12 "Historical Perspectives Reduced Incidence of Menstrual Toxic-Shock Syndrome—United States, 1980–1990," *MMWR* 39.25 (June 29, 1990): 421–423.

13 D. E. Marlowe, R. M. Weigle, and R. S. Stauffenberg, "Measurement of Tampon Absorbency Test Method Evaluation" (May 1981), BWHBC, Box 29, Folder 2.

14 Ibid., 1.

15 Ibid.

16 Ibid., 11–12.

17 An oral history of the Tampon Task Force is available in Vostral, "Toxic Shock Syndrome, Tampon Absorbency, and Feminist Science."

18 F. Alan Anderson to Patrick G. Laing, July 13, 1981, BWHBC, Box 29, Folder 2.

19 Ibid.

20 Wayne Ellis to Alan Anderson, January 22, 1982, BWHBC, Box 29, Folder 2.

21 Becky LeBuhn, email correspondence, 2017.

22 BWHBC, Coalition for the Medical Rights for Women, Empire State Consumer Association, National Consumers League, National Women's Health Network, and Woman Health International to Mark Novitch, Acting Commissioner FDA, April 16, 1984, BWHBC, Box 29, Folder 2.

23 David Swankin, interview with author, February 24, 2016, Washington, DC.

24 Esther Rome and Jill Wolhandler, "Regulation of Tampon Safety," in Alice Dan and Jan Lewis, eds., *Menstrual Health in Women's Lives* (Urbana: University of Illinois Press, 1992), 263.

25 Anderson to Laing, July 13, 1981.

26 Rome and Wolhandler, "Regulation of Tampon Safety," 270.

27 Larry Kobren, "Standard for Performance Characteristics of Menstrual Tampons," working document, September 24, 1981, BWHBC, Box 29, Folder 2.

28 Elayne Clift to Lillian Yin, June 8, 1981, National Women's Health Network, BWHBC, Box 29, Folder 2.

29 Memo recorded by Philip White, "Tampon Manufacturers/NCDRH Meeting to Discuss Progress of ASTM Tampon Standard," March 28, 1982, BWHBC, Box 29, Folder 2.

30 Consumer Representatives on the ASTM Tampon Task Force to Commissioner Arthur Hull Hayes Jr., January 20, 1983, BWHBC, Box 29, Folder 7.

31 Memo, "Consumer Members of Tampon Task Force," October 1, 1983, BWHBC, Box 29, Folder 2.

32 Ibid.

33 Memo, "Tampon Manufacturers/NCDRH Meeting."

34 Though the science was initially "undone," in this case the advocates' science was dismissed. See David Hess, "Undone Science, Industrial Innovation, and Social Movements," in Matthias Gross and Linsey McGoey, eds., *The Routledge International Handbook of Ignorance Studies* (New York: Routledge), 141–154.

35 Rome and Wolhandler, "Regulation of Tampon Safety," 270.

36 Nancy Reame, interview with author, April 6, 2016, New York City.

37 Nancy Reame, email correspondence with the author (January 30, 2017, and February 10, 2017).

38 Nancy Reame to David Swankin, May 23, 1983, BWHBC, Box 34, Folder 1.

39 Ibid.

40 Nancy Reame to Ray Sansone, ASTM Staff Manager/F4, March 20, 1985, BWHBC, Box 34, Folder 5. Later, this discrepancy fell under the term "precision," in which the variability increased with absorbency. Thus the test was less precise with higher absorbency tampons. See Emil Jebe to A. J. Houtteman, Director of Regulatory Affairs Personal Products, May 2, 1985, BWHBC, Box 34, Folder 5.

41 Esther Rome, Jill Wolhandler and Nancy Reame, "The Absorbency of Tampons," *JAMA* 259.5 (February 5, 1988): 686.

42 Consumer Coalition to Mark Novitch, April 16, 1984, BWHBC, Box 29, Folder 2.

43 Ibid.

44 Ibid.

45 Rome and Jill Wolhandler, "Regulation of Tampon Safety," 265.

46 David Swankin to Frank E. Young, November 16, 1984, BWHBC, Box 29, Folder 2.

47 David Swankin to Alan Anderson, May 31, 1985, BWHBC, Box 29, Folder 2.

48 M. Louis Arin, "Determination of the Fluid Capacity of Some Commercial Catamenial Tampons" n.p., n.d., BWHBC, Box 29, Folder 2.

49 Nancy E. Reame to John C. Villforth, March 20, 1985, BWBHC, Box 29, Folder 2.

50 John C. Villforth to Nancy E. Reame, April 25, 1985, BWHBC, Box 29, Folder 2.

51 Bendoraitis, "Tampon Regulation Remains Lax."

52 Rome and Wolhandler, "Regulation of Tampon Safety," 263.

53 Esther Rome to Kathi Anderson, January 14, 1985, BWBHC, Box 29, Folder 2.

54 Rome and Wolhandler, "Regulation of Tampon Safety," 266.

55 Ted Kennedy to Esther Rome, January 31, 1985, BWBHC, Box 29, Folder 2.

56 Public Citizen Press Release, "FDA Sued for Failing to Require Tampon Absorbency Labels," June 1, 1988, BWHBC, Box 33, Folder 11.

57 *Public Citizen Health Research Group and Public Citizen v. Frank E. Young (FDA), Otis R. Bowen (HHS), and James C. Miller, III (OMB)*, U.S. District Court for the District of Columbia, lawsuit, June 1, 1988, BWHBC, Box 33, Folder 11.

58 Ibid., 4.

59 Rome and Wolhandler, "Regulation of Tampon Safety," 267.

60 Docket no. 86-N-0479, Comments of Playtex Family Products, Inc. ("Playtex") to FDA's proposed rule for tampon absorbency labeling (published September 23, 1988, in the Federal Register), p. 4, BWHBC, Box 33, Folder 11.

61 Rome and Wolhandler, "Regulation of Tampon Safety," 267; Rovner, "Toxic Shock: Fighting over Tampon Labels."

62 Steven Fellman, phone interview with author, July 12, 2016.

63 Steven Fellman to Esther Rome, August 4, 1989, BWHBC, Box 32, Folder 2.

64 Esther Rome to Commissioner Young (draft), July 12, 1989, BWHBC, Box 32, Folder 2. In her essay "Regulation of Tampon Safety" (August 7, 1989), Rome lists the signed supporters as the BWHBC, National Women's Health Network, Consumer Federation of America, National Consumers League, Public Voice, Tambrands, Inc., Kimberly-Clark, Corp., and Sentinel Consumer Products, Inc.

65 Rome and Wolhandler, "Regulation of Tampon Safety," 268; Federal Register, Rules and Regulations, "Medical Devices; Labeling for Menstrual Tampons; Ranges of Absorbency," 54.206 (October 26, 1989), 43766-43775, BWHBC, Box 32, Folder 1.

66 There were many iterations of this scale, with Steve Fellman corresponding with Esther Rome on behalf of the other manufacturers throughout the summer of 1989, resulting in draft letters to Commissioner Frank Young. See Esther Rome to Commissioner Young (draft), July 12, 1989. See also the final Federal Register, "Medical Devices; Labeling for Menstrual Tampons; Ranges of Absorbency," 54.206 (October 26, 1989), specifically 801.430 user labeling, p. 43771.

67 "Historical Perspectives Reduced Incidence of Menstrual Toxic-Shock Syndrome"; Dixie Farley, "Preventing TSS: New Tampon Labeling Lets Women Compare Absorbencies," in *Current Issues in Women's Health: An FDA Consumer Special Report* (November 1991): 20–24.

68 Rome and Wolhandler, "Regulation of Tampon Safety," 270.

69 Jain, *Injury*, 33.

70 *Rinehart v. International Playtex*, U.S. District Court, Southern District of Indiana, Indianapolis Division, July 18, 1988.

71 Roger W. Shuy, *Fighting over Words: Language and Civil Law Cases* (Oxford: Oxford University Press, 2008), 111.

72 Ibid., 114–115.

73 Joan Fujimura, "Crafting Science: Standardized Packages, Boundary Objects, and 'Translation,'" in Andrew Pickering, ed., *Science as Practice and Culture* (Chicago: University of Chicago Press, 1992), 168–211.

74 Clarke and Fujimura, *Right Tools*.

CONCLUSION
1 Emma Gray, "The Removal of Rupi Kaur's Instagram Photos Shows How Terrified We Are of Periods," *Huffington Post*, March 27, 2015.
2 Alli Maloney, "Kiran Gandhi Discusses Free-Bleeding While Running the London Marathon, and Using the Period as Protest," August 11, 2015, http://nytlive .nytimes.com.
3 Emily Feng, "Uninhibited Chinese Swimmer, Discussing Her Period, Shatters Another Barrier," *New York Times*, August 16, 2016.
4 Email, SMCR to SMCR member email list, September 29, 2015.
5 On the "technological fix," see Lisa Rosner, *The Technological Fix: How People Use Technology to Create and Solve Problems* (New York: Routledge, 2004).
6 "My.Flow," accessed May 20, 2016, http://www.trackmyflow.com; Arwa Mahdawi, "The Connected Vagina: Monitor How Full Your Tampon Is—with a New App," *Guardian,* May 17, 2016.
7 "Bruce Dan, Who Helped Link Toxic Shock and Tampons, Is Dead at 64," *New York Times,* September 10, 2011.
8 Sam H. Au, Paresh Kumar, and Aaron R. Wheeler, "A New Angle on Pluronic Additives: Advancing Droplets and Understanding in Digital Microfluidics," *Langmuir* 27.13 (2011): 8586–8594.
9 Sam H. Au, email correspondence, May 2–3, 2016.
10 Patrick M. Schlievert, James R. Deringer, Michael H. Kim, Steven J. Projan, and Richard P. Novick, "Effect of Glycerol Monolaurate on Bacterial Growth and Toxin Production," *Antimicrobial Agents and Chemotherapy* 36.3 (March 1992): 626–631; Schlievert, "Comparison of Cotton and Cotton/Rayon Tampons," 1112–1114; Schlievert, "Effect of Merocel Vaginal Sponge."
11 M. Melish, S. Murata, C. Fukunage, K. Frogner, L. Matsuda, and D. Cole, "The Effect of a Surfactant Pluronic L92 (PL92), on TSST-1 Production in Model Toxic Shock Syndrome (TSS)," *Abstracts of the General Meeting of the American Society for Microbiology* 92 (1992): 67.
12 Pat Schlievert, email correspondence, May 31, 2016.
13 Shands, "Toxic Shock Syndrome: A Lasting Legacy."
14 Nancy Buc, email correspondence, October 21, 2017.
15 "Moderne Women Menstrual Tampon, USA, 1930s"; "*Fax* Menstrual Tampon, Chicago, U.S.A., Probably Early 1930s"; "Nunap Menstrual Tampon, U.S.A., Early 1930s," all at the Museum of Menstruation, www.mum.org; Harry Finley, email correspondence, October 28, 2017.
16 Code of Federal Regulations, Sec. 801.430 User Labeling for Menstrual Tampons, April 1, 2017, https://www.accessdata.fda.gov.
17 "Toxic Shock: Screening Too Costly?" *Journal of Commerce* (November 10, 1986): 12A.
18 Rana A. Hajjeh, Arthur L. Reingold, Alexis Weil, Kathleen Shutt, Anne Schuchat, and Bradley A. Perkins, "Toxic Shock Syndrome in the United States: Surveillance

Update, 1979–1996," *Emerging Infectious Diseases* 5.6 (December 1999); Code of Federal Regulations, April 1, 2017.

19 Schlievert, email correspondence, May 31, 2016.

20 Jeffrey Parsonnet et al., "Persistence Survey of Toxic Shock Syndrome Toxin-1 Producing Staphylococcus aureus and Serum Antibodies to This Superantigen in Five Groups of Menstruating Women," *BMC Infectious Diseases* 10:249 (August 23, 2010), doi: 10.1186/1471-2334-10-249.

21 Jeffrey Parsonnet, phone interview with author, June 14, 2016.

22 Marnie L. Peterson, "A Long Road to a Preventative for Toxic Shock Syndrome," *Lancet Infectious Disease* (June 10, 2016), http://dx.doi.org/10.1016/S1473-3099(16)30163-3.

23 Rob Stein, "Missing Microbes Provide Clues about Asthma Risk," NPR Shots, September 30, 2015, http://www.npr.org; Jennifer Brown, "Bacteria May Cause Type 2 Diabetes: Findings Suggest Anti-Bacterial Therapy or Vaccines May Be Able to Prevent or Treat Type 2 Diabetes," *Iowa Now* (June 1, 2015).

24 Ravi Manthra, "All about Bacteria," TEDxCoimbatore, accessed June 6, 2015, http://amara.org; "No *E. coli* in India, Thanks to Cow Dung," June 14, 2011, http://agrariancrisis.in.

25 Julia Scott, "My No-Soap, No-Shampoo, Bacteria-Rich Hygiene Experiment," *New York Times Magazine* (May 22, 2014).

26 Roderick MacPhee, Wayne L. Miller, Greg Gloor, John K. McCormick, Jeremy Burton, and Gregor Reid, "Influence of Vaginal Microbiota on Toxic Shock Syndrome Toxin-1 Production by *Staphylococcus aureus*," *Applied and Environmental Microbiology* 79.6 (March 2013): 1835–1842; Ed Yong, "A Grand Unified Theory of Unhealthy Microbiomes: The Anna Karenina Hypothesis Says That Every Unbalanced Microbiome Is Unbalanced in Its Own Way," *The Atlantic*, August 25, 2017, https://www.theatlantic.com.

27 Grady, "Shocking Diagnosis."

INDEX

absorbency of tampons: approval of final ruling, 165, 169; dual-labeling proposal, 162–63; lack of standards, 13, 139, 146–47; manufacturer changes after Rely withdrawal, 108; materials for, 24, 25; methods of measurement, 142–43; numerical rating proposal, 159–160, 162; relationship to TSS, 14; syngyna test fluid experiments, 156–57; warnings to use least absorbent tampon needed, 13, 16, 138, 146, 157, 169, 174. *See also* standards for tampon performance; syngyna test

Acdisol, 122

activism. *See* health activism

actor-network theory, 33, 196n41

advertising of tampons. *See* marketing of tampons

age, as factor in toxic shock syndrome, 15

agency: of bacteria, 33–39; technological, 33, 38, 47

agnotology, 43

A. H. Robins Company, 29, 30

Allegheny College, 97–98

Altman, Lawrence, 65

American Society for Testing and Materials. *See* ASTM

Am I That Name? (Riley), 18

Anderson, Alan, 150–51, 158

Angell, Marcia, 110

animal studies: CDC TSS study, 65; Rely tampon product testing, 130, 131–32

Annenberg, Walter, 99

antibiologism, 17

antibiotic treatment: scarlet fever, 65; TSS, 4, 99

antibodies to the TSS toxin, 16–17, 178–79

Arin, M. Louis, 159

ASTM (American Society for Testing and Materials): overview, 150; Tampon Task Force meetings, 151, 152, 154–56, 158, 159

Atkins, Bobby, 24

Au, Sam H., 175, 188

bacteria: agential power of, 33–39; effects on CMC, 121–23; interaction with the human body, 34–35, 37, 180–81; lack of liability of, 43; as users of technology, 38, 171, 182. See also *Staphylococcus aureus*

bacterio-technological relationships. *See* techno-bacteriological relationships

Barad, Karen, 34

BASF, 25, 174

Bashaw, Robert, 24

Bennett, Jane, 33, 47

Bennett, John, 64

Bergdoll, Merlin, 74–75

Bernstein, Joan Z. (Jodie), 85–86, 188

beta-glucosidase, 122–23, 124, 125

beta-lactamase-resistant antibiotics, 99

Betty (letter-writer), 99–100

bias, in scientific studies, 118, 119–120

biocatalytic technology: delay in recognition of, 48; development of term, 10, 37–39; lack of attention to effects of, 181–82; TSS as harbinger of future problems, 171, 182

biomedicalization, 108–9

GRID (gay-related immunodeficiency disease), as term, 57
Gruenenthal Group, 29
Gupta, Sanjay, 42

Haas, Earle Cleveland, 114
Haley, Stephanie, 80–81
Halsey, Neil, 64
Hanna, Bruce, 123
Harness, Edward, 72–73, 87, 93
Harper, Billy, 24
Harris, Patricia, 85–86
Harrison, Leo, 178
Harvey, Mary, 119
Hassing, Gordon, 71, 87, 144–45
Hayes, Arthur, 105–6, 153
headlines from early reports, 109, 203n16
health activism, 138–169; changing hospital admission procedures, 99; consumer group advocacy, 160–65; establishment of standardized labeling, 165; limits of labeling, 166–69; overview, 138–140; P&G modifications of syngyna test, 144–46, 147, 149; push for labeling, 99, 100, 157–160; shortcomings of syngyna test, 155–57; syngyna test development, 140–44, 146–49; Tampon Task Force, 139–140, 150–55. See also feminism and feminist health advocacy
healthscapes concept, 108–9
Helmreich, Stefan, 35–36
heparinized blood, for syngyna test, 155, 156–57
Hess, David, 156, 211n34
HIV/AIDS, challenges in identification of, 56–58
Homo microbis, as term, 35, 36
Horwitz, Ralph, 119
human body: feminist scholarship on, 17–18, 37; interaction with bacteria, 34–36, 180–81; need for understanding of, 171
Human Microbiome Project, 34

Imboden, Linda, 96
implantable cardioverter defibrillators (ICDs), 33
inattentional blindness, 43
indirect harm concept, 42, 45
inertness assumption about tampons: biocatalytic nature of injury, 42; faultiness of, 12–13; interactive nature vs., 10; prevailing notion of, 2; shortcomings of Medical Devices Amendment, 33; Tierno, Philip research, 121–24
injury. See gendered injury; risk and injury
in situ absorptive capacity measurement method, 142
Institute of Medicine, 8
institutional advocacy, 62–68
International Playtex, Inc., 25, 75, 167. See also Playtex Family Products
intrauterine devices (IUDs), 29–30
invisible gorilla perception studies, 42–43

Jackson, William, 65
Jacobs, John, 128–29
Jain, S. Lochlann, 41, 42, 166, 168
Jasanoff, Sheila, 89, 117–18, 135–36
Johnson, Russel L., 24
Johnson & Johnson, 23, 107, 152, 164
Jones, Colleen, 127
Journal of Infectious Diseases, 101
Journal of the American Medical Association, 119, 157
junior absorbency tampons, 164

Kapral, Frank, 59
Kaufman, Stephen, 121, 188
Kaur, Rupi, 172
Kehm, Michael, 113, 114–15, 128, 136
Kehm, Patricia: death of, 12, 111, 113, 136; trial discussion of menstrual cycle and use of Rely, 127–28

mutual bacterial-organism relationships, 35
My Flow monitor, 173

Nalbone, Angela, 96
naming, of the other, 36–37
nanotechnology, unexpected consequences of, 39
narratives: epidemiological, 57–58; origin stories, 58–62; shaping of TSS story, 109. *See also* technological progress narrative
Nash, Linda, 35
National Consumers League (NCL), 151, 152
National Institutes of Health (NIH), 34
National Women's Health Network, 152
NBC, 94
networks: importance in disseminating information, 11; role in identification of illness, 58–59; role in identification of TSS, 60–62
New Blood: Third-Wave Feminism and the Politics of Menstruation (Bobel), 18
New York Times (newspaper), 82, 86, 96
New York Times Magazine, 98
nonmenstruant, as term, 18
non-users of technologies, types of, 38
Norsigian, Judy, 100, 188
Novick, Richard, 178
Novitch, Mark, 157

Office of Management and Budget (OMB), 104, 105, 110, 163, 165
Okie, Susan, 80
Ong, Aihwa, 33
O'Reilly, Jim, 89
Oreskes, Naomi, 74
origin story of TSS, 58–62
Osterholm, Michael (Mike): case definition of TSS, 64; Chicago meeting participation, 87; oral history interview, 188; retrospective study, 101–2; TSS studies, 14, 177

the other: bacteria as, 36–37; HIV/AIDS affecting, 58
Oudshoorn, Nelly, 33
Our Bodies, Ourselves, 30, 139, 151, 164
outbreak narratives, 57–58
outbreaks, steps in identification of, 53–54
overmatching, 67, 68
oxygenation conditions, 14, 15, 16

pacemakers, 33
Paperwork Reduction Act, 163
Parsonnet, Jeffrey, 178–79, 188
patents on tampons, 23–25, 26
patient confidentiality concerns, 71, 72
Paxson, Heather, 35
peeling skin symptoms, 6, 7
pelvic inflammatory disease, from the Dalkon Shield, 30
Pendergrast, Mark, 53
Pennsylvania Department of Health, 56
perchlorates, regulation of, 42
Personal Products Corporation, 23, 75
Petroski, Henry, 40
pH of the vagina, 15, 16
the pill, feminist health advocacy for, 31
Pinch, Trevor, 129
Pines, Wayne, 84, 88, 89, 92–93
Pinkerson, JoAnn, 15
Playtex Family Products: labeling concerns, 162–63; lawsuits against, 111, 167–68; Tampon Task Force involvement, 152. *See also* International Playtex, Inc.
Pluronic L-92 lubricant, 25, 174–76, 194–95n21
polyacrylate, 24–25, 146
polyester, in Rely tampons, 15, 25, 27, 75, 131, 146
polyethylene glycol, 174–75
polyphenylene oxide, 175
polypropylene glycol, 174–75
polyurethane, in early versions of Rely tampons, 78–79, 131
Procter, Lita, 34

tampon-related toxic shock syndrome, as term, 7. *See also* toxic shock syndrome

tampons: consumer loyalty to, 45–46; exacerbation of TSS with frequent changing, 177; history of, 22–23, 177; identification of TSS link to, 66–68, 79–80, 82; inertness assumption about, 2, 10, 12–13, 33, 42, 121–24; limits of product testing, 129–134; medical device classification, 31; My Flow monitor, 173; patents on, 23–25, 26; as preferred method for managing menstruation, 4; questioning of efficacy of, 77, 86; recommendations on time limits for wear, 176–77; substantial equivalence application, 32; as technologies, 22–28; user concerns with, 96–100, 150–51; women's decisions in aftermath of withdrawal, 100–101. *See also* absorbency of tampons; labeling of tampons; *specific brands*; *specific manufacturers*

Tampon Safety and Research Act (proposed), 14

Tampon Task Force: creation of, 150–55; disbanding of, 160; establishment of, 139–140; health activist experiments, 155–57; request for FDA to propose labeling, 157–160

techno-bacteriological relationships, 21–47; agential power of bacteria, 21, 33–39; gendered injury from technologies, 28–31, 41; medical devices regulation, 31–33; overlooking of, 39; overview, 21–22; tampons as technologies, 22–28; trust in consumer goods, 43–45; unexpected nature of risk and injury, 39–43, 45–47

technobiological, as term, 22, 193n1

technological agency, 33, 38, 47

technological progress narrative: expectations of, 45; gains of 1960s and 1970s, 28, 55; illusion of, 5, 58

technologies: bacteria as users of, 38, 171, 182; co-construction of tools and scientific practice, 141; emergence of new menstruation management technologies, 173; gendered injury from, 28–31; tampons as, 22–28; unexpected consequences of, 45–47

testing of products, limits of, 129–134

thalidomide, 28–29

Thomas, Carolyn, 45

Thompson, Kyla, 94

Tierno, Philip, 14–15, 60, 120–25

Todd, James: case definition of TSS, 64; Chicago meeting participation, 87; concern about incorrect theories, 93–94; *Lancet* article, 59, 60, 61; media appearances, 95; naming of TSS, 59; P&G grant funding, 74; syndromes vs. diseases, 52; TSS research, 39

total immersion absorptive capacity measurement method, 142

tow tampons, 23

toxicity and teratogenicity, testing for, 129, 130, 131–32

Toxic Shock Syndrome (Chesney and Bergdoll, eds.), 75

Toxic Shock Syndrome (IOM proceedings), 8

toxic shock syndrome (TSS): background facts about, 50–52; as both technobiological and socially constructed, 18; case definition of, 64, 81, 115; clinical definition of, 5–6, 115; contemporary scientific explanations, 14–17; contradictory evidence for, 47; etiology and microbiology of, 7–9; exacerbation of, with frequent changing, 177; as health crisis vs. epidemic, 9; inaccurate theories of, 93; latent vs. open and obvious risk of, 167; medical vs. coroner's report in *Kehm* trial, 128; origin story of, 59–62; prevalence of, 4; prevention of, 171, 178–180; Public Health Service poster, 161; symptoms of, 6–7, 48, 49;

ABOUT THE AUTHOR

Sharra L. Vostral is Associate Professor of History at Purdue University, with affiliations in the programs of Women's, Gender and Sexuality Studies, American Studies, and the College of Engineering Education. She is the author of *Under Wraps: A History of Menstrual Hygiene Technology*.